BEHIND
THE
SHOULDER
PADS

*Tales I Tell
My Friends*

Also by Joan Collins

BEHIND
THE
SHOULDER
PADS

*Tales I Tell
My Friends*

Joan Collins

SEVEN DIALS

First published in Great Britain in 2023 by Seven Dials,
an imprint of The Orion Publishing Group Ltd
Carmelite House, 50 Victoria Embankment
London EC4Y 0DZ

An Hachette UK Company

1 3 5 7 9 10 8 6 4 2

A CIP catalogue record for this book is
available from the British Library.

ISBN (Hardback) 978-1-399-609-96-8
ISBN (Export Trade Paperback) 978-1-399-609-97-5
ISBN (eBook) 978-1-399-609-99-9
ISBN (Audio) 978-1-399-610-00-1

Typeset by Input Data Services Ltd, Bridgwater, Somerset

Printed in Great Britain by Clays Ltd, Elcograf S.p.A.

MIX
Paper from
responsible sources
FSC® C104740
FSC
www.fsc.org

www.orionbooks.co.uk

*To all my family and friends who may have heard the
stories before, thank you for your patience.
And for Percy, who is always there for me.*

Contents

Dear Reader,

I'm lucky to have an inexhaustible appetite for life, which often exhausts my husband, children and friends. To me, every day is an adventure in which I try to achieve something, learn something, and enjoy something. And most of the time, I succeed. I love writing as it also presents itself as an adventure – capturing my life and thoughts on the page is an achievement; I always learn something new about myself, and I so enjoy doing it. This will be my nineteenth book. Hopefully, it won't be my last!

I've had many amazing adventures in my life, which I have shared with you in my other books, I hope in an entertaining fashion. Some I share again, from a different perspective. Some stories, though, I have only ever shared with my friends . . . You've got to have a bit of mystery, so I hide a knowing smile behind my shoulder pads . . .

Make yourself a drink and read on for some of those secrets I said I would never reveal!

Love,
Joan x

I

Behind the Shoulder Pads

One of my favourite parlour games that we often play at our house in the South of France is called 'The Salad Bowl Game'. Each player writes the name of a famous person on a tiny piece of paper (ten names per player) which we fold up and toss into the big wooden bowl we usually use to toss salads. Hence, 'The Salad Bowl Game'!

We divide into two teams, and each person in the team takes a turn to pick a name from the salad bowl and describe that individual to their own team in as many words as they like. They each get one minute (with the opposition team timing) for their team to guess that name. This continues with other players guessing as many names as they can. For example, 'Famous Disney mouse' for Mickey Mouse would be disqualified while 'Blonde actress, sang Happy Birthday to JFK' to describe Marilyn Monroe is perfectly acceptable.

This continues until all the names have been used up, with the guessed names emptied into another salad bowl, whereupon the game resumes in similar fashion – only now the teams have only two words with which to describe that individual. This is more difficult than one might think. In the case of Marilyn Monroe, 'Actress/President' or 'Blonde/Kennedy' might help jog the memories of your team. It is a game of recall, after all.

But it's the third round which really gets things going, because to describe the famous name you can only use mime. And let's face it, most people are not Marcel Marceau in that department. This causes enormous hilarity! In a recent game, one friend picked up a piece of paper and said, 'Famous actress, has a famous sister, married several times.' The whole group looked at me!

'No – not Joan! Blonde hair, big boobs!'

'Oh, um, Joan Fontaine? Jayne Mansfield? Lana Turner?'

'Come on!' he said. 'Comes from Hungary. Calls everybody "darlink".'

Finally, a chorus . . . 'ZSA ZSA GABOR!'

Later in that game, Percy picked a piece of paper. Thinking it would be easy, he mimed large breasts.

'ZSA ZSA GABOR,' came the immediate reply.

He shook his head. He pointed at me and at his wedding ring and made a gesture that transmitted repetition, as in married several times.

'ZSA ZSA GABOR!' his team insisted. No, he mimed.

'Elizabeth Taylor? Liza Minelli? Arlene Dahl?' the team called out.

Frustrated, Percy finally pointed at me and mimed a pair of huge shoulder pads.

'JOAN COLLINS!' they yelled back triumphantly. Sigh of relief from Percy!

Sigh of mixed feelings from me. Must I always be linked to the shoulder pad?

Well, I reflect, it could be worse. I really do like the way most people look in them. After all, shoulder pads made our hips look slimmer, our waists look trimmer, and are more flattering than an Italian waiter . . .

So, whatever the latest fashion decrees, I shall continue to wear jackets and coats with shoulder pads. If it was good enough for Joan Crawford and Bette Davis in the 1940s, it's certainly good enough for me.

The great actress Claudette Colbert once said to me, 'In my thirties I adopted a hair style that suited me, and I have not changed it ever since.' Bravo, Claudette!

So, I shall continue wearing my shoulder pads, and let no man (or woman) put them asunder . . .

2

Where Did You Find Her?

I want to tell you the tale of two young English girls who, by dint of hard work, ambition, discipline and, yes, luck, would become internationally famous. This is how it all began . . .

I was born Joan Henrietta Collins on a warm May morning in a Bayswater nursing home, weighing in at almost eight pounds. My father was a theatrical agent and my mother was an ex-dancer, looking forward to being a full-time mother. When Joe viewed his firstborn, mewling in Elsa's arms, he looked nonplussed at the red-faced, squalling creature, then joked, 'She looks like half a pound of scrag end.' My father was never one for effusive compliments. But I soon became the apple of my family's eye, for, modesty aside, I was considered a gorgeous baby. I had big green eyes, fine black hair and Cupid's bow lips.

I didn't realise I was going to have a sibling to play with until I was whisked away one morning by Auntie Hannah to stay with my grandma in her house in Brixton. I was four years old and full of questions. 'Where's Mummy? Where are we going?' I asked fearfully as the taxi sailed through the familiar views of Bayswater, Park Lane and Piccadilly.

'It's a surprise,' said Auntie Hannah, making a 'shushing' gesture with gloved finger to mouth, 'you will love it.'

For three days I mooched around Grandma Hetty's cramped

flat, decorated with quaint Victorian antiques and bric-a-brac, with nothing but my Shirley Temple doll and a creaky old radio for company. But dear old Grandma, her music hall vibes still resonating, would sometimes teach me to join her in a 'knees-up' for which she had been famed in her day, when she entertained the troops during the Boer War.

I was bored stiff and missing my parents and my cat, so when Daddy turned up on the fourth day and announced he was taking me home and that I was getting a surprise, I was ecstatic.

'What's the surprise?' I asked.

'Just you wait,' he said. Then he opened the door to Mummy's bedroom and there, lying on a nest of white pillows, lay my beautiful mother holding in her arms a rather grotesque pink creature.

'Meet your new baby sister!' announced Mummy.

I stared in shock. 'Where did you find her?' I whispered.

Daddy coughed embarrassedly and turned to his beaming wife as if for an answer.

'God sent her to us,' said Mummy proudly. 'Come and say hello to your sister, Jacqueline Jill.'

What a stupid name, I thought, gingerly approaching the sleeping infant.

'Would you like to hold her?' asked Mummy.

'No thanks,' I said, backing away. 'Can I go and play with my cat?'

'Yes, yes, off you go,' said Daddy as a fierce uniformed figure who I took to be a nurse stepped forward to take the creature from 'its' mother's arms.

For the next few months I kept away from Jacqueline Jill, much preferring to play with my cat or Shirley Temple doll. But a few months later when I was sitting on the floor reading, Jackie turned to me in her little high chair and gave me the sweetest toothless baby smile. From that moment on I adored her.

In our childhood, we didn't have social media, Twitter trolls or smartphones, and we didn't read newspapers, so we didn't worry about anything. We were on holiday in Bognor Regis, staying with our maternal grandmother Ada, when the Second World War broke out. We had the most glorious weather on that day in September and I was playing with friends in a meadow. I was terribly excited to see a headline in the paper that war had been declared. I had just learned to read and, in my childish innocence, it seemed like some sort of game was afoot. I thought I must be the first in my family to know as I ran across the field to impart the news. Two-year-old Jackie gazed impassively from her crib as Mummy and her sisters pretended to be very busy setting out tea things and tossing off remarks like 'Oh, it's nothing to worry about' and 'It'll all be over soon, you'll see.'

So, dutifully we left it to our parents to worry about the war. My sister Jackie and I threw ourselves into just being kids, entertaining and amusing ourselves all through our formative years. Our parents were of the 'children should be seen and not heard' generation, so they left us to get on with our little lives and never felt the need to entertain us. I could walk to school through the streets of London without being knocked over by somebody on a bike with their nose buried in a smartphone – all we had to worry about was the bombs and the Blitz, but we were really too young to understand the true extent of that danger. Besides, picking up and collecting different pieces of shrapnel after the air raids was exciting. Ignorance was bliss for little Jackie and Joan during the Second World War.

Our innocence of the danger remained intact through the war years, even while we were repeatedly evacuated then returned to London when it was all clear. When the bombs came back to London, off we trundled again in Daddy's Rover, Jackie sitting next to me in the back seat, sucking her thumb and reading a book, and Mummy, Daddy and me singing inspiring songs like 'We'll Meet Again' and 'There'll Be Bluebirds Over the White Cliffs of Dover'. Bognor, Brighton, Chichester, Norfolk, Ilfracombe; back and forth we went, sometimes staying for six months, sometimes only six weeks. Each time, Jackie and I would be enrolled in a new school and, from being quite outgoing children, we became rather shy as the 'old girls' never took kindly to the 'new girls', especially being from London – we were mocked and bullied mercilessly. Nevertheless, the war was quite an adventure and we didn't feel even remotely scared, thanks to the calming influence of our mother, who never showed us a newspaper or let us listen to the radio news.

One morning, towards the end of the war, we came out of Edgware Road Tube station, where we had been spending the night safe from the bombing, only to find our flat in Maida Vale completely destroyed. Jackie started crying inconsolably about her toys being gone and I, the heroic older sister, did my best to comfort her while feeling the great loss myself, particularly of Shirley Temple.

As I entered puberty, I was appalled that I was expected to wear the tight girdles, itchy stockings and suspender belts that my mother wore. I preferred the corduroy trousers and loose shirts of Daddy's wardrobe. So, for a while I wished that I had been born a boy and dressed in 'tomboy' style. I even went to football games with my father, obediently spinning my ratchet and celebrating loudly when everyone else did, although I had little idea what was going on and, frankly, I was miserably bored. By the time I was fifteen I reverted to embracing my female side.

We little girls did what little girls did in those days – played with our dolls, collected paper cut-outs of our royal princesses, Elizabeth and Margaret Rose, and dressed them in the various outfits that came along with those cut-outs. I drew pictures of fashionable ladies and adored reading – I even taught my sister to love it too.

Jackie looked up to and admired her big sis. Despite my acting career taking off at age sixteen, when I was accepted at the Royal Academy of Dramatic Art and with a stint as an assistant stage manager at the Maidstone Repertory Company, Jackie and I were still were very close, still sharing a bedroom in our flat in Great Portland Street. The ceiling was painted like the sky, with white scudding clouds, and in the spring and summer months, when it was still light after we went to bed, we would stare at the beautiful ceiling and make up stories about what we would be when we grew up. I veered between actress, fashion designer and detective, but Jackie was adamant about only one thing.

'I'm gonna be a writer!'

Even as teenagers, Jackie and I had definite ambitions. After my dithering, I settled on becoming an actress – but an actress in the 'theatre' and not 'the films', heaven forfend! However, we both adored films and film stars, and spent endless hours cutting pictures of our favourites from magazines and pasting them into giant scrapbooks, as well as sending off to Hollywood for auto-graphed pictures from the likes of Gene Kelly, Danny Kaye and Tony Curtis, most of whom obliged. Jackie even stuck pictures of Tony Curtis behind her bed, while I had my picture of Irish film star Maxwell Reed under my desk at school.

Jackie started writing a series of amazing stories when she was only ten – sophisticated plots about teenagers in America and France with exotic names – under the umbrella title 'These Things called Teenagers'. The concept of a teenager had just been invented in the late 1940s. Prior to that, people were only known as babies, toddlers or adults, and the idea of a young person's options when coming of age was foreign. Jackie was very 'in vogue', even then. I was called upon to illustrate these gems which, thanks to a school course in art, I did well. Jackie's handwriting was beautiful and structured, as were her stories, and I cherish the originals I now have, which her daughters found after she died.

Jackie was tall and had developed a fantastic figure by the time she was twelve. When we went on holidays to France, boys would whistle and try to chat us up, and even follow us around the beaches and the streets of Cannes (sorry folks, this was the 1950s after all, when 'PC' only meant Police Constable). But Jackie was good-natured about it and neither of us allowed the boys to get too close – it was a far more innocent time.

We were on the beach at Cannes when I received the telegram telling me that I had passed my audition for RADA. Jackie was happily splashing about in the water with three young French boys. As I whooped with joy and ran down the beach to tell her, I realised a whole new chapter of my life was starting.

3

A Hollywood Affair

During my early years as a young contract starlet at Rank, the company founded by J. Arthur Rank, Jackie followed my career closely, pasting every single press mention of me in scrapbooks and writing captions underneath. I had a meteoric rise to fame. Starting at seventeen, I spent eighteen months at Rank learning my craft while under contract to the studio, where I made twelve films in three years. I worked with some brilliant actors but also earned the moniker of 'Britain's bad girl' due to the studio's penchant for casting me as either juvenile delinquents, naughty heiresses or baby jailbirds; early intimations of being known as 'The Bitch'. Then, at age twenty, I was literally 'sold' to Hollywood's Twentieth Century-Fox. I worked at Fox for seven years, scoring above the title credits and working with such luminaries as Bette Davis, Richard Burton, Gregory Peck and Paul Newman. Those were heady days for a young girl from Blighty and I learned so much from these amazing stars.

Watching old movies now, especially musicals from the 1940s and 50s, I'm always incredibly impressed by the artistry and imagination of the creators and performers. Esther Williams swimming underwater or diving from 200 feet into a pool surrounded by fire, Fred Astaire dancing on the walls and ceiling and Betty Hutton cavorting on an elephant. Have there ever been more talented song and dance men than Gene Kelly and Fred Astaire? Eat your heart out, contestants of *Dancing with the Stars*! Those two guys were magical.

In fact, the whole of Hollywood was magical. When I arrived as a young actress and saw the sprawling backlots of MGM and Twentieth Century-Fox, I couldn't believe it. They were a fairyland of ancient castles, old villages, New York streets and Midwestern American roads, rivers and, of course, swimming pools for Esther Williams ('Wet, she's a star. Dry, she ain't,' said Fanny Brice). Beautiful people strolled the lot in their screen costumes. When they weren't in costume, the men were always immaculately dressed and the women, be they in slacks, shorts or tea dresses, were all beautiful and glamorous with perfectly coiffed hair and great make-up.

Every weekend a different movie mogul threw a party either at their palazzos or the restaurants Romanov's or Chasen's, and if you weren't invited you were on the way down. Hollywood was a gossipy village where everyone knew everyone, and everyone knew everyone's business and where they stood on the totem pole of importance in 'this town'. I had three things going for me: youth, beauty and a movie contract. You couldn't buy these attributes, which were much in demand for certain occasions, like being invited to grand parties. Of course, there were many starlets with the two former attributes, but being under contract to a big studio made me special, so the party invitations kept on coming.

And those Saturday-night parties! Oh my God, I've never seen so much silk, velvet and brocade . . . and that was just the men.

I was strolling down Rodeo Drive on my way to the Hawaiian restaurant Luau for cocktails (as you do) when I spotted Fred Astaire strolling elegantly on the opposite side of the road. He was, as usual, impeccably but casually dressed and, although passers-by might have recognised him, they were sophisticated enough not to bother him. Imagine if Tom Cruise or Brad Pitt was spotted on the streets of Beverly Hills alone today, they would be mobbed by the selfie crowd.

One of the most original and versatile dancers ever to grace the movies was Gene Kelly. He always insisted on performing his own daredevil stunts and acrobatics, which absolutely fascinated me as a kid. Watching him jump from high buildings and castles in films like *The Pirate* and *Singing in the Rain*, and even dancing with an animated mouse was exciting. He was so innovative. He wanted to expand what the 'old-school' musical represented and broaden its horizons.

I first saw Gene Kelly in *For Me and My Gal* with Judy Garland. I must have been about eleven but I totally fell in love with him. Imagine how thrilled I was when, a decade later, my then boyfriend Sydney Chaplin took me for lunch to Gene's 'Cape Cod' style house on Rodeo Drive. I was overwhelmed, totally starstruck, almost tongue-tied. The group that congregated around Gene's volleyball court consisted of some of the most cultured, talented and interesting people in Hollywood: the actor, pianist and great wit Oscar Levant lounged in a deckchair laconically smoking a cigar and chatting to Adolph Green, one of the top songwriters of musicals in Hollywood, who I had met before. The very intelligent writer Harry Kurnitz chatted to Betsy Blair, Gene Kelly's very intelligent wife, and there were others there who I would get to know in the following months: actress Cloris Leachman and her husband, the producer George Englund (I would get to know him better a few years later!); tennis pro Jack Cushingham, who would soon instruct me in the intricate art of tennis; and a witty young man named Arthur Loew Jr, scion of the MGM founders. He was extremely attentive to me and since

I was too tongue-tied to converse with the intelligentsia, we hit it off. He made me laugh as he whispered pithy, slightly catty remarks about the group to me.

A year later I left Sydney, who was moaning a lot about not working and spending all his days drinking, golfing and playing tennis with Jack Cushingham. I had lent him my car to drive to Palm Springs for the weekend to meet Gene Kelly and the gang. I was to take a creaky old prop plane there, as I was shooting *The Girl in the Red Velvet Swing* on Saturday morning. Sydney promised to meet me at the airport.

Arriving at the Palm Springs airport in sweltering weather, I found no sign of him. There was no car, and no taxis were available either. Fuming, I called the Racquet Club. No answer from his room. Eventually a cab appeared and, sweating and hot, I got to the club where the desk clerk informed me that Mr Chaplin was in the bar. Oh, *really*, I thought.

How typical. In the bar, quite a pretty sight greeted my eyes. Syd, Gene Kelly, Greg Bautzer, Jack Cushingham and a few other cronies had decided to imbibe after-lunch liquors. They thought it would be fun to sample the bartender's selection alphabetically. Accordingly, they had gone from Amaretto to brandy to crème de menthe to Drambuie, and were obviously now on to V for vodka, when I appeared, flushed and furious.

'Sydney Chaplin,' I hissed, 'I let you borrow my car, I paid to fly on a bumpy two-engine plane to this godforsaken hole for ageing tennis bums. This was supposed to be a relaxing weekend, and you don't even meet the plane!' My voice started to rise to a crescendo, much to the embarrassment of Gene Kelly and company.

Syd, smashed as he was, managed to look sheepish but, unable to answer me, picked up his Smirnoff and downed it in a gulp, not meeting my eyes.

'Fuck you, Sydney,' I screamed. 'Fuck you. Fuck you. Fuck you. Fuck you!'

The select members of the Racquet Club looked aghast at such foul language coming from the lips of such a dainty English girl. Sydney turned slowly on his barstool to finally face me and staggered to his feet.

'And fuck you too,' he blurted out before keeling over, only saved from hitting the linoleum by his friend, Gene Kelly.

'Well, that,' I enunciated clearly in my best Royal Academy of Dramatic Art diction, 'will be the last time you will *ever* fuck me.'

Enter Arthur Loew Jr, age twenty-nine and very rich. As often happened in my life, someone had been waiting in the wings and Arthur became my boyfriend. We were happy for a year until a New Year's Eve party at producer Charlie Lederer's. We were dancing to the music, which was soft and romantic, but we were not. We were having another peevish row, quietly, so that the imposing array of distinguished guests could not overhear our heated discussion.

But they could not have failed to hear the following dazzling dialogue, which many people, including Gore Vidal, said they witnessed:

Arthur: 'You are a fucking bore.'

Me: 'And you are a boring fuck.'

And that was the end of that.

In Gene Kelly's living room the famous composer of musicals, Saul Chaplin (no relation), was often found tinkling at the piano, watched by musicals producer Roger Edens and his best friend Leonard Gershe. 'Lennie' would become my close friend a few years later, when I became good friends with Billy Wilder and his elegant wife Audrey. She gave wonderfully intimate parties in their tiny apartment on Wilshire Boulevard. Every surface was covered in unusual *objets*, as Billy was a dedicated collector of many things. There wasn't room to place your cocktail glass, but dinner at the Wilders' was a coveted invitation. With delicious food and brilliant conversations, I learned a lot from the Wilders and their incredible collection of talented friends.

As I left Gene Kelly's house, another massive talent came rushing through the door carrying a cranky child. 'Sorry I'm so late,' gasped the breathless Judy Garland. 'Liza wouldn't stop crying!'

I stayed in touch with Gene Kelly throughout the years, but he was an intellectual and I am not, so our paths didn't cross much. Besides, my life became a world of shooting movies, getting married, having babies and travelling constantly. But in 1983 I co-produced and starred in a long-form TV movie called *Sins*. I had control of the casting, except when I suggested Timothy Dalton to play my lover. The studio said he wasn't sexy enough, so he was cast as my brother instead. Ironically, he became James Bond a few years later!

The director Douglas Hickox couldn't think of who to cast as my character Helene's older piano-playing husband. He suggested John Forsythe.

'God, no! What about Gene Kelly?' I suggested.

'He's retired. You'll never get him,' said Doug.

'I will,' I said boldly.

I called the Hôtel de Crillon in Paris, invited myself over for a drink and gave Mr Kelly a heavy pitch.

'I love it. I'll do it. I love you, Joanie,' he winked.

A month later in the South of France we shot our first love scene. When it came time for a kiss, Gene gave it the full-on French. Coming up for air, he exclaimed, 'I've been wanting to kiss this little gal ever since I first met her!' What a guy. And I quite enjoyed the kiss from one of my childhood idols.

On a recent flight, I was watching *The Philadelphia Story*, Cary Grant sparring brilliantly with Katharine Hepburn. It was like taking a master class in comedic acting. Even the transatlantic turbulence was forgotten as I admired these two unforgettable icons. Cary Grant was an incomparable movie star. I truly believe there is no modern screen actor who comes close to him in terms of looks, humour and charisma. Certainly, there have been more talented actors – Brando, De Niro, Hackman – but Grant was, and always will be, in a magical class all of his own, particularly comedy.

4

That's the Way It Is

It was the act that dare not speak its name. None of the powers that be in Hollywood would break the conspiracy of silence that hung over the casting couch like a dreaded mafia blood oath.

I am a feminist and I have always been a feminist, even though for decades I didn't know the true meaning of the word. As a fifteen-year-old just hitting puberty, I despised being female. My bodily changes were embarrassing, and I had no desire to emulate my lovely mother or my six glamorous aunts. My tomboy phase lasted approximately half a year. But when I embraced my femininity and entered the tricky world of showbiz, I was stunned at the absolute misogyny that rained down not only on me, but on all the other pretty actresses, as well as many girls of the same generation working in fashion, retail, factories and hospitality.

As a seventeen-year-old actress playing my first lead role in a British film at Ealing Studios, I was subjected to a torrent of, at best, innuendo and lewdness and, at worst, physical and sexual harassment and abuse that almost overwhelmed me. But when I confided my fears to an older actress on the film, she told me, 'Unfortunately, dear, that's the way it is in the film world. I know they didn't teach you about that at RADA, but you'll just have to put up with it, I'm afraid. Like it or lump it – and be prepared to lose roles if you don't cooperate.' This was a daunting prospect, and one I was not willing to accept.

It's sad to say that male interviewers, and in general men who were in a position of power such as producers, directors, actors and CEOs, were sneeringly condescending and patronising towards young females, as were many of the attitudes expressed in newspaper articles and TV shows. Some men delighted in leering down our cleavage or patting our bottoms. Then there were the constant passes which, when rejected, elicited responses like, 'Are you frigid?' or 'A girl who looks like you should love it.' Or, my favourite, 'How do you like being a sex symbol?'

That's the way it still was when, shortly after arriving in Hollywood, under contract to Twentieth Century-Fox, I met Marilyn Monroe at a party at Gene Kelly's house. Every week he would host a party for an eclectic group of power brokers, stars, intellectuals and his many friends. You never knew who would be there, so I didn't register who the nondescript blonde sitting alone at the bar was until she turned to me and said ruefully, 'They wanted me to play the lead in *The Girl in the Red Velvet Swing*, but I'm too old.' This was my first starring role in Hollywood, and it suddenly dawned on me that this pale-faced woman was the fabled Marilyn Monroe, beautiful even without make-up and coiffure.

She was extremely friendly, so we started chatting just like girlfriends. After a couple of martinis, she poured out a cautionary tale of harassment and 'the wolves in this town'. I replied that I was well used to them after a few years in the British film industry – 'All of us had to put up with having our bottoms patted and men leering down our cleavage,' I told her.

'That's nothing compared to the studio power bosses, honey,' Marilyn replied. 'If they don't get what they want, they'll drop your contract. It's happened to lots of gals. Specially watch out for Zanuck. If he doesn't get what he wants, honey, he'll fire you. It's happened to lots of gals.'

'Well, thanks for the advice, I'll definitely keep away from him.'

But at the studio a few days later, Darryl Zanuck himself pounced on me, trapping me against a wall. Breathing cigar fumes, he hissed, 'You haven't had anyone until you've had me, honey. I'm the biggest and the best and I can go all night.'

I was so shocked I couldn't think of anything to say. I managed to wriggle free and ran back to the set. I'm glad I was speechless, because I heard that a starlet had recently been fired because when he said, 'Baby, I'm the biggest in the business . . .' she responded with, 'You better be, honey, 'cause you're only five foot two!' It was the stuff of legend that he had a golden replica of his manhood sitting on his desk as a paperweight. But it was true – I saw it once at his office. Ugh!

In the aftermath of the Harvey Weinstein scandal, the full extent of the depravity that pretty young actresses were forced to descend to for potential roles no longer continues, or at least is no longer accepted. I hope.

My first encounter with the casting couch was while testing for the juvenile lead in *I Believe in You*. One of the producers had made such obvious advances that I had to dodge him by hiding in a wardrobe in the costume department, helped by sympathetic dressers, and waiting until he left the studio before taking the bus and Tube home.

But after my third test he caught me and persuaded me to accept a lift home in his flashy Bentley. During the ride, he grabbed my hand and put it on his open fly. I screamed in horror and yanked my hand away. 'What's the matter? Don't you want the part?' he leered.

'Not that much,' I cried, childishly bursting into tears as I realised I had blown my chances. I'd never seen a naked man before, let alone felt one.

'Are you frigid?' he hissed. It was the first time I had been called that by a man, but sadly not the last. Men who, because they were rich or powerful, thought that women were playthings could be very cruel. I was also called a cock teaser, a shameless flirt and a cold, heartless bitch.

But the recent light that has been shed on the film industry has not just landed on the predatory institutional sexism of Hollywood – it's also been shed on any business run by ruthless, powerful and misogynistic men. And it's not just actresses who receive abuse – it's every girl, woman and sometimes man in a subservient position who are unfortunate enough to have to deal with them.

Power corrupts, and absolute power corrupts absolutely, and, thankfully, these monsters have crept off into the shadows . . . for now.

Luckily, this producer was overruled by the director and the head of the studio, so I got that role despite his threats. However, he still pursued me, and when I told him I wasn't interested and was still a virgin he called me a 'frigid little witch'.

It wasn't just producers who were predatory. Sadly, many of the actors I worked with considered it their divine right to have sex with their leading lady. At twenty-two, I had repeatedly said no to a handsome, if short, famous actor I was working with. One night after shooting, he followed my car, and when I paused at the Twentieth Century-Fox exit gate he shouted at the top of his lungs, 'You stupid cow – you'll be washed up by the time you're twenty-three!' Luckily, I was under contract and for a good salary, so I considered myself reasonably safe until I hit twenty-seven, which was widely deemed by studio bosses to be the age that women lost their sexual allure.

The studio bosses themselves were steeped in a time-honoured tradition – to screw, literally or figuratively, all the good-looking women they could. They were notorious for it! Harry Cohn at Columbia Pictures had no qualms about firing any contract starlet who rejected him. He was incredibly powerful and totally amoral. When his prize contract player, Kim Novak, had an affair with Sammy Davis Jr, who had recently lost an eye in a car crash, he threatened to have 'the other eye taken out' if he didn't stop seeing her. Cohn was so powerful that Sammy obeyed and immediately married someone else.

Jack Warner at Warner Brothers fancied himself an attractive bon vivant. He was a snappy dresser who gave glittering parties and was a massive flirt. My first Hollywood picture, a Warner Brothers epic called *Land of the Pharaohs*, was shot in Rome. But at one of his parties in Hollywood, Mr Warner propositioned me and was amazed when I didn't succumb. He openly bragged about his conquests, which seemed to include every other actress on the Warner lot and many from MGM too.

Three years later, when I was doing a press junket in New York, my agent secured me an interview with a very famous producer for a part I really wanted. I dutifully went to his office at 6 p.m., and when I arrived his secretary was just leaving.

'He's in there,' she pointed to a back room. 'He's waiting for you.'

I entered a bedroom and a voice called, 'Come on in,' from another door. I tentatively walked in and there he was, lying in the bath without as much as a bubble to cover his embarrassment, with which he was tinkering.

'Sit down,' he commanded, gesturing to the end of the bath.

'Oh, I'm fine, thanks. I'll stand.'

'Come on in,' he grinned. 'The water's fine.'

'Oh, ah, no, no thanks.' I tried not to shudder, nor notice what he was doing to himself under the soapy water. After a few minutes' chat about the film, which I argued was totally right for me as she was English, he agreed I would be perfect, and then again insisted I share his bath.

'I'm sorry, I have to go – I've got a date with my boyfriend,' I stammered, horribly aware that I wouldn't get this part now.

'Who's your boyfriend?' he asked.

'Oh, you wouldn't know him. He's a young actor – Warren Beatty.'

'What are you doing wasting your time with unknown actors?' he said, beginning to sound annoyed. 'C'mon, let's go to 21 tonight. I'm an important man, we can have some fun. By the way, how old are you?'

'Twenty-five,' I muttered.

'Twenty-five, huh? That's not young in this business anymore, sweetie.' I stared at his ugly fifty-five-year-old face, turned and left.

'You won't get much further in this business, kid, if you're going to behave like a high-handed bitch!' he called after me. American actress Kim Novak got the role of the cockney tart, but her accent left a lot to be desired.

Another role that I coveted around that time was that of the Egyptian queen Cleopatra. Both the head of Fox, Buddy Adler, and the chairman of the board – a Greek gentleman old enough to be my grandfather – had bombarded me with propositions and flowers, culminating in express promises to cast me as Cleopatra if only I would be 'nice' to them. They both used this euphemism, quite prevalent in Hollywood.

I couldn't and I wouldn't – the very thought of these old men touching me was utterly repugnant. So, I dodged and I dived and I hid around the lot and made excuses while the studio tested me for Cleopatra ad infinitum, with various actors who, to say they were wooden, would be unkind to trees.

At one point, Mr Adler cornered me to dance with him at a glamorous industry party. He told me I would have 'the pick of the scripts' after Cleopatra and that he would set me up in an apartment which he would pay for as long as he could come and visit me three or four times a week.

Having run out of excuses, I blurted out, 'Oh, Mr Adler, I came here with my agent, Jay Kanter. Why don't we discuss this deal with him?'

'Honey, you have quite a sense of humour,' he said.

'And a sense of humour is all you'll ever get from me,' I murmured as I left him on the dance floor.

Elizabeth Taylor got to play the part opposite Richard Burton, another predatory actor I had played opposite a few years earlier on location in Jamaica.

Richard had told me that if I didn't go to bed with him I would 'break his record'.

'What's that?' I asked.

'I've slept with all my leading ladies,' he bragged.

'Well, I'm not going to be another notch on your well-punched belt, so I guess I am going to break your record!' He barely spoke to me for the rest of filming.

Likewise, George Peppard. We were making *The Executioner* together and after attending a party to celebrate the start of filming, he dropped me off at my house in London, then tried to grab me. When I pushed him away, saying I was married and had two small kids, he accused me of being 'totally square' and then stalked off. He didn't speak to me for the rest of the movie, and since I had to do a couple of topless scenes with him, this was embarrassing to say the least.

*

I work in a profession where hugs, kisses and physical contact are the norm, but call me cold and aloof – and I try not to be – I don't willingly participate. How I admire the Japanese culture's sensible approach in which people just bow and nod their heads when they meet, be it friends, acquaintances, or strangers. They obviously know something about germs as they are often swathed in gloves and surgical masks, even before COVID!

Arriving at airports, I arm myself with enough hand sanitiser, nose-blocking gel and baby wipes to stock a corner chemist. Scared to get the flu even after having had the flu shot, I protect myself from the zillions of invisible germs that lurk inside airplanes, as they do on every surface from door handles, lift buttons and supermarket trolleys. But I believe the deadliest germ carriers are other people's hands and faces. I try not to shake hands whenever possible. Instead, I offer my jaunty closed fist for a gentle bump. This is usually met by a puzzled expression unless the recipient is approaching puberty. But the bane of my life is the bear hug followed by a sloppy kiss on the cheek from total strangers. As I was brought up at a time when you didn't kiss or hug anyone except your close family, and it was the norm to seldom receive much affection from your parents past the age of ten, this overt physical warmth is something I can't adjust to.

My mother was a germophobe long before it was trendy to be one. As I was firstborn, she figuratively wrapped me in cotton wool, constantly checking to see if I was too hot, too cold, too dry or too wet. When I went out in the pram, strangers would often coo over me and get far too close for her comfort, so she felt compelled to have a sign printed, which she put on the blanket covering her little darling, stating 'Please do not kiss me.' Unfortunately, I no longer have that sign with me, as it would still be useful.

It's interesting that the #MeToo movement and the circuitous and condescending new HR guidelines that proscribe the traditions of luvvie-land and make it verboten to get too close to your colleagues suit me fine, even if I disagree with the nannying. Now, after the curtain comes down, actors are not supposed to fraternise, presumably with each other and much less with the management and production staff. If those were the rules in 2000, I would never have been able to date my husband when we met in San Francisco and toured the US. Percy Gibson was managing the *Love Story* company and I was playing opposite George Hamilton. Luckily, George was not one of those actors who spray you with saliva when you have a scene in close proximity. Ever the gent, we worked together several times on television, and he has never parted his lips or done 'the French' during a kissing scene.

Sadly, that doesn't apply to some other actors. As soon as the director yells 'action' during a love scene, they become full on with the hands, the mouth and the dreaded tongue. Not to speak ill of the dead (but I will!), when I played opposite George Peppard in our little island epic *The Executioner*, shot in Malta, Mr Peppard proved an eager beaver in the amorous department. Wearing nothing but knickers and a sheet during our first love scene, I was at somewhat of a disadvantage as all six foot two of him was splayed on top of me. The wardrobe lady had swiftly pulled the sheet away at the last minute as he came in for the kill. I tried a closed-mouth screen-kiss, but he wasn't having any of that and attempted the full-on Frenchie. When I politely extracted his tongue from my throat for the fourth time, I became angry.

I protested to our director, Sam Wanamaker, while Mr Peppard looked on in amusement as the make-up department tried to reconstruct both our lipstick-covered faces.

'Just do it a little less forcefully, George,' said Sam persuasively.

'OK,' growled the great star, and off we went again.

Action! Sheet off, Peppard on, tongue in – ugh! Sam was finally satisfied and cried 'Cut'.

'Did you enjoy that?' smirked George.

'No, I hated it, and you didn't have to be quite so "methody",' I retorted as I struggled back into my robe to cover my nakedness, trying not to be the day's cabaret act for the crew.

'Oh, you're such a prude,' he sneered. 'Most actresses love it.'

'Well, I'm not one of them.' I stalked off, speechless with fury.

After this, George became so angry and petulant that we communicated only through our respective make-up people and during our scenes.

When George was cast as the lead in a new serial drama called *Oil*, he was so difficult that the producer Aaron Spelling fired him. They recast with John Forsythe, retitled it *Dynasty* and the rest is history. I don't think I could have stood nine years working with George Peppard. Another actor who some years later inappropriately kissed me was Gene Barry. You may remember him as Bat Masterson in the eponymous series. I played a wife pining for her lost, estranged husband, who appears to have been a double agent, and Gene was the spymaster trying to catch him out. In one scene, Gene escorted me to my front door after a platonic dinner date. He then leaned in for what was supposed to be an avuncular goodbye peck on the cheek but out came that tongue again. 'Oh, no, you can't do it like that,' I said, struggling away, 'I'm supposed to be grieving.'

'For chrissake, what are you? Frigid?' he demanded.

'Yes, I've had two kids and two husbands, and I'm frigid,' I replied sarcastically, but Gene didn't get the joke.

'Listen, honey. I'm Gene Barry. I'm the hero of this picture, so this woman's gotta enjoy kissing me or my fans will be disappointed!'

'Well, my fans will hate it. Why don't you go kiss them instead?' I hissed.

We were frosty to each other from then on, until he made a guest appearance in *These Old Broads* several decades later and recalled not the movie, but my appearance in *Playboy* magazine, which he remarked upon lasciviously!

Another memorable but distasteful kiss was on the superyacht of legendary producer Sam Spiegel, moored in a gorgeous bay outside Cannes. I was with Roger Moore and David Niven and their respective wives, looking forward to a birthday celebration for Sam. Twenty of us were seated on deck at a long table filled with flowers. Roger made a toast to the birthday boy, then added, 'And it's Joanie's birthday today too!'

'That's wonderful, congratulations, honey,' beamed Spiegel. 'And have I got a present for you, little lady.'

He lumbered up to me and plonked a tonsil-probing smacker, complete with snake-like tongue, on my lips. Roger thought it was hilarious as I sat there gobsmacked with a sickly smile on my face. The table whooped with glee as I surreptitiously wiped my mouth on my napkin. The following day I came down with a virulent strain of flu and had to spend the next three days in bed.

So, dear reader, if I don't accept your kisses, hugs and handshakes, it doesn't mean I don't like you, it just means I don't want to catch your germs.

5

Acapulco Adventures

'Come fly with me, let's fly, let's fly away . . .' So sang Frank Sinatra in his iconic 1950s album of the same name.

I was very excited when a girlfriend, Nora Eddington Flynn, asked me to accompany her to Acapulco for four or five days. Nora was the ex-wife of the notorious actor Errol Flynn, so I imagined she would know her way around all the hot spots of the jet-set world. Unfortunately, there was no jet or even a direct flight to Acapulco from LA in the mid-1950s. So, we had to drive to the tiny town of Tijuana in Mexico, then take a rickety propeller plane to Acapulco. It was a horrible trip, but when we arrived it was well worth it.

Acapulco then was a magical mirage of golden sandy beaches, clear turquoise water and cloudless blue sky, which apparently the locals were lucky enough to experience for 350 days of the year! Nora rented a car and we drove through tiny streets hemmed by glowing bougainvillea, up and down little hills, passing donkeys laden with produce, until we arrived at a delightful boutique hotel called the Villa Vera, where we were greeted by a charming middle-aged man called Teddy Stauffer.

'He was an absolute stud and man-about-town in his day – married to Hedy Lamarr, among others – and all the girls adored him. He was quite a guy,' whispered Nora. And Mr Stauffer soon lived up to his notoriously rakish image.

'I'm going to show you the *real* Acapulco,' he announced a few days later. And so he did!

First, he took me to the La Quebrada restaurant to watch the fantastic young fishermen who dived from the great height of the cliffs into the water. I was enthralled by the bravery of those men and boys. It was a deliciously balmy night at the outdoor restaurant, and the atmosphere was electric.

'This started eighty-five years ago,' said Teddy. 'It's one of Acapulco's biggest tourist attractions.'

'Well, I can understand why,' I replied, gasping at the daring divers who seemed to dive far too close to the rocks. 'Don't worry, they never miss,' said Teddy. The guacamole was spicy and delicious, the margaritas perfect, and it was an unforgettable night. I was only sorry that Nora had wanted an early night, so I was alone with our gracious host.

After several margaritas, Teddy said, 'Now I'll show you *another* side of Acapulco. Are you game?' he added with a grin. We had been joined by two friends of his, men in their forties, which to me at twenty-two seemed ancient!

'Of course,' I said, with the misplaced confidence of youth. 'I'm always up for new experiences.'

We drove through dark scented streets, then more insalubrious ones, until we came to a building with a discreet black door.

'Are you feeling adventurous?' asked Teddy.

'Yes,' I replied. 'In your twenties, life should be an adventure.'

'Are you ready for a totally new experience?' He looked deep into my eyes.

'Err – maybe. What is it?' I asked, slightly apprehensive after all these questions.

'Sshhh.' He put his finger to his lips as a flashily dressed lady in red opened the door. She seemed pleased to see Teddy and greeted him warmly. The two men went upstairs, and Teddy introduced me in Spanish to the woman.

'This is the most famous lady in Acapulco,' he told me, then, smiling in an avuncular way, added, 'You will either love this experience or you will not.'

Oh God, I was becoming a bit scared now. I was alone with Teddy and this rather intimidating 'famous woman' who was wearing more make-up than Ru Paul. She led me upstairs to a bedroom, the walls of which were hung with faded red velvet and pointed towards the bed on which lay a naked young girl.

'You like?' she smiled, revealing a large gap in her dentures.

'Good God – NO!' I attempted to leave the room, but she held me by the wrist and gestured to an armchair. 'Now, now then. Just sit and enjoy the show. I think you will like it.'

She left the room in a cloud of cheap scent and, at that, one of Teddy's friends strolled in, totally naked. He started to make love to the girl on the bed and, for a few seconds, I sat rooted to the spot (as you do!) in horror.

This was all so vile that I regained my senses and rushed to the door and down the stairs to where Teddy was sitting at the bar.

'I've never been so embarrassed in my life,' I cried. 'How could you do that to me?'

'I thought you were a modern girl,' he smiled. 'Adventurous, believing in equality to men – no?'

'Yes – I mean no. I've got to get out of here. That is NOT my scene, Teddy. Not at all.'

'Nora said she thought it would amuse you. Most of my lady friends love it,' he said as we walked to the car. 'Some even join in.'

'I was not amused,' I said in my best Queen Victoria voice. 'She's spent too much time with that bloody Errol Flynn!'

Despite this egregious incident, I still adored Acapulco. I

moved to a smaller hotel and during the following weeks I lived a healthy and absolutely fabulous life.

Every morning I would hit Caleta beach, where I became great friends with the local boys who rented boats and water skis. They taught me to ski around the clear azure waters of Acapulco Bay, and I loved water skiing so much that eventually I graduated to a mono-ski and would skim along the bay for hours.

After Nora returned to California, a whole bunch of actors arrived from LA, one of them a young actress called Vicki. I was grateful having a fellow female my age. We hung out together with the guys and after lunch lazed on what they called Hornos beach – the afternoon beach – and in the evenings the whole gang would dine together again and party until dawn. Talk about flaming youth – we practically set ourselves on fire! Little did I know that magical Acapulco would feature so heavily in my future.

6

Non, Je Ne Regrette Rien

I believe that if women ruled the world there wouldn't be so many wars – and if men got pregnant and had to have babies, there wouldn't be nearly as many people in the world.

I screamed in rage at the TV when I heard the news that the majority of justices in the US Supreme Court (mostly white men) had passed an amendment withholding and banning a woman's right to an abortion, even if it was by incest, if she had been raped, or was a minor. Even though it wouldn't be law in all US States, it was a gross affront to all females.

These legal dinosaurs have curtailed the freedoms and rights of women that our female ancestors fought and died for, and which girls and women all over the world have experienced for fifty years. It's completely misogynistic, inhumane and cruel. I can't imagine the fate of an underage girl, raped by her father or a relative, her life ruined, another unwanted child entering this already overcrowded world.

Maybe these old men should now ban Viagra so men can't have fake erections. It seems the power of the penis trumps women's rights. Why do so many women have to suffer, when *we* are the ones who usually have more empathy, humanity and compassion?

Childbirth is an arduous and painful experience which men have little knowledge of. A woman who doesn't want a child should never be forced to give birth to one. This whole new scenario is reminiscent of the TV series *The Handmaid's Tale*, in which fertile women are forced to give birth to multiple babies.

A long time ago I had an abortion. I was living with my fiancé Warren Beatty; a young, unknown actor then; and even though I was careful, I fell pregnant.

'I think I'm pregnant,' I said, coming into the kitchen one day, where he was preparing one of his health concoctions in the blender. He stopped slicing bananas and pouring wheatgerm, took off his glasses and stared at me. Without his glasses he was quite myopic, and I wondered why he didn't want to look at me.

'Pregnant?' he asked in his puzzled little-boy voice. 'How did that happen?'

'The butler did it,' I said sarcastically, 'or maybe it's an immaculate conception.'

'This is terrible,' he said, putting his glasses back on and looking at me as if for the first time. 'Terrible!'

'I know,' I said in a small voice. 'I'm sorry.' But why was I sorry? He was just as complicit.

We sat on the faded red sofa in the living room of the apartment I had rented in New York. I had a stiff vodka, he had his health drink, and we discussed what to do. Abortion was a dirty word in the early 1960s. In fact, so was sex. Even living together as Warren and I were was considered sinful. Abortions of a kind were available, but I shuddered at the memory of the screams of pain of my friend in Tijuana.

The previous year I had travelled with my married friend Susan and her married lover Nicky to a revolting hovel in Tijuana. I huddled with him in the connecting room while Susan's body was put through the most invasive and agonising procedure to rip out the foetus. I had listened, horrified, to her screams of agony as a Mexican 'doctor' performed the operation without an anaesthetic. I cried bitterly for her pain but understood that this was a last resort for her as she already had four children and she and her husband were no longer cohabiting.

Warren and I were engaged, so we could get married, of course, but I was not in favour of 'shotgun' weddings. The few times we had discussed marriage we had both decided that we were too immature to make it work. He was only twenty-three, a struggling wannabe actor with a potentially great career as a sex symbol ahead of him if the future movies he was angling for came to fruition.

As a successful twenty-six-year-old actress under contract to Twentieth Century-Fox, having a baby out of wedlock would have been career suicide. Fox would have immediately dropped me as an immoral whore, my acting career would be over, and I would spend the rest of my life raising and supporting a child I was not ready for – at that time. I had recently turned down a very good role in *Sons and Lovers* because Warren thought the script was 'crap'. I was in the middle of finishing shooting a rather exciting film noir called *Seven Thieves*, and potentially lined up by Fox was a movie in Italy called *Esther and the King* in which I would play the lead role. After that I would hopefully be starring opposite Bob Hope and Bing Crosby in *Road to Hong Kong* in London. My future was looking rosy, but not if I would be expecting a baby.

I would obviously have to return to London, my real residence, and hopefully back into the bosom of my family home. There, I would raise the baby – if my parents would forgive me for this terrible deed. I think Mummy would have had sympathy for me and welcomed the child, although she was suffering with breast cancer. Nevertheless, I felt sure she would forgive me and even help me raise the child. I think my father would reluctantly have allowed me and the baby to stay in his flat in Harley House with my fifteen-year-old brother Bill, but it would have been troublesome as my father was always worried, in his Victorian way, about 'what would people think'.

I would have had only a little money left over from my Twentieth Century-Fox career, not enough after paying for the birth to afford an apartment or even a child carer. I would probably have loved the child, but that would have precluded me from meeting Anthony Newley in 1962 and having Tara and Alexander, which means they would never have been born.

So, getting married wasn't an option for either Warren or me. And having a baby was definitely out. There was only one solution.

I didn't want to throw my whole future away for a baby, but thinking about two of my friends who had gone through illegal abortions made me shudder. The early 1960s were dark days for women and girls. Abortion was illegal practically everywhere, even though the new popular freedoms of expression in music, fashions and attitudes were raising their head in the UK. And women had 'The Pill', a revolutionary if controversial way of avoiding pregnancy. But gay sex remained illegal until 1967. We were still in the Dark Ages.

When I was at RADA a few years earlier, my classmate Jacqui had gone for a backstreet termination in East London. Her description of the agony and humiliation she suffered as a result, not to mention the fact that, because it was botched, she was never able to have children, chilled me to the bone. I did not want that to happen to me. Although I wasn't prepared for motherhood now, nevertheless I felt that one day, if my maternal instincts rose, I wanted to have my options open.

With the two frightening examples of Jacqui and Susan in my head, I still knew I must get rid of these few tiny cells which, if allowed to blossom, would potentially ruin my life and my career. I couldn't possibly think of it as a baby or even a human being as I had only been aware of it for less than a week.

We had heard that an abortion could be performed in clinical circumstances without any risk to health. Accordingly, Warren contacted a sophisticated man of the world who, with great secrecy and a lot of my money, arranged an appointment with a highly recommended ex-surgeon who worked in New Jersey. I would not consider a Tijuana-type operation.

That morning I woke up trembling with my oldest and most frightening nightmare. It was as terrifying as ever. I was walking alone up a very dark and winding staircase. The stairs creaked and the wind howled outside. In the distance, I heard dogs barking and an owl hooting, and then silence – only my footsteps, which went faster and faster up the crumbling stone stairs. Rats and mice scurried ahead of me, their tiny, furry bodies brushing my bare legs. Suddenly, I heard breathing. 'It' was behind me. 'It' was getting closer. I ran faster and faster up the endless stairs, hearing the breathing getting closer all the time. And then I came to the top of the stairs to a door that said 'Doctor'. I rapped furiously. The footsteps were gaining behind me. Slowly the door opened. A grinning old man stood there, his white apron covered with blood, a bloody knife in his hand. He came towards me to take me by the hand. Behind me I heard the moans of a woman. I stepped back. A hand grabbed my arm and swung me backward. 'I've got you at last, little girl,' screamed the man dementedly, his face a mask of cruelty, his eyes those of a madman. 'Now you'll really get cut up and carved up, and no one will ever look at you again!' He raised the bloody knife in his hand to bring it slashing to my face. I screamed. It was the face of my first husband.

'What is it, what's the matter?' Warren, groggy with sleep, asked, as I sat up sobbing, the vivid dream still gripping me.

'I can't go through with it,' I sobbed. 'I can't, I can't. Please don't make me go there, Warren, I'm scared – I'll have the baby, we'll get it adopted – but I can't go there.'

He comforted me as I sobbed hysterically. It was true. It's an ironic fact of life that the metabolic and hormonal changes that women go through when pregnant bring them closer each day to a protective feeling towards that life inside them. I had been feeling – perish the thought – broody for a couple of weeks, almost accepting what was happening to me, and now that it was going to be taken from me, I wanted to keep it.

'Butterfly, we can't, we can't do it,' Warren said helplessly, trying to comfort me. 'Having a baby now will wreck both of our careers. You know it will.'

He was right and I knew it. Ingrid Bergman, a far bigger star than I, had almost wrecked her career by having an out-of-wedlock child by Roberto Rossellini. It was a very serious and far-reaching step. There had been rumours of various actresses throughout the years who had disappeared for several months, and a few months after their reappearance had 'adopted' a tiny baby, but it was all extremely hush-hush.

With the eyes of the gossip columnists on us, nagging in print for us to 'tie the knot', it would have been an impossibility. So, I dried my tears, putting Warren's ambition and my career first, and mooched about until it was time to drive to New Jersey.

I wore thick black stockings, a sweater and a full plaid skirt. 'Don't wear slacks,' I had been told by a sterile, sibilant voice over the telephone when I received my instructions. My eyes, which were swollen and red from crying, were covered by my biggest black sunglasses, and a headscarf covered my untidy hair. I did not wish to be recognised by anyone. I chain-smoked as Warren drove a rented station wagon to Newark. We spoke little. He glanced at me with concern several times. I suddenly wished I could keep the baby. Practically, though, I knew it was impossible. *But I felt no support coming my way.* He was a man. He took none of the responsibility for me becoming pregnant. That was the woman's department. But pre-Pill, however careful one was, accidents happened, and the female was the one to face the emotional upheaval that pregnancy causes – and then the unbearably ambivalent feelings it generates.

I tried to convince myself that we were doing the right thing as we entered the Holland Tunnel and Warren started consulting a piece of paper on which were written the directions. I had just turned twenty-six. I had a thriving career, which, if not exactly to my liking as far as the roles I was playing were concerned, was still lucrative and rewarding in many ways. A baby would change all that. I would have to stop working. Fox would suspend me, and definitely fire me. I might lose my figure. I might be a lousy mother. He and I were not suited to each other in the long run. Was our love just a physical thing? We were both selfish, care-less, argumentative, combative, and just plain immature. It was stupid to think otherwise. Thus, I convinced myself – while my mind shrieked 'No!'

I dried my eyes and blew my nose as the car drew to a halt in front of an ominous-looking maroon high-rise apartment building.

'We're-um-here,' said my fiancé, nervously wiping his glasses on the sleeve of his tweed jacket, his face covered with perspir-ation. He was probably more scared than I was. We looked at each other and I swallowed hard.

'If anything goes wrong—' I started to say, but he interrupted me, almost screaming.

'Nothing's going to go wrong. Nothing. He's the best doctor around for this. Don't even think about that, Butterfly.'

He was close to tears himself. My maternal instinct went into comforting him, and hand in hand we walked to the green paint peeling elevator.

I awoke to hear someone pounding on the door.

'Are you still there?' yelled a coarse voice. I looked at my watch. It was one o'clock in the afternoon. I pulled the covers back over my head and tried to sleep again. The voice kept on yelling.

'Open up in there. I've gotta clean the room.'

'Oh, go to hell,' I yelled back. 'I don't want it cleaned. Leave me alone.'

The voice sniffed, 'If that's what you all want, you just go ahead and sleep all day, see if I care.' It shuffled down the corridor and left me in peace.

I tried to go back to sleep. Warren had gone to rehearsal, and I didn't want to think about what had happened last night. It was too vivid and too painful. We must get out of this fleabag hotel and find an apartment, I thought as I drifted back to sleep.

The next day I felt much better and full of energy again. I pushed the horrifying abortion out of my head. Done. Over. Forgotten. That was yesterday – no point in brooding about it, and oh, good – I didn't feel maternal anymore. Not even to Warren. I called a house agent and went apartment hunting. It was a beautiful, clear, crisp day, rare in New York. I felt newborn myself, as though a great weight had been lifted and I could get back to living.

I was lucky to have had an expert doctor. I had no pain and recovered within two days and was able to get on with my life. This may make me sound callous, but I just thought of the episode as a delayed period and put it to the back of my mind. The scenario of what my future life would have been like if I had gone to term and delivered a child was too depressing. I would have been vilified by the press and my career absolutely ruined.

Since I have strong maternal instincts, I would certainly have grown terribly attached to the child and in its early days devoted myself to its welfare, much as my *Dynasty* on-screen sister Kate O'Mara did when she gave birth to a son while unmarried in the mid-1960s. Once Kate had Dickon, she became devoted to him and let her career slide.

If I had had the baby, I wouldn't have married Anthony Newley, and I wouldn't have had my children Tara and Alexander. I would never have met his friend and tailor Doug Hayward, who introduced me to Ron Kass in 1970. So, I would never have married Ron, nor would I have had my beloved daughter Katyana.

The ramifications of 'what if?' go on and on. If I was lucky, I would probably have eked out a career in the British theatre, but certainly my movie career would have been *kaput*. I know I will be judged by many for having an abortion, but my three wonderful children and four fabulous grandchildren would never have been born if I hadn't, so, in the words of Edith Piaf, *je ne regrette rien*.

7
Family Matters

Jackie came to Hollywood to stay with me a couple of years after I arrived. Almost as soon as she touched down, however, I had to leave for Jamaica to shoot *Sea Wife* with Richard Burton, so I gave her the keys to my apartment and to my car! There was four years' age difference between us, which was only vast when you're a child. As she got older, she became more bookish, while I was more outgoing. She had a marvellous time, driving my pink Thunderbird around Beverly Hills and Sunset Boulevard and hanging out with other teenagers, who were more fun than the British teens. She adored the American way of life – hamburgers, drive-ins, chocolate malts. When I returned, she then hung out with me and my more sophisticated friends like Paul Newman, Sydney Chaplin, Gene Kelly and Marlon Brando, who she worshipped.

Marlon's brooding, sensual looks mesmerised everyone. James Dean, seven years Marlon's junior, worshipped him to the point of adulation and every young actor in Hollywood was influenced in some way by his mystique. He was, and remains, a lord of language and his seduction techniques were unparalleled. When he had his prey within his sights, he was unstoppable and irresistible, and women fell like ninepins.

At a party at Arthur Loew's one night, everyone watched

Marlon zero in on a shy teenager, new in town and evidently a virgin. Within an hour he had seduced her with his eyes, his charm, his magnificent voice, and his fund of anecdotes. Shortly thereafter he gently led her by the hand upstairs to the master bedroom.

I'd been out by the pool smoking while this was going on, so it was only when I returned and asked, 'Where's Jackie?' that I was told what my little sister was up to.

'Oh God! Mummy will kill me!' I attempted to dash upstairs to stop the seduction but Arthur, my current boyfriend, stopped me.

'No, don't go. Jackie will kill you if you break this up. Let's face it, if a girl's going to give up her virginity, who better to lose it to than Brando?' he grinned.

'But surely she won't let him go all the way . . . I hope?' I said with hope vanishing and reflecting on my promise to Mummy to 'take good care of Jackie and see that she doesn't get into trouble'.

But I was pleased to see that the pair of them looked delighted and dazed when they surfaced later, hand in hand, beaming like honeymooners.

Jackie never told me what happened, nor did she ever confess to her daughters, and so the Marlon Brando event remains a fascinating secret.

Hollywood in the 1950s was unbelievably glamorous. Most of the women were always painted and coiffed to the nines, even for tennis or shopping, and as for the parties – they were packed with the most famous and gorgeous stars and powerful heads of studios. I was invited, and took Jackie, to many of these soirées, given by the likes of moguls Darryl Zanuck and Ray Stark. I would gaze in awe at Lana Turner, Susan Hayward and Elizabeth Taylor in their prime and pimped to perfection.

Not having too many glamorous outfits when I had arrived, I hit Saks and I. Magnin's regularly, and soon attained my black belt in shopping. I also started designing many of my cocktail and evening dresses and had them made by a tailor to my specifications, something I still do today.

But most evenings we spent at various friends' homes where we played charades and word games, and Jackie and I dressed in jeans. In fact, I was so casual that sometimes I didn't even wear make-up, which the powers that be at Fox considered a heinous crime. I was reprimanded by Daryl Zanuck's second-in-command Lew Schreiber, and by powerbroking gossip columnist Hedda Hopper, when she wrote that I 'looked like [I] combed my hair with an egg-beater'.

Regular visitors to the house I shared with Arthur included Marlon Brando, who would raid the fridge and eat all my ice cream, and the equally talented James Dean.

One night a group of us were dining at Don the Beachcomber's on Hollywood Boulevard and Jimmy Dean offered to drive me home.

'I've got a new car,' he said, proudly showing me a fierce-looking Porsche. 'It goes really fast.'

Arthur tried to stop me. 'He drives too fast,' he warned. 'He's going to kill himself one day.'

Never one to heed advice, I jumped into the passenger seat and Jimmy went from zero to eighty in about four seconds. By the time we arrived at our destination I had been frightened senseless as he zoomed in and out of traffic. 'Never again,' I said to Arthur.

In late September 1955, I was staying at a hotel in New York on a publicity tour for *The Girl in the Red Velvet Swing* when an ashen-faced Arthur knocked on my door.

'Jimmy's dead, killed in his Porsche,' he said. I was so shattered. I cried all day. I have never liked going in fast cars since then.

*

Jackie was summoned back to London in the early 1960s by our father. Our mother was gravely ill, and Daddy was at his wits' end, finding it hard to cope with her illness and our younger brother Bill, even though he was no trouble at all. (Bill's favourite story recalls a dinner hosted by Arnold and Anne Kopelson – famed producers of *The Fugitive*, *Platoon*, *Murder at 1600* and other blockbusters – when controversial comedian Don Rickles turned to Percy while standing in line for the buffet and said, 'Percy, watch out! That brother of Joan and Jackie Collins is behind you – his name is Bill but don't turn round. No one sees him – they usually keep him locked up in the basement!')

I stayed behind in Hollywood, having to complete my contract, and Jackie put aside her writing ambitions to look after Mummy. It was during that time that she too started acting. I encouraged her acting ambitions in Hollywood, introducing her to casting directors and producers, taking her onto the set and showing her the way around and some of the tricks and tips of the trade. She featured in several British films and TV shows and toured the UK as MC of 'Carroll Levis Discoveries' on the variety stage, which was a sort of early version of *The X Factor*. But Jackie was furious that she was billed as 'Joan's younger sister'.

In the meantime, I went to Barbados to film a movie about interracial tensions called *Island in the Sun*. The stunningly handsome Harry Belafonte immediately showed an interest in me but, even though I was attracted to him, I was cautious about men who oozed sexual power. He had been idolised for years for his fabulous singing and he was also a terrific actor, and a staunch activist. The English crew took bets on whether I would surrender to his cool, sophisticated charms, and they were sorely disappointed when I didn't . . . then. An interracial relationship in the 1950s would have caused a massive scandal and probably hurt my career. But three months later, after attending one of Harry's sold-out shows in Los Angeles, I changed my mind!

In 1960, Jackie married Wallace Austin, a clothes manufacturer who had wooed and quickly won her in spite of the many swains who still clustered around her. By this time I was planning my second marriage, to Warren Beatty. My first marriage at eighteen, to Maxwell Reed, had lasted eighteen months and was utterly intolerable.

Warren and I attended Jackie's lavish celebration at the Grosvenor Hotel in London with my parents and a host of friends and celebrities like Joyce and Lionel Blair, Roger Whittaker, Frankie Howerd and Roger Moore. Mummy looked radiant and I hoped she was getting better. Sadly, that was not the case.

After my seven-year contract with Fox ended, I moved back to England, to Harley House and to my childhood bedroom, alone. Jackie was married and I was starring opposite Bob Hope and Bing Crosby in *Road to Hong Kong*, filmed at Shepperton Studios. My engagement to Warren Beatty had bitten the dust, and I was now dating the West End star of *Stop the World: I Want to Get Off*, the supremely talented Anthony Newley.

It was during this time that Mummy died. Daddy, Bill, Jackie and I were completely shattered. She was the sweetest, kindest, nicest person – a true lady, a loving, caring mother, and everyone who met her adored her. Such was his grief that Daddy refused to speak of her again, flying into a rage if anyone mentioned her name. So we never spoke about her, and our friends weren't allowed to speak of her. It was very strange, as though she never existed. I was involved in a blissful new relationship with Anthony Newley so I buried my head in the sand to try not to think about her as it made me too upset.

Jackie threw herself into married life with zeal, even though Wallace was less than perfect. I thought he was a bit of a psychopath, frankly. During a visit to his clothes showroom he knocked eight months pregnant Jackie to the ground. I lashed out at Wallace, screaming, 'How dare you hit my sister, you bully!' I'm not a physical person but this was the first (and last) time I ever slapped anyone. (Well, except for Linda Evans and Diahann Carroll in *Dynasty*.)

Not surprisingly, their marriage didn't last. He was not a good person and, I suspected, very dependent on substances. I begged Jackie to end it earlier, but she felt she had to stay with him for the sake of their baby daughter. Eventually, she did kick him out, but he continued to torment her until one day, a year after their divorce, he drove into the Black Forest and took an overdose of pills, ending his life.

Jackie had been writing for years at this point, but now she needed to make it work monetarily for her. She had several letters of rejection from publishers, but she kept on writing. 'Never give up' was our motto, I guess unconsciously formed during the war years. We had become even closer after Mummy died in 1962 and while I lived at my father's flat. Bill, now fifteen, had moved in with Jackie, and she became like a second mother to him.

I had fallen hard for Anthony Newley and seeing Jackie with her baby daughter Tracy made me start to pine for children of my own. I decided that Tony would make a great father, and Jackie agreed, for she adored him. Tony loved Jackie too, and had lent her some much-needed cash after Wallace had left her practically bankrupt.

We married in 1963 in New York, with my best friend Cappy Badrutt as my maid of honour, and actor Michael Lipton, Tony's best friend, as his best man. We had a 'quickie' wedding ceremony followed by a 'quickie' champagne breakfast, then Tony rushed back onto the Broadway stage to give his evening performance in *Stop the World*, which had moved there after its successful West End run.

In October of that year, my adorable Tara Cynara Newley was born, and I gave up all thoughts of acting and a film career. Besides, at twenty-nine, I was now considered too old!

Jackie came to stay with us in our palatial New York apartment and we had glorious times with our two little girls, Tracy and Tara. Jackie was now happily married again to the wonderful Oscar Lerman. They had recently been married in our house, with Tara and Tracy as tiny bridesmaids. The Lermans returned to London, where Jackie's first book *The World is Full of Married Men* became an instant bestseller and her shining career took off.

Twenty-two months after Tara, my second child Sacha Newley was born, and I thought my family was perfect and complete. How wrong can a girl be?

In November 1963, when the beloved president of the United States John F. Kennedy was assassinated, Tony decided he didn't want to live in America anymore. So, after a gypsy existence which took us to France, Switzerland and New York, Tony and I finally put down roots (which I desperately wanted to do) in a beautiful house in Beverly Hills. I was thirty-two, with over seventeen years of acting experience and practically non-stop work in movies, TV and theatre, but I had absolutely nothing to show for it except for tons of clothes and a car. No home of my own, no furniture, paintings, or cash and just a few pieces of jewellery, mostly bought by Tony. The kids were starting nursery school and kindergarten, Tony was beavering away writing all day and getting ready for a movie, and I started to miss acting.

Only an actor can know how much the 'smell of the grease-paint and the roar of the crowd' means to them. Even though it's the world's most overcrowded profession, it's in my blood. I discussed going back to work with my sister. 'Go for it,' Jackie insisted. 'You're still young, you've got your whole life ahead of you. You must do what your heart tells you.'

'OK for you,' I grumbled. 'You're writing and getting published. I've no career and it seems my marriage is going nowhere.' Tony was spending most of his time in his office writing. He was an absent father and barely saw his kids or me.

'Then why don't you get an agent?' she replied.

So I did. Since my previous agent, the formidable and famous Sue Mengers, had told me I was 'too old to get parts', I switched over to the equally redoubtable Tom Korman, who had moved away from Sue to open his own company. Tom started to find me guest-starring roles in many popular TV shows like *Batman*, *Star Trek* and *Police Woman*.

Tony and I separated in 1970. I couldn't have lived with him anymore after seeing *Can Hieronymus Merkin Ever Forget Mercy Humppe and Find True Happiness?* – his semi-autobiographical movie. It bleakly told the slightly dramatised story of Tony's life in which he had affairs with every female that crossed his path. I had too much pride to swallow this. I had never been unfaithful but in a tiny revenge I had a fling with a handsome TV actor. It was a pyrrhic victory. I was desperately sad for Tara and Sacha, that they didn't have much of a father figure as Tony was always working.

Jackie was delighted that I was moving back to London. She spent weeks helping me find the right house for my family and was glowing with the ongoing success she had with her novels, plus she and Oscar were expecting their first, and her second, baby.

Back in the UK my career suddenly had a renaissance, for lack of a better word. I was cast in several scary thrillers, and I became 'Queen of the Horror Flicks'. At least it was commercially viable work, and I was getting well paid. I was also working with some big names – Christopher Lee, Peter Cushing, Ralph Bates, Richard Harris, Larry Hagman . . .

'I'm not forgotten, after all,' I said to Jackie as we sat on the spacious terrace of her flat in Roebuck House, watching our four children play games together.

'You never were,' she smiled.

8

Hard Times

Jackie's husband, Oscar Lerman, owned Tramp, the trendy disco-night club in Jermyn Street. Every night, Tramp was packed with the movers and shakers of the early 1970s. Michael Caine, Rod Stewart, Mick Jagger, gorgeous models and all the Beatles were regulars, as were Oscar, Jackie, brother Bill and me. Disco music was in its ascent. Marvin Gaye, Gloria Gaynor, and the Jackson 5 were turning out incredible dancing beats and we all hit the floor every night. Once, I was sitting with my sister and another girlfriend, telling them that I was 'off men', and definitely off marriage for the rest of my life. Jackie suddenly gave me a nudge and said, 'Look! Over there, look!'

I followed her eyeline as in walked a tall, golden-haired young man who, from his elegant confident manner and, dare I say, sense of entitlement, had obviously been educated at Eton.

'That's Theo Fennell, the hot new jeweller,' whispered Jackie.

I studied him for a second then, in my most commanding voice ordered Johnny Guido, the maître d', to 'Bring him to me!'

Theo shuffled over, now not looking so sure of himself and slightly shy. I asked him why he looked so lost and he said Guido had a penchant for playing practical jokes and he wasn't sure if this wasn't one of them. I asked him what had made him fall for it, and he said, 'Guido said if I didn't come and sit with you, I may not get out alive . . .'

We danced and chatted – he was extremely charming and funny and good-looking and basically everything a woman recently divorced would like. However, he told me he was married and that's a line I will never cross again. But he and his wife Louise became very good friends, which we still are today.

After the success of Tramp London, Oscar and co-owner Johnny Gold opened Tramp LA, at which I was a frequent visitor. One night I visited with my PR Jeffrey Lane, when in came Elizabeth Taylor with George Hamilton. They sat next to me. Johnny came to greet us and that's when we realised the entire room was staring at us and the only noise was coming from the music still pumping away. Then we saw a member walk in the door, stop dead in his tracks at this tableau, exclaim 'Only Johnny Gold!' and walk out again. This greatly amused us.

That reminds me of the very first time I ever met Elvis Presley, at a costume party thrown by Rock Hudson in the mid-1950s. I was dressed up as a cowgirl and Elvis was a gorgeous vision in complete white, his outfit accentuated with rhinestones as a sort of glamorous version of the Lone Ranger. We exchanged pleasantries and he was incredibly polite, a real old-school Southern gentleman. We had a photo taken and went our separate ways. I didn't see him again until some years later, in August 1969, when I made Johnny Gold fulfil a promise he had made to my then-husband, Tony Newley.

Johnny promised that if Tony ever played Las Vegas, he would come and see him. 'You're coming to stay with us in Beverly Hills and then we'll go to Vegas,' I told Johnny. I picked him up in a limo the day he arrived, and we all enjoyed the beautiful drive through the dreamscape of the Mojave Desert, ending up in the mock-Roman opulence of Caesar's Palace, where Tony was to play and where we had an endless suite of rooms.

Tony's act was great. He had cleverly studied other Vegas acts and knew just the right combination of strutting his stuff and connecting with the audience. Johnny and I had a wonderful time. Every night we went to see a different show and, one particular evening, I announced, 'Great news, we're going to see Elvis tonight.' Johnny was reluctant as he wasn't a great fan, preferring the Stones or the Beatles.

'Oh, come on. We're going. Stop being a boring old fart,' I insisted.

I dragged Johnny to see the show and he quickly changed his mind, because Elvis was utterly fantastic. It wasn't just a performance: it was the magical experience of being in the same room as a consummate performer who, in a subtly astute manner, managed to take the mickey out of himself and still be worshipped. I went crazy with the rest of the audience, who were standing on the tables and hollering for more.

Sadly, only a few years later, when I went to see Elvis with Ron Kass, it was so different. Elvis at forty was pale and wan, puffy-faced and puffy-bodied. Although he still had energy, and the fans whooped and cheered, and girls threw their knickers at him, I realised his heart wasn't in it anymore. Two years later, I heard the tragic news that Elvis had 'left the building'. He was only forty-two. Gone, but certainly not forgotten. I only wish I could find that photo of us together from the fifties somewhere!

Jackie was brilliant at staying up until 1 or 2 a.m. and still getting the kids up for breakfast and school, then writing all day, her stories no doubt inspired by her nights at Tramp! At teatime she would often pick up my kids too as I was now the sole breadwinner and working hard on TV shows and movies, which often kept me away from home for 12–16 hours a day.

During this time in my life, I met a new man, American

producer Ron Kass, who was president of The Beatles' company, Apple Records.

Ron and I were married when The Beatles broke up, and Ron went on to head Warner Brothers Records UK. I remember going up to the roof at Abbey Road in 1969 for their last concert, when they played 'Get Back', but leaving before I succumbed to a contact high from all the marijuana being smoked. Besides, I had to pick up the children from school. But my career seemed to be on an upwards swing, with several TV and movie roles. My beautiful daughter Katyana Kass was born in London shortly thereafter, and Ron and I bought a lovely summer house in Marbella for holidays with our six children (Ron had three from his previous marriage), all under the age of twelve! Jackie's tribe and our tribe would often spend Easter and the summer holidays together in Marbella and France, and it was an extremely happy time. Everything seemed to be going swimmingly in my life, career and marriage. Until Denis Healey came to power in the Treasury, promising to squeeze the rich 'until the pips squeak'!

Ron insisted we all move back to the United States, where he had signed on for yet another job as president of Sagittarius, a movie company established by Edgar Bronfman, scion of the Seagram's fortune. Ron became Edgar's rock, holding his hand through the incredible ordeal of having his eldest son kidnapped. Edgar was Katy's godfather, and he asked us to throw his second son, Edgar Jr's twenty-first birthday party at our house in LA. Not only did I have to organise and invite all the high and mighty of show business, but, despite assurances that Edgar would 'foot the bill', I also had to advance the money for the party from my personal account. The party was an immense success, with the likes of Dionne Warwick, Kirk Douglas, director Dick Donner, Rod and Alana Stewart and many others all at the height of their power and fame.

On the day after the party, basking in my laurels as congratulations and flowers arrived, Ron walked into our bedroom and announced sadly, 'Edgar's fired me.' I couldn't believe it. After weeks of preparation, after years of friendship and business partnership, after schlepping our family across the Atlantic, his boss had fired him only a few months after Ron had taken the job. I don't think Ron ever fully recovered from the trauma, pain, and shock that Edgar Bronfman caused him. Certainly, this became a turning point in our up-to-now happy marriage.

We started by selling the Beverly Hills house and downsizing to a smaller one and living off the proceeds, but that wasn't going to last indefinitely. Plus, it wouldn't be fair to the children to move them all over Los Angeles making them change schools and find new friends, so the prospects of downsizing indefinitely were limited.

So, now it was time for me to once again take on the mantle of being the sole breadwinner. I decided to take any and all work that would come my way – guest roles in *Starsky & Hutch* and *Baretta*, and any offers that might come through the door. But despite my appearances, I had lost my profile after years away from the Hollywood circuit. 'Joan who?' was the phrase I most heard during my rounds of the casting directors' and producers' offices.

When the parts dried up, I even ended up at the unemployment office to collect the benefits that Samantha Eggar told me I was due after decades of paying taxes. As I handed in my application to the teller, she exclaimed, 'Joan Collins??? Didn't you used to be her??'

'I still am,' I replied coolly.

Well, at least she recognised me.

I've always felt I was born to be a gypsy, but in the 1970s life became one long plane ride. For the next decade, I flew back and forth between California and London, wherever my career took me. It was great to be in California because Jackie had moved there with Oscar and her three children, and she was churning out bestselling novels, one after the other. And I always felt equally at home in London or LA.

But I was feeling massively anxious about our finances. I suggested to Jackie that her novel *The Stud*, set against the backdrop of the disco world of the mid to late 1970s, would make a wonderful screenplay. 'It's set in a disco owned by a glamorous rich socialite who is sexually liberated, it has lots of disco music – wouldn't I be perfect to play Fontaine?'

'Well, I'll give you the rights and then you can see if you can get it made,' she said airily. 'I'll even write you a script.'

I was long established in the film industry so I still had many well-known and powerful friends. So much so that some celebs asked me to throw parties for them so they could guarantee they would be star-studded. I could have been a Dolly Levi!

When *Saturday Night Fever* came out, the industry wanted to piggyback on its projected draw. I was promoting the ghastly *Empire of the Ants* at a lunch in Cannes when I met George Walker, a distributor of B-flicks in England. I gave him my pitch, which had been rejected by everyone else I'd approached, and George fell in love with Jackie's script. Within four months we were shooting *The Stud* at Tramp and on location.

As a producer, George Walker was famous for yelling 'Fuck creativity – that doesn't sell. Tits and ass do!' At a meeting with Jackie, Oscar and Ron, he insisted I do a scene where I cavort, topless, on a swing over a swimming pool. I did not want to do this scene unless I wore a bathing suit or some sort of covering, but he was horribly insistent. 'You've gotta do it. It's in her book,' he barked.

'I have three children – it's too embarrassing,' I retorted

helplessly, looking to Jackie, Oscar and my husband for support, which was not forthcoming. 'The kids will hate me.'

'Glenda Jackson's done nudity, Jane Fonda . . . and even Diane Keaton in *Goodbar*,' Ron replied.

'They don't have kids,' I retorted.

After several days of fierce arguments with all of them, I agreed, reluctantly, to do the nude scene, but I had to get drunk first. The whole thing was a blur, but the film was a huge success and I garnered a great deal of attention, not least because a woman in her forties was not supposed to look that good or have sex appeal. However, despite the column inches and the apparent box office success, receipts into our account were not forthcoming and to this day I have never understood why. Some kind of convoluted book-keeping, I believe. In the wake of its success, I made another little gem from Jackie's pen – *The Bitch*, a sequel to *The Stud*. I can't remember much about the movie except that I wore a corset, black suspenders and had to seduce the chauffeur. I played opposite an unknown Italian actor who insisted on being naked under the bed covers for one scene. I hated him doing this so I wore jeans and long socks. After my wardrobe assistant covered me up, she whispered, 'I've seen bigger things crawl out of cabbages.' And that was the beginning and the end of *The Bitch*.

9

Stamping My Stilettos

I adore acting, it has always been my number one passion. I've been fortunate enough to have had a theatrical and film career that has spanned more than seven decades which, if I may brag, is one of the longest careers of any British or American actor or actress. I consider myself a working actress now, with my fair share of 'resting days'. I believe that an actor is like a library book on a shelf, waiting for the world to take interest in you again and 'check you out'. Like miniskirts or low-rise jeans, you can be 'flavour of the month' for a while and then quietly disappear again. The key to survival in this business is longevity and patience!

There's absolutely no question that the popular and iconic series of *Dynasty* changed my life. I was on a holiday in Spain when I received a phone call from Tom Korman, my LA agent.

'Do you know what *Dynasty* is?' he asked.

'A Chinese restaurant?' I replied.

He sighed, 'It's Aaron Spelling's new TV show. His answer to *Dallas*. It's been on air for a season, but the ratings keep dropping and they've written in this mysterious new character called Alexis, hoping to pep it up.'

'Love the name. Can I think about it?' All my thoughts were with Katy at this time, in the aftermath of her accident.

'I'll fax you a couple of scenes,' he said.

'How long is the gig?'

'Maybe one season,' he replied. 'Call me tomorrow. ABC has got to know fast.'

LA sunshine and a steady pay cheque were strong incentives to make the move. I read the scenes and loved them, and within two weeks our whole family was back in LA, in a rented apartment in Century City, and I started shooting the second season of *Dynasty* just down the road at my old stomping ground – Twentieth Century-Fox Studios.

It was unbelievable how quickly Alexis Carrington took America by storm. Within two weeks of the premiere episode of season two airing, the ratings zoomed and by January 1982 it was rated as one of the top ten most popular shows in the US. I was inundated with interview requests and cover shoots and soon I became the world's favourite 'bitch'.

Although I was initially signed to the ailing TV show for just a season, I had a sneaky feeling that *Dynasty* could be a game changer for me. Consequently, I stamped my stilettos right at the beginning to forge the way to create Alexis Carrington and make her an unforgettable character.

In my first scene on the stand, being cross-questioned by the prosecutor, played by the great actor Brian Dennehy, the entire *Dynasty* clan sat in the courtroom looking me up and down. I knew they were all commenting sotto voce to each other about my face, my figure, my acting and my attitude, so as I sat in the witness box I was glad I had totally memorised the fifteen pages of dialogue and understood the backstory.

I caught the eye of Blake Carrington (John Forsythe), who gave me a grim smile. I wondered whether he was acting or if he hadn't enjoyed his breakfast, but I hoped the former as I was directing hate-filled looks his way, as Alexis despised Blake. Krystal Carrington (Linda Evans) smiled at me sweetly but then

I recalled what her ex-husband, John Derek, had said about her: 'Every time I see Linda she smiles at me as if I were the only person in the world she wanted to see. Then one day I realised she smiled at everyone that way.'

My 'children' – Steven (Al Corley) and Fallon (Pamela Sue Martin) – stared at me ambiguously. The friendliest face of all in the spectator section was Jeff Colby (John James), who gave me a secret wink and 'thumbs up'. John and I actually became the best of friends during the nine years of shooting and still keep in touch.

During Blake's trial for manslaughter, I had to testify that he fought with my lover, Ted Dinard, who subsequently died. I put plenty of sugar-coated venom into my speeches about Blake and I could see that the cast and director seemed intrigued.

The following day, Nolan Miller, the designer of the fabulous *Dynasty* duds, told me that when he, Aaron and several suits from ABC watched the first day's dailies, everyone gasped when I took off my sunglasses and raised the veil.

'Put a lot of hats on that gal,' Aaron instructed Nolan, 'She looks great in hats.'

I wore so many different outfits in *Dynasty*, it's hard to pick out any particular favourite. However, my least favourite was the cheap polyester black and white dress made for me for the scene where Krystle pushes Alexis into the lily pond. Because the director didn't know how many takes would be required, wardrobe made four identical frocks – each more hideous than the last. It was very unusual to see these limp rags hanging in my dressing room, as the quality of my costumes had always been first-rate. But I guess Aaron Spelling had put them on an austerity kick, which he frequently did. Less flowers! Less caviar! Let's have smoked salmon instead.

As the dress material was so cheap and the wardrobe department hastily slung each dress into the dryer after each take, naturally all the polyester garments shrank. They came out two sizes smaller and shrivelled. After four takes we ran out of fresh dresses, so for the close-ups in the pool I had to squeeze myself into a frock that would fit an eight-year-old.

By the way, although I always say I don't do stunts, when I fell into that pool and my hat came off, that was me, not a double! Check it out on YouTube!

The costumes were all created by the talented and super-elegant Nolan Miller. I first met him when I had my initial fitting for *Dynasty*. This tall, handsome man stood watching me while I was being fitted for the identical suit and hat that another actress had worn in the final episode of *Dynasty*'s first season. The studio had wanted Elizabeth Taylor or Sophia Loren to play the ex-wife of Blake Carrington. Those stars had vacillated and asked for tons of money. But Aaron Spelling, who I had known since the 1950s when he was married to Carolyn Jones (who played my best friend in *The Opposite Sex*), wanted little me! And he finally got his way after a fight with the network, who still didn't want me.

With the exception of Alexis's first outfit – a monochrome suit and big hat when she enters the courtroom to take the stand and condemn her ex-husband Blake Carrington – my outfits became more and more stylish, yet often bizarrely over the top. The wardrobe department initially presented me with a choice of little Chanel-type skirt suits, tweed jackets, pastel slacks, and blouses with pussycat bows. I eschewed them all, much to the dismay of 'wardrobe', and asked if it was possible to have modern haute couture outfits.

'Alexis is an international jet-setter,' I told them. 'She can't wear clothes that look like they came from Bloomingdale's. She's been living in Paris, New York, Acapulco, the South of France, so her personal style must reflect an elegant lifestyle.'

'But we can't get haute couture in Hollywood,' sniffed the first lady of the wardrobe department.

'Yes, we can,' said a cultured voice, and into the changing room stepped designer-to-the-stars Nolan Miller, a 6' 3" vision in a perfectly tailored suit, a crisp pink shirt and a Charvet tie. And that was the beginning of a beautiful friendship and a fabulous collaboration with that gorgeous man.

I had noticed that the actresses who played Krystle and Fallon were of the gabardine slacks, silk shirts, blow-dried hair type. 'That's not Alexis,' I told Nolan. 'I want her to have big hair, big sleeves, and big bling! After being banned by Blake from ever seeing her two children again, the first Mrs Carrington has been living the jet-set lifestyle for the past sixteen years, so we must reflect that in her clothes,' I said.

'Well, Southern California is a long way from the ateliers and haute couture houses of Paris,' said Nolan, 'But we can design them for her.' I was thrilled to realise the great Nolan Miller shared my views and we began feverishly collaborating on what would come to be known as 'The Alexis Look'.

Nolan was a close friend of Aaron Spelling and his co-producer Douglas Cramer. He had been brought on board – like me – to spice up the second season of *Dynasty*, which needed a kick up the backside. Nolan often quoted Barbara Stanwyck, who he adored for her pithy comments about life and Holly-wood. Stanwyck and Lana Turner had once had a confrontation over their affairs with Nolan, which ended when Barbara smirk-ingly looked Lana over and said, 'You know what your problem is, Lana? There's no such thing as a seventy-year-old sex symbol. It's time to get over yourself!'

Encouraged by Cramer, who was gay, Nolan was tasked

with making Alexis Carrington a world-class fashion icon. He grasped this opportunity with both hands, and, with my input and support, he proceeded to create the most stunning wardrobe for me since Bob Mackie famously transformed Cher in *The Sonny and Cher Show*. And how we loved doing it.

We studied *Vogue* and *Harper's Bazaar* and every outfit worn by Princess Diana, then Queen of the Tabloids, blatantly copying many of them. Of course the other actresses followed suit, and eventually it would be hard to tell the difference between Stephanie Beacham as Sable, Kate O'Mara as Caress, and even Diahann Carroll as Dominique, who all craved the same look. Diahann loved being referred to as 'The first black bitch on TV', with furs and turbans sometimes even more OTT than those worn by Alexis.

In the 1980s, Nolan commanded a magnificent team of cutters, seamstresses, hand-beaders and embroiderers, many of whom had worked in the Hollywood film studios since the 1940s, and boy, were they experts in their craft! They could run up an outfit for Alexis practically overnight, and after a few weeks they often had to do so without so much as a fitting. Since new scenes kept on being written for me, Nolan often went over-budget and had to go cap in hand to the producers for more money. Aaron would usually say, 'Hey buddy, that's OK. I want Alexis to be the envy of every woman and look fabulous.' As it turned out, by the end of season two the team had succeeded.

Nolan was as obsessed with old films and glamorous movie stars as I was, so we clicked as co-conspirators in designing for Alexis. If we couldn't find something suitable, Nolan would design it, so the outfits became even more stylish, outré, and some would say camp. But I loved these clothes, and I loved Nolan, and over the years he became so like my 'other brother' that it would sometimes annoy my real brother Bill.

During one of our early fittings, Nolan was kneeling pinning my hem when an assistant rushed in and whispered something in his ear. Nolan looked flustered and, apologising to me, said, 'I have to go, right now.'

'Why?' I asked.

'It's Sandra. She's ovulating. I've got to go and fuck her. I guess I'll just have to lash it to a toothbrush!'

'That's a bit rude,' I coughed, but I couldn't stop laughing at this reference to his well-known bisexuality. Although linked to affairs with Barbara Stanwyck, Lana Turner and Joan Crawford, Nolan liked to 'bat for the other team'. He also loved giving parties – the more lavish the better. On one notable event in his lovely mansion on Whittier Drive, it was covered in roses and gardenias from top to toe, silver urns of caviar adorned each of the twenty tables, and at each table a major star commanded. I chatted to Elizabeth Taylor, who adored caviar as much as I did and was eating it with a mother-of-pearl spoon, directly from the urn. We chatted about a mutual friend who she had been dating.

'Why won't you do my show?' Barbara Stanwyck demanded as I stopped at her table. She was a beautiful but intimidating presence, having appeared in countless movies and won multiple awards over her sixty-year career. She was a total icon, but faced with money problems she was now starring in *The Colbys*, the rival show to *Dynasty*. I was embarrassed to be put on the spot, but flattered that she cared.

'Miss Stanwyck . . . I . . .' I started.

'Oh, please call me Missy,' she smiled.

'OK,' I said, falteringly at first. 'Well, I feel that the *Colby* show will take a lot of interest and many of the fans away from *Dynasty*, and I don't want to do that. They have already got John James, John Forsythe, Linda Evans and several others, but they're not gonna get me. I'm loyal to *Dynasty*.'

'I admire your loyalty,' she smiled. 'It's rare in this town.'

'Don't I know it,' I replied, relieved.

A massive presence who was sitting at 'Missy's' table called out to me, 'Well, I'm gonna do your show, kid, if you're not gonna do ours.'

'You are?' I gulped, as 'Moses' himself stood up to his full 6' 5" to shake my hand in his great paw.

'He certainly is,' beamed Aaron Spelling from the next table.

'If the mountain won't come to Muhammad, Muhammad will come to the mountain,' boomed Charlton Heston, king of kings. 'And I'm delighted to support you, kid, I love your show.' And so he did! What an epic day that was! I hadn't been so intimidated since my early days at Gene Kelly's house.

In readiness for God's arrival, a giant director's chair was delivered to the set. It was twice the size of a normal one. It had a table, a place for scripts, another section for drinks and on the back Charlton Heston's name was inscribed.

I passed the table of Lana Turner, gorgeous in pale-pink chiffon, deeply tanned and in conversation with my pal George Hamilton. 'I think I may also be joining *Dynasty*,' George whispered.

'That would be great,' I said. I adored George, who I'd known since he first came to Hollywood soon after me. He was nineteen and insisted on driving me around proudly in his vintage Rolls.

Then a cocky little guy patted me on the bottom (so politically incorrect these days) and said, 'Hey, didn't we used to be married?'

I looked down to see a tiny, wrinkled Mickey Rooney, the biggest box office star of the 1940s in the Andy Hardy pictures. He had also famously been through four or five marriages.

'Did we?' he grinned, 'Did we . . . do it?'

'Do what?' I asked.

'Get married,' he grinned.

'No, we did *not*,' I replied frostily.

I had to admire the gall of this five-foot individual, who apparently started in films at a very early age. I asked him if it was true.

'You bet,' he said proudly. 'The pic was called *Ermine and Orchids* and I was five years old. They stuck a moustache on my lip and a cigar in my mouth and everyone called me a midget!' He guffawed with laughter.

'You can't say midget now, Mr Rooney,' I said.

'But it's the truth,' he grinned. 'Now, are you sure we never even got it on?'

I laughed at his moxie and walked over to Liza Minnelli, who held court at her table, surrounded by a host of young gay men.

'Baby!' she yelled – she called everyone baby even though she was younger than most people – 'Come and sit down, baby! I love you!'

She patted her black Halston-clad lap, but I laughingly declined. I hugged her and went over to Nolan Miller, who was standing at the bar talking to his young acolyte Mark Zunino.

'This is the most fabulous party I've ever been to,' I gushed.

'Better than Jack Warner's or Darryl Zanuck's?' he asked.

'Just as good as,' I said, and it certainly was.

Nolan gave so many parties and he was so profligate and generous that when he divorced Sandra a few years later, he had to sell the gorgeous Whittier Drive house and many of the beautiful antiques in it. But he was extremely happy doing *Dynasty*. We attended loads of events together for which he always designed a spectacular dress for me.

The Carousel Ball was a biannual event thrown by the legendary Barbara Davis, widow of Marvin Davis. As we stood at the bar checking everyone out, Nolan talked about how Marvin had bought Twentieth Century-Fox and all the surrounding acres of land and turned it into a shopping mall and a 'mini-city' with hotels, skyscrapers and apartment buildings, as it still is today. Nolan recounted sadly how distressed he was when he saw props and costumes from Twentieth Century-Fox movies thrown into a skip in the lot, only to be burned in the incinerators.

'I tried to save some of the costumes,' he said. 'I saw a show-girl outfit with Betty Grable's name on the label and a hat with fake fruit and feathers that said Carmen Miranda and I pulled them out. It was shocking how callous the Fox bosses were to throw away thousands and thousands of iconic, one-of-a-kind pieces from their movies and not save them for posterity or a museum.'

I agreed, as Nolan went on: 'Debbie Reynolds was so upset when she heard about this. She was trying to create a Holly-wood Museum, but sadly the top people in Hollywood wouldn't support it. No sense of history – they just destroyed it all. Thank God we have the films to remember things by.'

'And this dress,' I said. I was wearing a white beaded gown Nolan had copied from one that Bette Davis had worn in *Now Voyager*.

'It was all so stylish then,' he said mournfully, 'Hollywood sure has changed.'

We went back inside to join the jolly group at our table, my sister Jackie, her fiancé Frank Calcagnini, George and Jolene Schlatter and George Hamilton, in the brilliantly decorated Hilton Hotel. Then emcee Jay Leno came on to introduce a new young singer called Beyoncé.

'I think this gal has a future,' quipped Nolan.

I was devastated when Nolan died, even though he had been ill for some time.

He spent his final years in the Motion Picture County Home, a charity hospice for actors and industry folk.

'He does nothing all day but stare at the ceiling,' said Mark Zunino sadly. 'He won't even play the CDs or videos you brought him. I think he wants to die.'

On his death in 2012, Nolan was immediately cremated. Shortly after, Mark and his business partner Rene Horsch came to visit us in Ramatuelle, bringing with them Nolan's ashes in a beautiful urn.

'He wanted them scattered in the Venice canals,' said Mark. 'But they refused to let us do that, so we brought him here. Maybe we can put him in the Mediterranean.'

'Oh, I think it's illegal here too,' I said.

The following week, we all took a day trip on our friends Joyce and Simon Reubens' lovely boat. I noticed Rene had brought a very heavy knapsack with him. I asked what was in it, and he whispered, 'Nolan's ashes. I thought we could scatter them off the back of the boat . . .'

'You've got to be kidding,' I hissed. 'First of all, the environmental police are all over the bay and will come down on you the moment they see anything being thrown overboard and, secondly, the wind could scatter his ashes all over the deck and onto our lunch!'

Rene said despairingly, 'I just don't know what to do with them!'

'I have an idea,' I said. 'Come to lunch tomorrow.'

The following day the boys arrived with a couple of other friends and the urn. After lunch, we had a little funeral ceremony in the rose garden in our villa, then Nolan's ashes were buried in the warm Provençal soil. Whenever I pass our rose garden, I think of my dear friend and almost brother who died much too soon but left a legacy of gorgeous and beautiful clothes.

*

I was able to make my mark on the show once again in season four when Aaron Spelling called me in my dressing room one day.

'We've got three guys to play your next husband and I want you to meet them.'

'Oh! You mean I get to choose?'

'Of course you do,' said Aaron. 'You're going to be spending a lot of time with him. You'll marry him eventually, but you'll have some ups and downs along the way.'

'I just hope he's more sympathetic than Blake . . .' Blake, played by John Forsythe, was the family patriarch and Alexis's first husband, and they were constantly at each other's throats.

'I'll bring the new actors onto set tomorrow morning,' said Aaron.

So, the next morning, five youngish actors slunk onto the set accompanied by an assistant director, and I was told to have a brief conversation with each of them. The first one seemed like a dolt, the second one was too short, the third one I don't even remember, the fourth was Jon Erik Hexum, who I went on to co-star with on *The Making of an American Model*, and who I rather liked – but not as much as the fifth one, who I thought was mind-bogglingly handsome.

'Hi, I'm Mike Nader.' He smiled a charming lopsided smile and I noticed he had a tiny scar above his lip, which made him even more attractive. He was tall, but not too tall, he had black hair, but not too much of it, and he had a *machismo* that was what I thought would blend well with Alexis's feisty temperament.

Aaron called me after lunch. 'What did you think?'

'Well, Nader is head and shoulders above the others.'

'Great,' said Aaron, 'I was hoping you'd say so.'

Two weeks later, I worked with Michael for the first time.

Although he was visibly nervous, he managed to control it enough to be fascinating in our first scene together.

From the moment Dex first saw Alexis, he was in love with her. When we were filming the first scene, the door to Alexis's office was flung open and he entered, as Alexis demanded, 'What are you doing here? Who are you?'

'I'm Farnsworth Dexter,' he said, 'call me Dex.'

'I'd still want to know why you're here,' Alexis replied.

Michael advanced towards me provocatively as we played our scene, which I thought went really well, as we seemed equally matched. Then, at the end, he plunked a kiss on my lips which was not in script and took me by surprise. He winked and sauntered off the set.

Aaron called me that night. 'You think he's good enough for Alexis to marry?'

'I think he's great!' I said. 'I think he's one of the best-looking men I've seen in a long time and he's a very good actor. I think that our female fans are going to absolutely love him. I just hope you're giving us some juicy scenes together.'

'Just you wait,' said Aaron.

Within a couple of weeks, Dex relentlessly pursued Alexis and, foolishly, she did not give in. I never understood why it took so long for Alexis to fall head over heels for him. He was so charming and attractive, it just didn't seem right that she constantly rejected him. But such is the magic of soap operas. Once they have a fascinating plot point that will make viewers tune in, they will milk it for all it's worth!

This cat-and-mouse game between Dex and Alexis continued for almost the rest of the season until she finally relents, and we have an amazing love scene. However, Michael got carried away by the passion. He kissed me so forcefully that he bit my lip and blood was smudged on both our chins.

'You bit me. It's blood!' I wailed.

'It's just lipstick,' he laughed nervously.

'Doesn't taste like any brand I wear,' I retorted, running to my trailer to apply astringent.

I really liked Michael. He was amusing and we had an easy off-set relationship. He had a good sense of humour. One April Fool's Day, Michael and I were rehearsing yet another passionate love scene. Dex comes close to Alexis who is wearing a gorgeous silk dressing gown and suggests, smoothly and sexily, 'Alexis, aren't you going to open your surprise present?'

Alexis is meant to slide the dressing gown off his shoulder equally smoothly and sexily, gazing seductively into his eyes until his naked chest is revealed – but Michael was wearing a white Wonderbra! I couldn't stop laughing and flubbed my next line, 'Look here, Dex, I'm a *very* busy man.' The crew got more than they hoped for!

Despite some ribbing from several of the cast and crew that our relationship was more than friendship, Michael was married and I was married, so it was purely platonic. However, on the set it sizzled! I loved our scenes in the bath together where I would be covered in soapsuds protecting the bare necessities. When the director yelled, 'Cut!', Michael would try to scrape the suds off me, but it was all done in good fun.

Michael once said, 'Joan and I are kindred spirits. There was chemistry between us when I auditioned, and when we talked I discovered what it was – we were both driven to succeed.' He added, 'If the relationship between Joan and me [hadn't been] easy, I would have been written out of the show a long time ago.'

I once asked him how he got the facial scar, which reminded me of one that Gene Kelly also had, and he told me that he was hit by a drunk driver when he was six years old. He also talked about his uncle, who was a famous actor in the 1950s called George Nader. During the second series of *Dynasty*, he admitted to having a drug problem. I knew he drank heavily, but since all the English actors on the show were fond of the bottle, we didn't think it was a problem. Regardless, he was always on time, knew his lines and was a consummate professional.

Finally, Alexis and Dex were married in 1984 on the show and we had a couple of seasons more or less happy. But we were always sparring with each other, as Alexis would never let any man get the better of her, and he wouldn't let any person of whatever sex get the better of him. Then, a shocking thing happened: Dex had an affair with Alexis's daughter Amanda (played by Catherine Oxenberg). Naturally, Amanda and Dexter had sex because they were trapped in a hut by a blizzard in New Mexico, but Amanda always had her sights set on vengefully taking Dex away from Alexis. I was quite upset about this as I thought it would destroy our on-set love affair, but Aaron was adamant that this would bring in more viewers.

'We've already got tons of viewers, and they love the two of them together!' I pleaded, but my words fell on deaf ears.

Michael and I both commiserated with each other, but I was given a vast selection of lovers too: tennis players, oligarchs, kings, detectives and, finally, the worst of all, a mysterious woodsman (at least, he was always chopping up trees – I have no idea what else he did). This was Sean Rowan, played by unknown actor James Healey. I thought he was a most unpleasant actor. It was hard for me to profess passionate love for this oaf, who boasted of being close friends with Sir Laurence Olivier. It was even harder to look ecstatic when Alexis married Sean. After the end of season eight, the producers finally sensed that Mr Rowan's popularity with the fans was at a low ebb, who were all furious, as was I, that Alexis had lovingly given full control of her massive empire and fortune to the dastardly Sean – I mean, why? I yelled at the writers about this idiotic twist in the tale, but they did not care and, soon, neither did the viewers. So, with great fanfare they had Sean Rowan killed and finally allowed Dex and Alexis to reconcile at the beginning of series nine.

But sadly, the end was nigh for those star-crossed lovers. Dex, in his foolish one-night fling with Alexis's arch enemy Sable, had impregnated her, thereby dooming the Alexis/Dex relationship. But I felt *Dynasty* was doomed too by now, with its ridiculous plot lines. ABC pulled the plug on the show at the end of season nine, right at the moment where Sable reveals the bastard issue, whereupon Dex and Michael get into a fight, break the banister of the second floor stairs, causing Dex to fall down one flight – along with Alexis, who happened to be next to him, much to the fury of the millions of fans who were left with this ludicrous cliff-hanger. Did they die in a Romeo and Juliet embrace, or simply twist an ankle?

And so ended the romance that kept viewers glued to their TV sets every Wednesday for several years. The last time I saw Michael, Percy and I were on a New York rooftop celebrating New Year's Eve with some friends. Michael looked frail and had lost his hair, but he still had that spark and charm. Of all my *Dynasty* husbands, he was by far and away the best-looking, the best actor and the most charming, and I was extremely happy to have married him. (Sorry, Percy!)

I was really sad when Michael Nader died far too young in 2021.

10

Ripped Off

'The Alexis Look' took off worldwide, and suddenly I found myself on every magazine cover, from *Harper's Bazaar* to the *National Enquirer*. And how that supermarket rag loved to gossip about me! Doug Cramer made sure the tabloids couldn't tell the difference between Alexis Carrington Colby and Joan Henrietta Collins by inventing juicy stories to leak to the press. And they printed them! Much of what was written about me was quite hurtful, and a lot of it was totally fabricated, but the public ate it up and developed a love/hate relationship with my character, which spilled over onto me. This, of course, was quite upsetting. I would read that I was having multiple affairs. If I went out with my gay agent I'd be 'in a relationship' with him. If I spilled a glass of wine in a restaurant, I'd be accused of throwing it in a waiter's face because he had served the wrong vintage. And, worst of all, they sometimes accused me of being a bad mother, which is about the most terrible thing you can say about a woman who has children, particularly if she is the breadwinner of the family. The life of a mother who is also a working actress is one of being a pawn on set, where your time is accountable to others.

But whatever was said about, or gossiped about, or rumoured about Alexis, the fact remains that I adored the character. I loved playing Alexis and, even though she often did dastardly deeds, as an actress I could always find a way to understand her reasons. When the great actor Laurence Olivier couldn't get to grips with his character, Richard III, the distinguished director Tyrone Guthrie told him, 'My dear boy, if you don't find things to like and admire about the role you are playing you will never be believable. You must learn to love that person, as you would love yourself.' Great words of advice, and ones I try to live by when I act.

Despite the adulation, when *Dynasty* finally ended I was somewhat relieved. It had been a long slog. Nine years of rising at 6 a.m. and working twelve- and fourteen-hour days practically every day, not to mention every weekend being taken up with fittings, interviews and photo shoots. Now I was ready to fulfil my life's dream: to appear again on the West End stage in my favourite play, *Private Lives*. I would leave Alexis behind forever.

But I never could. The character haunted me – and many other people, too. Even today I am remembered by middle-aged mums and dads who tell me, 'Ooh, I watched you every week when I was little and wanted to be like you when I grew up'! Even some millennials have caught the *Dynasty* bug and are enthralled by the glamour and elegance of that bygone era of the 1980s.

I only wish I had some of Alexis's grit, determination and bravado in my own character. If I had, I wouldn't have been so stupid as to marry one man who was obviously a sociopath and a user, nor to stay in relationships that had worn themselves out. Leaving school at fifteen to go to RADA and having attended at least ten schools because of being moved around England as an evacuee during the war, my education had been sketchy, to say the least. Arithmetic, algebra, and anything financial was beyond my comprehension, but I was tops in grammar, liter-ature, and writing. (I wonder if they still teach those subjects in school these days?) In my career I was ripped off financially several times by business people I trusted. Foolish girl. Alexis trusted no one. Clever girl.

When I look back at the list of my financial disasters, it is quite alarming, and what happened to me is quite shocking. I can only attribute my mistakes to naivete, work strain and ignorance of the dubious business connections of my advisers. But clever Alexis would never in a million years have allowed her counsellors to take such control of her life.

At the age of twenty, and on the advice of Twentieth Century-Fox, I entrusted all my money and business dealings to a financial guru who I will refer to only by his initials, E.B. Each month I met with him and signed cheques, but I *never* checked my bank balance. What an idiot I was. This man was entrusted to invest my earnings wisely but I never checked up on the money. I was told it was all 'going well' and I would eventually have a pot of gold. Ha! At the end of my contracted seven years, I asked E.B. if I could buy a small house for $50,000. He informed me that, except for a few thousand, all the money was gone.

'But how? Why?' I asked. 'I've always been reasonably frugal.'

'All those trips to London and Acapulco. All your clothes, and that Thunderbird you drive – and of course taxes,' he replied smoothly. It sounded fishy, but what could I do?

So, having made hundreds of thousands of dollars in my twenties, it had all been spent by my 'advisers' and was gone with the wind by age twenty-eight.

I felt I had been ripped off, which of course I had, thanks to dodgy investments and sharks taking advantage of my naivety. Alexis would never have allowed that to happen. Nor would she have let some smooth-talking lawyer convince her at the end of *Dynasty* that the show would never go into syndication.

'Serials never do,' he lied to me. 'People aren't interested in re-runs, so residuals would be paltry. Take the buyout – the entire cast already agreed. You're the hold-out and they're starting to resent you for it.' So, reluctantly, I did, as I had no choice.

Alexis would have fought like a tiger to get her fair share of the proceeds from *Dynasty*, little caring that John Forsythe, Linda Evans and the rest of the cast had meekly accepted this edict. She would have taken it to court – and won! And had she done the same, Joan Collins would today be massively rich from the billions of dollars that *Dynasty* has made in syndication, instead of still being a working actress. But don't get me wrong, I still love working.

Jackie loved the Alexis character as she said it was very similar to her favourite 'kick-ass' heroine Lucky Santangelo. In 1983 I won a Golden Globe for Best Actress in a TV show and Jackie's latest novel was Number 1 on the *New York Times* bestseller list. We sat in her living room, eating popcorn surrounded by our children, and watched a tape of a *French & Saunders* sketch that a friend had sent us from England. Jennifer Saunders played me, complete with massive hair, huge earrings and gargantuan shoulder pads and Dawn French played Jackie, pulsating in animal prints and cats-eye sunglasses. We watched transfixed as the two comediennes ruthlessly satirised our perceived public personas and laughed out loud when both looked at the camera sultrily and announced, 'For we are those lucky bitches.'

'I guess we made it, sis,' said Jackie.

'I guess we did,' I laughed. 'And against all odds!'

II

An Affair of the Heart

I first set eyes on Percy Gibson in April 2000 in New York City.

I was doing a book signing at Rizzoli's, the high-end bookstore, before going to San Francisco to start a short tour of the two-handed play, *Love Letters*. Although I was only fifteen minutes late, I was disappointed to learn that Paul Newman and Joanne Woodward, two of my oldest friends, had popped in at six on the dot. Since the Newmans were not only show business royalty but also adorably nice – 'We were here, where were you?' wrote Paul – I was sad to have missed them. After half an hour of signing, Jeffrey Lane, my press agent, said there were two young men from the *Love Letters* company who wanted to meet me. In the corner, next to the psychology section, stood two good-looking guys in their thirties. I greeted Max Torres, the stage manager, and then shook hands with Percy Gibson.

He was tall, dark-eyed, handsome and well-dressed, with good shoes and shirt, but sporting a rather unfortunate mustard-coloured jacket! I thought he was American, and I also thought that he would be better-looking if he let his dark hair grow a trifle longer as he had almost a crew cut, never my favourite look. But he was extremely attractive and had a wonderfully endearing smile.

I remarked to Max, who looked rather like Matt Damon, 'You look awfully young.'

'How about me?' asked Percy.

'Oh, you'll do,' I smiled.

'Good,' he smiled back endearingly. 'How are you liking your hotel?'

'It's the pits,' I said. 'The bedroom's the size of a dartboard, there's no closet space and no room service either. I can't even order coffee in the morning.'

'I'm so sorry.' Percy seemed genuinely concerned. 'I'd been told you were happy there.'

'We'd better get back to the signing,' interrupted Jeffrey, grabbing my arm hastily and whisking me back to a queue of eager book-buyers.

'Bye, guys, I'll see you in San Francisco,' I waved.

I first laid eyes on Joan Collins in April 2001, at Rizzoli's bookstore in New York City.

She completely ignored me.

She had landed in NY the evening before and been met by her publicist, who took her to her hotel and settled her in after a tiring trip from London. The next day, among various press engagements for her new book, she had a book signing only a few blocks from our office.

'Hey, Percy,' said Max, our stage manager. 'Shall we go meet our star?'

We went into the bookstore and had to elbow our way among the throng, finding an oasis of calm towards the back, and we waited until the tumult receded, which took well over an hour. I entertained myself watching her greeting friends and attending to fans, very animated and obviously happy and excited to be there. As the crowds cleared out, her publicist brought her over to where Max and I were standing and she was introduced first to Max, but we didn't get beyond that. She immediately launched into a delightful story about her own forays into the world of stage management. Then she was off as quickly as she arrived, greeting another friend, attending to another fan.

I have to admit that I walked out of that bookstore with a silly grin on my face. She was enchanting.

'She's a lady broad,' was how Max summed it up.

The Phillips Club, where I was staying, was indeed totally unsuitable for what I was doing – promotion and publicity for *Love Letters* and my book *My Friends' Secrets*. This involved several media events every day, so I needed many changes of photogenic outfits and – since there was no room to swing the proverbial cat at the Phillips, let alone see yourself in a full-length mirror – I was understandably frustrated.

'Of course, Diahann would never have stood for this sort of accommodation,' teased Jeffrey, somewhat undiplomatically, the next morning as we were crossing the George Washington Bridge to yet another TV interview. Diahann Carroll was one of his clients and my friend from *Dynasty* days. We had great fun being the politically incorrect 'black bitch' and 'white bitch', slapping each other's faces and screaming insults at each other, to the amusement of the crew.

'She's very insistent on only being treated like a star,' he continued.

'Why didn't you tell the producer's people – that Percy guy we met – that I wasn't happy in the suite?'

'I did, but they said there was nothing they could do about it now.'

'Never mind.' I leaned against the cool leather of the limo and gazed down at the tumbling iridescent river. 'I'll be in San Francisco in a couple of days. I hope the accommodation is better there.'

A few months before I met Joan, I had taken a 'sabbatical' of sorts to look after my mother, who had recently moved back to Glasgow and was showing signs of dementia. As I'm an only child, it wasn't like I could 'delegate' this. But I was getting nowhere with my attempts to create a protective cocoon around her before things got worse.

'Don't rush it,' the doctor kindly said. 'At some point she'll do something and then the protective arm of social services will take her in hand. The NHS is a slow lumbering beast, but it does eventually get there.'

Hmmm, I thought to myself. I hope it gets there before she gets run over by a bus.

As I sat stewing, my phone rang. It was a general manager I had worked with several times on Broadway.

'Are you done "finding yourself" or whatever you're doing there?' he boomed.

'Erm . . . taking care of my mother . . .' I didn't even get a chance to get that far – he just talked over me.

'How would you like to do a tour with Joan Collins and George Hamilton?'

I was dumbfounded. I had no idea if they'd been on stage before. I had no idea if they'd experienced the strain of North American touring. I was wary of the wear and tear that a theatrical tour can take on body and soul. I had serious concerns about the rumours of large egos and diva behaviour. I really thought this was a bad, bad idea.

Which is why I said, 'I'd love to do it!'

That evening, I was channel-surfing on TV and, as if

by fate, Joan was on Graham Norton. I thought perhaps this could give me a glimpse into her character. The programme that night featured her and Richard Wilson, of Victor Meldrew, *One Foot in the Grave* fame.

Graham in those days included an outrageous 'variety act' at the end of his programme. As I recall, it was a Russian circus performer whose speciality was shooting ping pong balls from a certain part of her anatomy onto a target about ten feet away. She was remarkably accurate. Richard was true to Victor Meldrew form as he evinced embarrassment at having to watch this, but Joan laughed uproariously. My concerns over touring with this lady started to dispel. She was a 'theatrical'.

Never let an experience pass you by, I had been taught. You never know how it's going to turn out . . .

Katy was my companion on the tour and we were met at San Francisco airport by Percy (still wearing the mustard jacket!) and Charles Duggan, the producer of *Love Letters* – a great friend who had also produced my US tour of *Private Lives*. We chatted happily in the car, and I gently admonished Charles about the fact that he wouldn't let me change my hotel in New York.

'That's not true,' said Percy. 'I called your press agent several times to see if you were happy there, and each time he said you were fine.'

He looked quite concerned, and Charles piped up, 'I heard him saying that to Jeffrey on the phone.'

'Well, never mind.' I smiled at Percy, whose concern and sincerity were touching.

'We hope you'll like this one.' He smiled back beguilingly.

The hotel was fine – simple, spacious and close to the theatre. Contrary to some people's opinions, I don't go for the overdone

and over-decorated deluxe suites and prefer more homey surroundings, especially since Katy was my companion on this tour.
So the two-bedroom suite with a little kitchenette to make coffee
and breakfast was perfectly OK. The kitchen had been stocked
with groceries, cookies and wine, and my favourite Casablanca
lilies were on the table, as were the English newspapers, which
Percy had detected I liked to read every morning.

'He is so considerate,' I remarked to Katy, as we unpacked.
'And cute, too!' she giggled.

The second time we met, this time on tour in San Francisco,
I was waiting by the theatre for the arrival of Joan and
George in tandem. In my naivete, I had booked a massive
limousine thinking that's what film stars were accustomed to.

'This car is so vulgar,' a voice from within the car intoned. It was much too high-pitched to be George.

She emerged and sized me up. I was wearing a pale-
yellow blazer with light blue checks which had belonged
to my grandfather, and I thought was quite chic in a retro,
'edgy' sort of way. After all, it was vintage.

'Nice blazer,' she said simply, with a slight moue.

I took it as a compliment and quickly grabbed her lug-
gage, leaving George behind with his ten garment bags.
I was always fascinated by how many clothes George
ended up bringing to the theatre. His dressing room started
bare and by the end of the week resembled the showroom
at Brioni. I helped him with more garment bags than I ever
did for Joan.

'Don't worry, I'll be fine,' I heard George's weak voice
squeak behind me as I struggled to catch up with Joan,
who had set a sprinter's pace.

The next night, we repeated the performance. Out she

came with a 'Can't we get a normal car?' and a 'Hmmm, that's the same jacket.' Slight moue, grab bags, sprint, George in dust.

By the third night it finally dawned on me that she didn't really think the jacket was the height of trendy fashion that I thought it was.

The fourth night I wore my brand-new Saks blue blazer. 'Now that's much better.'

I passed my first test.

The two-week stint with George Hamilton as my co-star at the Marines Memorial Theatre in San Francisco sped by. George is one of the funniest and most amusingly self-deprecating of actors. Backstage at the interval, Percy, Max, Katy and I would be in fits of laughter as George regaled us with his endless supply of anecdotes and jokes, and more seriously his exceptional knowledge of all things medical. How he kept his tan during those cold April months, I'll never know, but keep it he did.

The second thing that most attracted me was her laugh. George was always 'entertaining the troops' backstage, and Joan would sit by her dressing room door, perfectly coiffed and 'stage ready' (while George barely did up his suit as we walked to the wings), and laugh.

It's difficult to describe her laugh. I guess 'bewitching' would be one way. It's a deep rolling outburst which is ever so slightly accentuated by a nasal aspiration and ends up with a slightly girly giggle, a little hand to the mouth and a slight wink in the eye. It's entirely honest and supremely infectious and devoid of any airs and, over these twenty years, it's one of the things I'm blessed to be able to hear on a regular basis.

Love Letters is a light, two-handed play in which the actors are seated next to each other at a table, reading their love letters from one another from the time they were teenagers until the death of my character, Melissa. There were some sweet laughs, but audiences usually went to the touring show just because they had been told that it was amusing and because many famous names had performed in it all over the US – Charlton Heston and his wife Lydia, Robert Wagner and Jill St John, Larry Hagman and Linda Gray, Jessica Tandy and Hume Cronyn, and Uncle Tom Cobley and all had played, often to packed houses. The actors liked it because they didn't have to learn lines and there were minimum rehearsals (one day for us). It was an easy gig and a quick way to pick up a few bucks.

On our first matinee, George, Percy and I were sitting backstage at the interval, lamenting the lack of audience laughter.

'You know why they're not laughing,' I said gloomily, 'because this play's not fucking funny!'

Percy laughed uproariously at this and later told me that he thought that I was very funny and quite adorable. (The feeling was becoming mutual.) As the tour continued, it became clear that we were very compatible, and Katy absolutely adored him.

During the run in San Francisco, George was dating the novelist Danielle Steel, who lived there, so Katy, Max, Percy and I usually went out to dinner together after the show. As often happens on theatrical tours, we all bonded together like a family and exchanged many confidences.

In a misguided attempt to make everything 'friendlier', the producer had actually suggested that George come to pick me up in the limo arranged by him so we could both arrive at the theatre in time for the 'half', which is the traditional theatrical term for the time that actors are supposed to be at the theatre.

Percy and I were wary about this arrangement, but he had to follow Charles Duggan's instructions to save money, and I didn't want to risk being considered 'difficult', so everyone agreed. This worked for a few days, until George began arriving in the limo later and later. I started calling Percy, calmly at first.

'It's seven twenty-five' – the half was at seven thirty – 'and he's *still* not here.'

'He'll be there, don't worry. He called, said he was in traffic,' Percy would calmly assure me.

The next night: 'Where the hell is George? It's seven thirty-five!'

Again the diplomacy at which Percy excels came to the fore. 'Don't worry, he's pulling up outside now.'

Jumping into the car, I berated George for his tardiness. 'You *can't* arrive this late. You've got to let me get to the theatre by the half – I must.'

But George didn't quite get it, 'Your hair and make-up is done – all you've got to do is change. Why do you need half an hour?'

I stared at him bleakly, realising this was going to be a very long engagement.

But I have to say George more than made up for this exasperating tardiness by being charming, witty, supportive, and generous.

I love George, I think he's just wonderful. Endlessly entertaining, he had us howling with laughter backstage telling us stories about his time in Mexico shooting *Zorro: The Gay Blade*, switching seamlessly between English and surprisingly excellent Spanish. He had an endless trove of anecdotes and was engaging, energetic and convivial.

What he wasn't was punctual. Almost every night I would get a call from Joan saying, 'George is not here. It's already the half hour.'

'He'll be there soon, I'm sure,' I said, none too convincingly.

Preparing a theatrical tour requires a vast amount of logistics and politics while keeping a keen eye on the budget. Actors must be transported, housed, fed, watered, and generally kept happy. This sounds like I'm talking about actors as if they were circus animals but, then again, if you've ever eaten with one, the analogy fits.

I was worried about a particular stop in Houston, Texas. The hotel was apparently 'across the street' from the theatre.

'We don't need a car. She can just walk,' Charles Duggan announced airily.

'Does she walk?' I asked. It wasn't a joke – it was a serious question.

Actors have to go through a fair bit of stress having to give a great performance every evening, day after day, eight times a week, sometimes twice a day, and they only get one day off. They get tired, they get careless, accidents happen. Crossing the street can lead to a cancelled performance. With actors of a certain profile, who have fans waiting at the stage door willing to distract them for the sake of an autograph or a selfie, or just want to speak to them, crossing the street becomes a Via Crucis.

So no, she can't walk.

'OK but we'll only order one car to save money. It can pick George up first and then pick Joan up,' he countered.

Out of arguments, I relented.

The arrangement did not last long. Joan and George came in different cars from there on . . . and Joan was always on time.

George gave me a memorable seizure one day. I didn't expect him at the allotted 'half hour' but I did sort of expect him to show up before we started the show. With five minutes to spare, after I had been pacing the sidewalk nervously, smoking a pack of cigarettes for the last ten minutes, a 1980s Cadillac Seville screamed to a stop in a manoeuvre worthy of an episode of *Starsky & Hutch* and out jumped an unexpectedly dishevelled George. A very attractive woman was driving the car. I later found out it was Danielle Steel.

'Good on you, George,' I thought to myself.

Percy Michael Jorge Gibson was born in Lima, Peru, to a Peruvian father who was fifty-five at the time (and whose great-grandfather was Scottish – hence the surname) and a Scottish mother, Bridget Monahan, a schoolteacher who was forty-two. Theirs was a tempestuous yet loving relationship, for Bridget was feisty and opinionated and Jorge was the typical South American macho man – the boss and the breadwinner with a temper and a touch of chauvinism thrown in. In this respect, he would not have been unlike my own father: a strict, hot-tempered, Jewish chauvinist born in 1902, just a few years before Jorge Gibson.

So Percy and I had much in common, for our fathers were of the same strict intransigent generation. There were more than thirty years between Percy and me, but that didn't matter one whit as the camaraderie between us flourished on tour.

After two weeks, George's temporary contract ended so he left the company, and in San Diego Stacy Keach joined us to play the male lead. As is common on tours, heavy press duty was required upon arrival at each town. Often, I had to rise at dawn to prepare for early-morning talk shows. The first morning in San Diego, bleary-eyed and with badly applied make-up, I stumbled into the lobby to meet Stacy with the local press agent.

There, to my surprise and delight, sat Percy, who had not only long ago ditched the mustard jacket for a cool-looking navy blazer but was offering us two containers of steaming Starbucks latte. 'It was too early for room service, so I got you a latte. I know you like it with four sugars.'

'You didn't have to do that,' I said, thrilled by his thoughtfulness. 'You don't have to be here.'

'I know, but I just want to make you happy,' he smiled.

I felt a great wave of warmth for this handsome young man who was so completely dedicated to his job and to making his stars feel good; quite unlike most company managers I had known.

'He's the best company manager I've ever worked with,' said Stacy. 'Percy always goes above and beyond the call of duty, and that's rare in our business.'

At one of these press events, I realised I'd run out of eyeliner. 'I'll get you some,' offered Percy. When he returned, I opened the package to find a mascara wand.

'Oh, no!' I said.

'Isn't that it?' he asked, a bit confused.

'No,' I smiled. 'I guess you're not gay.'

'Afraid not,' he smiled back.

And that, as Claude Rains said to Humphrey Bogart in *Casablanca*, was the beginning of a beautiful friendship.

The third thing that impressed me most about Joan was her resilience.

The tour was not a success, and I had a larger than usual contingent of producers that I had to answer to, all with different needs and demands: 'Can you tell us how many of the half-price tickets you sold? How many of the new promotional tickets? Can you enact a new advertising campaign for radio listeners? Can you track tickets based on age? Can you divide the number of tickets by Pi and explain the theory of relativity?' It was getting silly, and all that really mattered was making sure the actors were comfortable and the show went up on time.

If I may take a paragraph to explain why the tour was not a success. The play that the tour had originally advertised was a new play called *If Memory Serves*, which had a short run off-Broadway with Elizabeth Ashley. I had, before my sabbatical, prepped that show, which was perhaps why I was called to manage this tour. As I understand, the playwright and the original producer had not seen eye to eye on the Broadway production, so *If Memory Serves* had to be replaced with another vehicle, and *Love Letters* was chosen. Now, *Love Letters* is a satisfying and wonderful show, but in America everyone and their mother has seen it, so much so that Jesus himself could descend from heaven and he'd still have trouble filling the theatre.

So, while we had decent houses in San Francisco, by the time we got to San Diego and Phoenix, we struggled to sell half the tickets. Every day Joan would ask me, 'How's the house?' and I would come up with the usual excuses, which are time-honoured in our profession: 'It's dreadful weather outside, no one wants to come out' or 'It's a beautiful sunny day, no one wants to be stuck in a dark theatre.'

Pretty soon Joan caught onto my act. 'No one wants to see this tired old play with us tired old actors, do they?' It was more the former than the latter, but there were no flies on her, and no ego either. Stacy Keach had by now replaced George and the play was hauntingly moving. I felt so bad for her and was determined to do what I could to make sure her experience was as liveable as possible.

Now, as I said earlier, I was fed up with more producers than I had actors onstage, and who were more demanding than the actors who, I felt, had a right to be demánding since they had to do the show. Plus, I was struggling to even give away tickets. Every day I was on the phone to various charity groups, offering tickets so we had a decent house for the actors who were turning out their fine performances, night after night. Otherwise, we might as well pack it up. So, naturally, I quit.

'OK, but you'd better explain it to Joan, because she's grown quite fond of you,' said Charles Duggan, the main producer.

That evening, Joan showed up and asked the inevitable, 'So, how's the house?'

'To tell you the truth, Joan, it's not good, and it's not going to be good for the rest of the tour. I'm sorry but that's the truth.'

I paused, she paused. I was about to launch into a long explanation of why I had to leave because I felt so embarrassed about not having given her the wonderful experience that their performances deserved, when she suddenly blurted, 'OK. Best pull our socks up, then!'

What a trouper.

I called the producer the next day and told him I would stay.

Percy had been legally separated for a year after an eight-year marriage. In his generosity, he had let his ex-wife have their New York apartment and furniture. He had then taken a sabbatical to look after his mother in Glasgow. She had been taken ill and he had seen that she was settled in a home for Alzheimer's patients before returning to New York. He had been working in theatre since college after he left Peru and was a very well-respected company manager who had worked on many shows in New York and on tour.

Although Percy was not seriously involved with anyone at that time, I was in a relationship with the art dealer Robin Hurlstone, which was frankly going nowhere. As our tour continued in Houston, Phoenix and Austin, Percy and I became so close that I started calling him my 'Latin from Manhattan'. In Austin, Texas, we dined one night with Charles Duggan, Stacy and some other friends, and Michael Caine joined us for coffee. He was shooting the movie *Miss Congeniality* with Sandra Bullock and was in fine, funny fettle. Percy, Charles and I were limp and exhausted with laughter as Michael, in his inimitable deadpan way, told us anecdote after anecdote. Afterwards Michael said, 'That Percy is a really nice young man.' And I started to realise that, more and more, he was becoming more than just 'nice'.

After the tour ended a series of coincidences occurred – it seemed that every time I was in any city, Percy was also there. When I was in London, he was en route to visit his ailing mother in Glasgow; when I went to New York to film a commercial, he was in rehearsals with Jean Stapleton for *Eleanor*. Some people would call it fate, or 'kismet'. Arlene Dahl, the famous 1940s actress who had been a lifelong friend and had turned astrologist, said we had known each other in another life – I was a queen and, as Percy likes to joke, he was my cat.

I wanted to see some shows, so we went to see *Kiss Me Kate* together, one of the most romantic stage musicals, at the Martin Beck Theatre, directed by Michael Blakemore. When the Broadway stars Marin Mazzie and Brian Stokes Mitchell each sang 'So in Love', Percy's and my eyes met, and I felt the sort of butterfly frisson in my stomach I hadn't felt for years. He looked into my eyes, and I looked into his, and we both knew that there was something more to our relationship than just friendship. Yet because he was much younger than I was, I knew I shouldn't consider those thoughts. I knew Percy found me attractive, as many a long night on tour we had talked and philosophised about life and our feelings. As a South American Latin male, he had none of the hang-ups that North American and British men have about age. 'If a woman is beautiful, it doesn't matter if she's young or old,' he told me. Well, I was firmly in the second category, and he was only thirty-four, but by now I liked him enormously and was extremely attracted to him.

In August 2000 I started rehearsing a movie musical in LA, *These Old Broads*, with Elizabeth Taylor, Shirley MacLaine and Debbie Reynolds. It was huge fun but hard work as I had to learn several musical numbers with Debbie and Shirley, who were both professional hoofers. I was not.

And who should be in LA at that time, company managing *Eleanor* at the Canon Theatre, but Percy. He visited me on set, and we often had lunch or dinner together and went on to a couple of parties. We talked about everything, like current affairs, our love of musical theatre, writing novels. My single girlfriends thought he was very sexy and quite adorable. 'Does he have a brother?' several of them asked.

'Unfortunately, not. They broke the mould when they made him,' I would reply, laughing. Actually, I wanted to keep him to myself because I knew the truth: I was falling hard for Percy Michael Jorge Gibson.

In January 2001 I was still renting an apartment at the Sierra Towers, a ritzy building on Sunset Boulevard, and desperately trying to finish my fourth novel, *Star Quality*. Since I had not yet entered the twenty-first century in terms of computers (I still can't type and I use Siri to text or email), all my manuscripts were written in longhand, so had to be typed and printed. The woman who usually did this for me in LA was not available and I was frantically trying to find someone who could decipher my hieroglyphics, when Percy suggested that he could easily do it.

Every day he came to the apartment at ten o'clock and, while I wrote, he transferred everything to his computer.

I had appeared in an episode of *Will & Grace* a couple of years back and they wanted me to do another one, but they refused to send me the script although the start date was imminent.

The script finally arrived the night before the first table read and it was dire. I'd wanted to do *Will & Grace* because it was a terrific show and I'd enjoyed my previous experience, but to play a character who insists on having an operation to get her shoulders extended by eight inches was frankly ludicrous.

'I can't do this,' I wailed to my agent, Alan Nevins. 'They want me to play a woman who gets shoulder transplants to extend them, for God's sake. It's utterly ridiculous, but I want to do the show. Do you think they'll rewrite it?'

Alan spent a morning of fevered talks with the *Will & Grace* producers, but they flatly refused. The gist of the conversation there with Alan was, 'Who does Joan Collins think she is? She's not doing *Dynasty* anymore and we're a hit show. We're hot and she's not. Tell her we won't rewrite and she's gotta do it the way it is.'

When Alan told me that on the phone I became extremely upset and broke down in tears. Mercifully, Percy was there with a tender shoulder to cry on. Before we knew it, we were in each other's arms and what we had both been thinking about for the past seven months finally happened. It was the moment I had always felt would occur one day, and it was just wonderful.

Love Letters ended, and I was immediately thrown into another show, this time taking Jean Stapleton around the country in her one-woman show based on the life of Eleanor Roosevelt. Why was I suddenly getting all these offers to go out with female stars? I had turned down an off-Broadway show with Morgan

Fairchild because I was getting tired of New York, and this was an easy tour with several weeks of shows in one town. Besides, it was going to be a warm and sunny tour: it started in Palm Beach, Florida, went to Austin, Texas and ended up in Los Angeles – and who would be in Los Angeles, but my good friend Joan?

We had kept in touch after *Love Letters* and I'd seen her a couple of times in London, en route to see my mother. She came to New York once and asked if I knew what good shows were on, so I took her to see *Kiss Me Kate*. She adored it. I hadn't realised how knowledgeable she was about musical theatre. She knew practically every famous song and what musical it was from. She even hummed along with the score that evening. I thought it was enchanting. We shared so many likes and dislikes and she made me laugh. I felt a great deal of 'simpatico' with her and it didn't hurt that she was always turned out beautifully. She was stylish, she was gorgeous, her make-up was perfect, her expressions charming, her manner feminine or girlish as the mood required, her legs were spectacular. She was every inch my ideal of femininity. Too bad she had a boyfriend, because otherwise I would have made a pass at her.

I had told her I'd be in LA early next year, and she told me she was also there because she had to shoot an episode of *Will & Grace* and had to finish her book, and would I mind transcribing her chicken scratches into my computer? We had started this working relationship on tour, when she had a couple of articles to do and I would lend a hand transcribing, editing and sending them, and this had continued remotely by fax. There was almost nothing to do on the tour as Jean was staying at her home, so I would spend my mornings heading over to Joan's apartment in LA, spending a few hours transcribing, making a few modest suggestions, and printing them out for revisions until it came time to pick Jean up for the show.

One morning, I came over to find Joan in floods of tears. I coaxed out of her that it had to do with the script for *Will & Grace*, which she hadn't received until the night before and had objected to because the premise was a silly attempt to ridicule her personally. She had a 'right of first refusal' in her contract, which meant she could pass if she didn't like the script, which is exactly what she had done. But her agent and the producer of the show got into a massive catfight and the producer had uttered those fateful words: 'Who does she think she is? She's nothing in this town, and I'll make sure she never works again!' which Alan Nevins had inexplicably related verbatim to her! No wonder she was a mess.

I felt so sorry for her, and I had no idea what I could say to make her feel better, so I did the only other thing I could think of, which was to hug her. I had never properly hugged her before, or shared any physical closeness at all, come to think of it. Our previous greetings and farewells had mainly consisted of chaste air kisses or hand waves. I think it took us both by surprise, but once entwined, we did not want to let go.

Now, I was having a fully fledged passionate affair with Percy Gibson, who was quite honestly sweeping me off my feet. It was giddy, it was fantastic, it was all the romantic fairy tales that young girls dream about, but I was not a young girl. I was a woman in her sixties in love with a man in his thirties. We tried to keep it a secret, but a few of my friends started to suspect, as we both had that heady glow that comes from being in love. He was the best lover I'd ever had, and I knew that the kind of passion we had for each other was terribly special – truly once in a lifetime.

By now Robin Hurlstone was eager to visit me in LA, even though his mother was still not well, but I kept putting him off. I had the perfect excuse in my looming deadline for *Star Quality*, so I told him I was writing morning, noon and night and that Percy was putting it all on the computer for me. But Robin decided to come anyway. I was in a frightful bind. Should I tell him before he flew to LA? Should I wait until he arrived? Should I not tell him at all and continue the deception? He solved it anyway. He and Charles Duggan flew out to surprise me. They had only told me the day before that they were coming, so I was in a state of high anxiety.

The night they arrived, Nolan Miller gave a screening of an early print of *These Old Broads* for twenty of our friends at his LA apartment. Robin and Charles came, as did Percy. It was an interesting evening, to say the least, particularly when the two first met and sized each other up and I sensed that male feeling of two stags at bay. I was completely agitated as I tried to concentrate on the movie, sitting between Gore Vidal and George Schlatter. (Gore was a very good friend, and I was proud to be one of 'Gore's Girls' – which was what he used to call me, Claire Bloom, Susan Strasberg and Joanne Woodward.)

The next afternoon, Charles, who suspected the relationship between Percy and me, came to my apartment for drinks and I bustled about fixing them for him and Robin, being cheerful and chattering away. I mentioned several times how well the book was going and how helpful and wonderful Percy had been, when suddenly Robin fixed me with a beady, accusing eye.

'This Percy fellow, you seem to talk about him a lot. Have you got a crush on him?'

'A crush? Don't be silly.' I literally felt my face flame. I don't think I had blushed since I was a teenager, but blush I did, and it was a hot crimson-faced one.

'My God, you're blushing! Look, Charles, she's blushing, it must be true, then.'

Charles was not that surprised, as he had remarked on our friendship several times. 'She sure is,' he said, laughing. 'Maybe it's just the wine.'

Later that night, after Charles had left, I confessed everything about Percy and my relationship with him to Robin. It was one of the most difficult things I have ever had to do. For someone who hates confrontation and hates hurting people close to me even more, it was intensely traumatic. It was appalling and it went very badly. Robin screamed and yelled and called me names, it was horrendous in every way. A lot of people today dump by text – Rupert Murdoch dumped my friend Jerry Hall by text message! But I feel that I faced the lion in his den rather bravely.

The following afternoon, I left for New York, as I had to do press for *These Old Broads*. Robin stayed behind in Los Angeles, in my apartment. Producer and sports promoter Jerry Perenchio had offered me a ride on his beautifully equipped private plane that had been remodelled and decorated to seat thirty passengers in total luxury. Although Jerry wasn't going to New York, there was a group of his American football associates on board. When I boarded, the flight attendant escorted me to a palatial state-room with a double bed and huge TV. 'Mr Perenchio wanted you to be comfortable,' she smiled.

I relaxed with a Bellini and rang Judy Bryer, my closest friend, to tell her the events of the previous night. It had been extremely distressing to confront Robin with the news that I had become seriously involved with Percy, but I have always tried to be honest with people and tell the truth. I could never do what a famous actor-friend of mine had done when he wanted to end his long-term relationship: he told his agent to 'Tell her it's over and give me back the keys.' Much as I loathed hurting people, it was clear to me that the Hurlstone relationship had been frozen in a not very mutually rewarding rut for several years and that Percy and

I had fallen madly in love. I didn't know what the future held, but I felt so strongly about him that nothing else mattered.

As the plane took off and I saw the shoreline of Santa Monica far below us, I noticed a stream of yellow fluid coming out of the plane's fuselage. 'The plane looks like it's sprung a leak,' I joked to Judy. Then there was a knock on the cabin door and an agitated attendant stammered, 'We're sorry, Miss Collins, but we've developed engine problems and we have to dump fuel over the ocean and go back to base.' I was so horrified that, coupled with my emotional state of mind, I burst into terrified tears.

Back at the terminal we were told that the plane couldn't function and we were to be put on a smaller plane as Mr Perenchio was 'very upset, and doesn't want to ruin your trip'. I called Jerry, who was absolutely mortified. 'We've never had any problems with this plane in the ten years I've owned it. I guess I'll just have to buy another one,' he joked. And even though I was upset, he made me laugh. I've always loved how the truly rich live, especially when they appreciate it.

Jerry's stand-by plane to New York was quite small and, as I sat between his football friends, I couldn't stop crying; I had hated hurting Robin and I felt I was being unfair to Percy with my vacillating and refusing to commit. After all, he was in his mid-thirties, I was in my mid-sixties. This was a very big step for both of us. The football pals asked me if I was OK and, drying my eyes with my second box of Kleenex, I assured them it was just a bad case of hay fever.

It was the first time in my life I'd had an affair, much less with someone famous. We would go off to lunches and dinners incognito, trying to find the most unlikely places. One of them was a charming restaurant called Il Piccolino, long before it became the famous Il Piccolino. It was just down the street from Nolan Miller's atelier, so I would drop Joan off at their parking lot and speed off before being seen, and then she would ask to be dropped off at the restaurant. If we went out at night we'd try to find off-the-beaten-track restaurants.

To make matters worse, the only car I could get from the rental agency for this visit was a white open-top jeep. It was hip, but a disaster on any coiffure. However, Joan didn't mention a thing about it and gamely went along with me. One night we went to a friend's house for dinner. She introduced me as the company manager who had accompanied her on the tour of *Love Letters* and who, as fate would have it, was in LA doing another show, so was her 'plus one'. We later heard that the entire fiction fell apart the moment she got on my rental and waved goodbye to them. 'They're in love,' said her agent, Alan Nevins, as he watched us bounce down his driveway. 'She'd never get in that open-top car unless she was.'

But, like all fairy tales, or any kind of tales for that matter, it came to an end at the close of January. Joan and I had not discussed our future. Fate would make that decision. Her boyfriend had twigged that something was amiss, and she had to come clean. Taking her phone call the next day, when she was about to board a plane back to London, was painful. I have no idea how she made it through the previous evening. She was sobbing, and I would have given everything I had to be next to her, consoling her. To make matters worse, she called me a few hours later. The plane she was on had returned to LAX. She couldn't possibly go home, where her boyfriend was staying. She didn't know what to do and I was in an open top jeep in the middle of a Los Angeles boulevard with very choppy reception.

Half an hour later she called again – she'd been re-booked on another plane and was heading to New York on her way to London. I wished her another tearful good-bye and wondered when I'd ever see her again.

A week later, I met with Robin in my London flat to reiterate that I wanted to end our relationship. He did not take it well, becoming upset and insulting about Percy and me. I decided to go to Forest Mere, a health farm, and retreat for the weekend to make the final decision about what to do. After three days of staring zombie-like at the ceiling and thinking back over my years with Robin, and what kind of future I had with a man who not only couldn't stand most of my friends, my family and my children, but who made me feel insecure, I made the decision. Robin Hurlstone packed his toothbrush (which is all he ever kept at my flat), and shortly afterwards Percy and I left London to begin our new life in New York City.

12

The Organic Actor

I've been lucky to work with some amazing actors in my life, all with different ways of getting into character. I'm sure have heard of the phrase 'method acting', where an actor so commits to a part that they keep in character the entire time you're shooting.

One of the greatest actors I had the pleasure to work with was Sir John Gielgud – an utter professional – on 'Neck', an episode of Roald Dahl's *Tales of the Unexpected*. I had been an admirer of John Gielgud's since my student days at RADA, when three of the most promising students had been selected to visit Sir John and Pamela Brown at the Queen's Theatre where they were appearing in Jean Anouilh's *The Lady's Not for Burning*. After a few days of shooting on 'Neck' I reminded Sir John about this meeting but, understandably, he did not recall what had been a red-letter day in my student life.

Sir John, as the cast deferentially referred to him, was exceedingly charming and witty, with exquisite manners and the ability to recall in minute detail the most interesting anecdotes about every actor and actress he had ever worked with. Since this was 1978 and he had started his career in the 1920s, he had fifty years of memories with which to regale us. 'Neck' was directed by Christopher Miles, brother of Sarah, and also starred Michael Aldridge, Peter Bowles and a young actor called Paul Herzberg, who so admired Gielgud that he kept a small notebook into which he inscribed Sir John's every bon mot.

My first meeting with Sir John took place one windy autumn morning in the unit car outside the hotel in Weston-super-Mare, across the road from the amusement pier. Cockney mums and dads in beach gear with assorted children and dogs and buckets and spades and picnic baskets struggled down to the beach, oblivious to the great actor who sat in solitary splendour smoking cigarettes in the front seat of the car.

'Good morning,' I mumbled shyly, falling into the back seat, a morning wreck as usual in jeans and T-shirt.

'Good morning, my dear,' he twinkled, turning his head around and extending a well-manicured hand. He was dressed impeccably in that elegant but slightly faded style that becomes actors of the old school. Grey flannel trousers, highly polished shoes – years old, but obviously of the best quality – a Tattersall shirt, a tie, a pullover and a good tweed jacket. Elegant. So unlike most actors I've worked with, who usually look like slobs in the morning. Never at my best at the crack of dawn, I tried to keep up my end of the conversation during the twenty-minute ride to Greystone Manor. He, unfazed by my mumbles and ineffectual chat, told several amusing anecdotes, culminating in a Noël Coward-ish 'Very flat, Norfolk,' when I remarked at the prettiness of the surrounding countryside. I enjoyed his company, and our off-set chats, which were extremely stimulating.

One day a reporter was interviewing me as Sir John and I sat on canvas chairs in the garden of the manor. The journalist asked the usual boringly predictable questions, finishing off with his pièce de résistance, 'So how old are you really, Miss Collins? We never seem to read the same age twice for you in the papers.'

Considering the negative attitudes associated with age, I've always believed that an actress should have the right of privacy on that subject. So did Sir John – he looked at the journalist and said, 'If an actress looks twenty-five but is in fact thirty-five, there is no reason why she should have to play the latter age on screen.' Unfortunately, with the press and public mania for knowing ages, this secret becomes almost impossible nowadays. In 2023, ageism is the ugly fact of life for most actresses over fifty.

Gielgud also gave me some insight into an actor's ability to project other areas of himself. I had given him a copy of a script I was interested in doing, asking him to read the part of a retired Italian gardener living in a home for old men. He returned the script to me, regretfully declining the part on the grounds that it was too much of a stretch for him to be believable.

'But you're such a marvellous actor, you can play any part,' I exclaimed.

'Not true, my dear. Look at my hands. They are not the hands of an ex-gardener.' I looked at them. They were upmarket hands. 'Ralph Richardson could play this part very well,' he said. 'He could look like a gardener with his gnarled old hands. I could play a gentleman fallen on hard times, of course, but you must remember that usually an actor is the victim of his or her own physicality, and one must take this into account when choosing the roles one does or does not accept.'

I nodded. He continued, 'You, for example, could never play an unattractive woman, because you bring to every role your physical presence and it would be difficult for you to play against that, unless you used a great amount of make-up and costumes to disguise the fact.'

Wise words, Sir John.

Shortly after the tragic events of 11 September 2001, and the year following *Love Letters*, I was decidedly less lucky in the leading man I was starring opposite. I opened in an extremely physical comedy called *Over the Moon* in Guildford. It was a tough play for me because Frank Langella, my co-star, who described himself as an 'organic' actor, changed his lines at will and hurled himself around the stage with no consideration for any actor who got in his way. Since he was 6' 4" and looked like he weighed 270 pounds, we all took to watching him warily.

Two actors – Rob Fitch and Cameron Blakely – had received sprains and cuts rehearsing fight scenes with him, because he liked to make them 'as realistic as possible' (although, strangely enough, he was never hurt). When he fought with them onstage, he was unable to pretend to fight – he really went into no-holds-barred combat. One night, he was rumoured to have hit the then seventy-five-year-old Moira Lister so hard on her head with his elbow that she almost fell over. She complained to our director, Ray Cooney, who begged Frank to hold back. He did not.

'I'm an organic actor,' he huffed. 'I have to feel everything from my gut.'

'It's big enough,' said Moira, sotto voce.

In one scene, Frank's character gets drunk and collapses into a chair. I had to shake and push him, pull him up by his shirt, pummel his chest and look as if I'm roughhousing him to bring him back to sobriety. One night his head started lolling from side to side as sweat poured from his face and neck. Since I have a bit of arthritis in my thumbs, I had to be extremely careful and I had told Frank several times, 'Please don't squeeze my hands.'

'Oh, you're so delicate, you English roses,' Frank mocked.

'Well, you're not delicate at all, you're like a big clumsy old carthorse,' I answered snippily. 'Look what you've done to Rob and Cameron, they're covered in bruises and cuts!' He simply laughed.

After the Guildford opening, Frank started to further pad out his dialogue, becoming even more uncontrollable onstage. He insisted on doing it his way. He stepped on other actors' lines and laughs and was manhandling all of us in his scenes.

All we could do to protect ourselves was not to get too close to him, which, when you're working together onstage, is impossible. One night over dinner at a restaurant, I regaled everyone with a story of a fight scene with Robert Mitchum in *The Big Sleep*.

'He threw me over his shoulder onto a sofa, he slapped my face and spanked my rear, but in take after take of this scene he treated me as gently as a china doll. Although through the camera's lens it looked as if he was really roughing me up, he wasn't at all. That to me is a real actor, one who's totally considerate towards his fellow actor.' I smiled at Frank defiantly.

'Well, honey, you're not a china doll and I'm not Mitchum,' he laughed. 'I'm a real actor.'

'It takes a great actor not to hurt another actor in a fight scene,' I riposted.

Unfortunately, Frank was anything but considerate and even though our producers and director complained to him constantly about his antics onstage, he never changed, just continued bleating, 'But I'm an organic actor, that's how I have to work.'

One night, during his drunken scene, when I was trying to get his attention by roughing him up and pulling his face round to listen to me, my hand inadvertently slipped on his sweat and I accidentally slapped him on the cheek. His eyes blazed and I mouthed, 'I'm sorry.' In the interval, I quickly scribbled an apologetic note, which I asked Percy, who was the company manager, to give to him. *Darling Frank, terribly sorry, slapped your face accidentally, didn't mean to. Hope you're OK.* Frank didn't acknowledge my note and at curtain call, when I asked him if he was OK, he glared at me venomously, touched his cheek, which had no mark on it at all, and mimed wincing with pain.

The next day when I arrived at rehearsals, Ray told me that Frank was furious because I hadn't apologised for slapping his face.

'But I did! I wrote him a note. It was an accident,' I said. 'You know I hate any fighting; I can't even fake the knock-out with Moira properly, I would never hit anyone deliberately. Not even Linda Evans,' I laughed.

'Well, he's really pissed off with you,' said Ray. 'I'm going to tell the company that we've got to sort out a little problem and they should go and have a cup of coffee in the meantime.'

Rehearsals were put on hold. The cast was sent away and Ray, Frank and I sat in the auditorium. 'So what is your problem, Frank?' I asked.

Frank glared at me balefully and snarled, 'Honey, you hit me hard, and it hurt.'

'I didn't do it deliberately. My hand slipped, and I sent you a note after to apologise.' I replied.

'You should have apologised *in person*,' he insisted. 'You slapped my face, not once, but twice.'

'Look at the *size* of you, Frank – you're six foot four, and Joan's five foot five, how could she possibly hurt you?' Ray asked. 'You're being ridiculous.'

'I don't give a shit what you say. Joan Collins slapped my face, hard.' He then turned and hissed at me, 'And you slapped it twice. And you didn't apologise *enough*.'

I was so distressed by this ludicrous accusation that I burst into tears – highly unusual for me, but being accused of deliberately hitting someone was a new and excoriating experience.

Frank stared at me contemptuously and said, 'Stop being such a fucking baby and quit bawling. Grow up, woman, and admit you slapped me on purpose.'

By now, to say that I was furious and upset would be putting it mildly. Having worked with some difficult actors in my time, this one topped the charts. I ran to my dressing room to call my agent. He was already aware of the situation because my colleague Moira Lister had told him that she'd never seen a leading lady treated as badly by a leading man as I had been by Frank Langella. Ray came in and begged me to have a rapprochement with Frank so that we could keep this show running, so I had to do it. Frank was unhappy about being in England because of the terrible events of 9/11 and he really wanted out, to go back to New York. So, I swallowed my pride and apologised, *again*.

Frank and I then went through an uneasy truce, even though I found it extraordinary that *I* had to be careful not to hurt *him*, yet his massive elbows, arms and feet flailed about constantly, so that everyone onstage had to really look out for him. When my agent came to see the show, he said, 'It looks to me like you're frightened of him.'

'To be perfectly honest, I'm terrified,' I said.

A week later, in Bath, one of the set doors stuck shut when an actor slammed it on his exit. Stage doors are only made of plywood and not as strong as the real thing: walls get easily twisted, and doors and windows get stuck. It's just what happens, and many times leads to audience hilarity. But Frank thought this was unforgivable. He immediately ran at the door and threw his 270 pounds against it several times. Rob and I stared at each other in horror as the entire set started to tremble, and the various pots and pans and other paraphernalia placed on shelves to resemble the backstage of a theatre rained down around us like hailstones.

Then Frank walked downstage and broke the fourth wall, the imaginary boundary between the audience and actors, and announced to a stunned audience, 'This is what happens when you work on a Bill Kenwright production.' Then exited stage left. To say Rob and I were gobsmacked was putting it mildly, but we, like good little troupers, found a way to stumble back onto the thread of the play until the end of the act.

I decided to just try and get on with my job as best I could, with great support from Percy, who also had a tough job since he had to keep the peace between Frank and the rest of the company and keep his opinions to himself. I kept saying to myself, 'When you get lemons, make lemonade,' which is what I tried to do, in spite of the fact that, by now, I knew Frank absolutely detested me, that he was trying his best to undermine not only my performance but everyone else's and consequently the play. I also think he resented the fact that Percy and I were a couple. Percy only told me after Frank left the company that he said to him after the Guildford 'slap incident': 'If your fucking girlfriend *ever* touches me again, I'm gonna throw her through the fucking wall.' Charming.

After opening night in London at the Old Vic Theatre I kept as far away from Frank in the physical scenes as possible, and treated him with kid gloves. Several critics mentioned our lack of chemistry together. I'm not surprised. They hated us, the play, everything. *Over the Moon* went under the scalpel.

The reviews made Frank even more despondent and his behaviour more erratic. Our stage manager, our director Ray Cooney and Percy met together and decided that Bill Kenwright, our producer, should come to the theatre and stage an intervention. Bill was told: 'Handle it with kid gloves. He's obviously very unhappy here and the events of 9/11 have not helped at all. We hear he misses his friends, his girlfriend in New York, he's very homesick.'

On the day of the 'summit', Kenwright arrived and Percy escorted him to Frank's dressing room, knocking gingerly.

'Come in,' Frank growled.

Percy opened the door cautiously and made way for Kenwright to come in.

The first words out of Bill Kenwright's mouth were, 'What's the matter, you cunt?'

Bill told him, 'The bad reviews have hurt bookings, and I can't keep the show open unless everyone takes a salary cut.' I had agreed, because I wanted the play to run, I wanted everyone, including Percy, to stay employed (for some of the younger members, this was their big break) and because shows all over the West End were folding like packs of cards due to the events of 9/11. In fact, everyone agreed to take cuts, except Frank Langella. So, Bill had to recast him.

As usually happens towards the end of an unsuccessful run, the script and the direction went out of the window so we all started to extemporise. During one of Frank's final performances, I made my nightly exit with the line, 'Goodbye, George, I'm leaving you.' Frank immediately ran off the stage after me, grabbed me with his enormous hands and dragged me forcibly back onstage, glibly improvising, 'No, Charlotte, I love you, you can't leave me.' It was a ghastly moment, an actor's nightmare, but luckily I managed to wrench my arm free, ad-libbing a line to the effect that I was definitely leaving and that I hated him (didn't take much acting there), and immediately exited again. Stunned silence greeted this exchange, from an audience that had no clue what was going on.

Backstage, Percy and five actors stared at me in goggle-eyed shock. 'That's probably one of the most insane things I've ever seen,' said my colleague Paul Bentley grimly. 'We're not going to let him get away with that again, Joan.'

At curtain call, Frank sneered, 'Did you like me dragging you back onstage?'

'No, I did not like it at all,' I hissed coldly.

'Good, then I'll do it again tomorrow,' he grinned malevolently.

The next night, after the same exit, Paul stood backstage wearing dark glasses à la *Goodfellas* and holding a fake machine gun menacingly in Frank's direction. Several of the other actors and Percy, arms folded, were wearing sunglasses and looking tough. The organic actor took one look at this tableau, burst out laughing and obediently nipped back onstage. I belatedly realised that not rising to his bait was the answer to Mr Langella's 'organic' antics.

Touched by the show of solidarity, Bill Kenwright decided that the show would continue and that he would pay full salary to Frank until such a time as he was able to replace him. We were pleased, although the prospect of Frank for an indeterminate period of time was a gloomy one indeed.

Frank continued behaving like a naughty schoolboy, throwing in lines that weren't in the script and being terribly rough in the fight scenes.

Towards the end of Frank's tenure, I asked Rob if he saw me slap him that day in Guildford. He said, 'To tell you the truth, I didn't see you slap him at all, I just saw your hand slip when he moved his face.'

'Why didn't you tell him that then?' I asked.

'Well, it was early days, so I didn't want to make waves,' he confessed.

Michael Cochrane took over Frank's role and we limped along for about four more weeks, but eventually it had to happen. Sadly, *Over the Moon* – an unfortunate title, considering what the critics had to say about this comedy – closed on 1 December 2001, amid much press speculation about the reasons. Joan and her co-star Frank Langella are 'not getting along' seemed to be one of the main ones, followed by snide comments about me 'parading around in my underwear'. But despite internal problems, we were rewarded by massive laughs from appreciative audiences each night. Making people laugh is not as easy as it looks, and sometimes the laughs come unexpectedly.

Being funny is not a joke – as the venerable Edmund Kean lay on his deathbed a young actor knelt by his side and whispered softly, 'Sir, what is dying like?' 'My boy,' boomed the old performer, 'dying is easy – comedy is difficult.'

However, as the Bard has said, 'All's well that ends well.' A few years later, Percy and I were staying in Palm Beach at our friends Joyce and Simon Reubens' apartment when Princess Firyal asked us to lunch with them and 'a surprise guest', smiled Joyce.

Lo and behold, at the pool restaurant, a beaming Frank Langella stood up from the table and smiled.

'I'm really glad to see you, honey. I know I behaved like a prick,' he grinned.

From then on, we've been friends, and I have to say that you would struggle to find a better dinner companion than Mr Langella – he's funny, gossipy and very *au courant*.

I even have him on speed dial now!

13

After Four Misses, I Finally Got a Hit

We thought long and hard before Percy and I came out as a couple, and about how the rest of the world – and our families – would react to our relationship. In the final analysis, it was Percy who made the decision. He wanted to be with me forever and he didn't care a hoot about what people would say. Being half Latin-American, Percy wasn't concerned about the age difference at all. In fact, because I have great vitality and enthusiasm for life and all it has to offer, Percy often admits that I can wear him out!

We were so compatible on every level that we had a strong foundation for a really good relationship and a happy marriage. We discussed getting married several times in early 2001, but I didn't want to ruin our great relationship and, having tried it four times before, I was wary. But in London after watching the ghastly events of 9/11 in New York unfold on TV, we held each other closely. Percy, realising that he had been called for jury duty in New York on that day, and that he would have had a very close call had he been there, said that life is short and we should be together; that he wanted me to be his wife and for us to be married for as long as we shall live. And I agreed.

My gorgeous wedding to Percy in 2002 at Claridge's was one of the highlights of my life. I had never felt happier or more secure with any man before. When the band played our favourite song, 'The Way You Look Tonight', and Percy and I took to the dance floor, I looked into his eyes whispering, 'I finally got it right.'

After being happily married to Percy for over twenty-one years, I realise what true love really is; the happiness, contentment and mutual respect we have for each other has been totally fulfilling. Percy is brilliant with my kids and people and helps me all the time with everything in my life. We are each other's best friend and accomplice.

He has become the glue that binds our extended family together. Tara and her children simply adore him, as do Sacha's. My daughter Katy and Percy will spend hours on holiday chatting and playing games with everyone, even helping sometimes with homework or job problems. Not only is he completely dedicated to looking after me, but he cares so much about Katy, and is always available to solve the myriad problems that technology has brought into our lives. My sister Jackie loved him, as do my brother Bill and his wife Hazel. In fact, Percy is that very rare person – a truly good man.

I know a lot of people envy the joy and contentment we have. We can spend twenty-four hours a day together and he is unutterably considerate and caring to me always. We have our rows and disagreements, of course, but I believe they are part of an honest relationship. He had an excellent relationship with his mother so is always respectful and gallant towards women. I know he loves me for who I am and not the 'Joan Collins' some people think I am.

And when people say to me, 'What about the age difference?' I blithely reply, 'Well, if he dies, he dies!'

Contrary to superficial belief, Joan is all about family. I would say that far and beyond personal ambition or accomplishments or accolades, she'd put her children first no matter what. I've seen her turn down work – really good work – because she promised that she'd be with her children and grandchildren on holiday. Sometimes, that's not possible. Money must be made, but if there's any wiggle room at all, she will fall on the side of family. And friends. She is the most loyal friend anyone could ask for. She is constantly on speed dial with all those closest to her, checking in regularly and arranging to see them. Rarely have I seen her choose a social event that could be advantageous to her career over going out with her friends. Yes, we have a busy social life, but that's because she loves her family and friends.

This quality extended to me and my mother. She was constantly encouraging me to visit her or bring her down to visit. She'd come with me too, which I thought was not normal for someone who is going to be noticed flying up to Glasgow or going to a tea shop and hanging out with a mother and her son. I don't know if she realises how much I appreciated that, and how much it raised her in my estimation, which was already quite high.

Joan suggested I bring my mother to spend Christmas with the family. My mother had not long been installed in a home after having been rescued a few times walking disoriented late at night in the streets of Glasgow – exactly what I had been trying to prevent. I decided that the best course of action, in order to cause her the least amount of confusion, would be to rent a car and drive her from Glasgow to London, rather than put her through the rigmarole of travelling by plane or train.

Yes, in my wisdom, I figured that a nice eight-hour drive with a person who had no idea who I was, and where I was taking her, would be far more pleasant.

If I sound disrespectful, please understand that this is the kind of back and forth my mother loved, and we had been exchanging it all our lives.

When I broke the news to my mother, in a slightly trepidatious voice, that I was 'going out with' Joan Collins and that she'd likely read it in the papers the next day, she paused for a few moments and said, 'You know the thing about being your mother, Percy? You've never bored me.'

So, as we approached Joan's flat, and my mother looked in wonder at the imposing facade of the Belgravia mansion, she said, 'Oh dear, I'd better watch my language around here.' I assume she meant Glaswegian, in all its colourful width and breadth.

As we mounted the stairs to the flat, I could hear Joan talking on the phone. As I put the key in the lock, my mother and I looked at each other in wide-eyed amazement because what was being said on the other side of the door was worthy of a sergeant major ripping into a green recruit. Her agent had obviously tangled her into a bad deal, and she was letting him know it.

'I guess I needn't worry about my language,' laughed my mother.

Of course, my mother and our entire families on both sides were de rigueur at our wedding. The night before was my bachelor party, which I really decided would be more of just a party for all who had come from far and wide to celebrate with us. I understand Joan had a competing 'hen night', which was far more ribald. But it can't have been that much fun, because she and all her friends decided to crash my party.

We drank for England – and Scotland, Ireland and Wales – and when we were leaving, we were faced with a barrage of flashbulbs from a phalanx of paparazzi that had congregated outside.

'I can't see!' I exclaimed.

'I can't walk,' she retorted.

And that's what the headlines quoted the next day: 'I can't see, says the groom, I can't walk, says the bride.'

I had the most debilitating hangover the next day. My best man had to practically pour me into my kilt, which I had decided in a moment of madness would be *the* thing to wear at my wedding, and I had convinced many of my friends to follow suit. As much as it was a splendid sight to see all those colours festoon our wedding congregation, the sight of the patterns was making my already queasy stomach lurch in protest.

People said that I looked so sweetly nervous at the altar but, believe me, it was the shakes. I did my best to follow the service but frankly it was taxing. It took all the strength I had just to stay upright. The registrar had read the vows that we had chosen and was talking about what marriage meant: 'Marriage is love, patience, understanding, friendship and, sometimes, marriage is having a sense of humour.'

A sudden eruption came from the wedding party behind us. What had been said, we wondered? It subsided and the registrar went on. My wife, of course, was flawless and looked angelic, and I managed my bit with, if not elan, at least an effortlessness I did not feel. 'I pronounce you man and wife' came and we, thankfully, were allowed to sit and sign the wedding banns.

I finally had the opportunity to ask what had caused such an outburst of mirth as we had said our vows. It turns out that, when the registrar said that marriage requires a 'sense of humour', my mother had blurted out, 'Well, she must have a sense of humour to marry him in that kilt.'

We went to Theo Fennell for our wedding bands, because he's a dear friend, and when we described exactly what we wanted he insisted on us making several visits to see the rings' development and have fittings.

We liked the idea of having the whole event at Claridge's because it would protect us from the press. That way we could have the ceremony, reception, dinner and dancing at the same place, but unfortunately this meant we were extremely limited to the number of guests. Our original list was over three hundred people, but because of space constraints we had to cut it down to one hundred and eighty. This was rather upsetting to several of our acquaintances, but not nearly as upsetting for us when two of the guests who had accepted didn't show up at all, leaving two empty seats next to Cilla Black, of all people!

Our wedding went off without a hitch because we'd planned it so meticulously and given ourselves time on the day of the wedding to deal with last-minute emergencies. Six weeks before the event I started arranging the placements in my head. Then, into a four-hole binder, I wrote out the complete guest list on page one: Roger Moore, Shirley Bassey, Cilla Black, Rupert Everett, Ruby Wax, Conrad and Barbara Black, Charles and Pandora Delevingne, Theo and Louise Fennell, along with a hundred other friends and family.

I then added twelve numbered pages to represent tables and started mixing names on them, making sure the people would be compatible with each other. I think one of the successes of our wedding was that dozens of people told us, 'Oh, I was at the *best* table. It was so much fun.'

We planned our colour scheme in great detail. I chose to wear a lilac silk dress which I designed myself with Nolan Miller and Mark Zunino, so I wanted the colours and flowers in the dining room to complement the dress.

We decided to have purple silk tablecloths and silver bamboo chairs with lilac velvet seat covers; the white napkins were tied with lavender ribbon; the menus were on deep lilac paper printed in silver ink, and the name cards were also purple and in tiny silver frames which everyone was given as a keepsake.

I disliked the idea of tables being numbered (because those on No.1 think that theirs is the best while those on No.15 think they're in social Siberia), so instead we decided to give our tables flower names: Lily of the Valley, Gardenia, Poppy, Orchid, etc. It was quite original, and everyone seemed happy with where they sat.

I gave much thought to my bridal bouquet. After telling our excellent florist Steel Magnolias what I wanted, they sent over two different options to try out the week before, along with two options of table centrepieces as well. This way I was able to sit with the florist and add and subtract flowers and get the exact effect I wanted, both for the bouquet and the table centres.

My bouquet was exquisite, consisting of white lilies, freesias and lily of the valley, which is my favourite flower. Around the base I wrapped an antique white lace handkerchief a dear friend had given me, which was my 'something old'.

Over three thousand blooms filled Claridge's reception rooms on our wedding day, and as Nolan Miller remarked, 'There can't be a single lily or orchid left in Europe!' The subtle scent of flowers filled the air throughout the night and when I entered the room where we were to be married, I was stunned by how gorgeous the effect was.

After the wedding we were so pleased we had decided to have everything videotaped. We particularly wanted the video cameraman to shoot our guests arriving at Claridge's and at the reception when Percy and I were having our pictures taken. That way we were able to later see so many things we had missed at the time. The videographer also filmed Percy getting ready with his best man, Chris Pennington, and myself with my matron of honour, Judy Bryer, my daughters Tara and Katy, hairdresser Hugh, dressmaker Mark, and various girlfriends in my room preparing for the ceremony.

Because I wanted to oversee every single thing, I had stayed at Claridge's the night before so that when the flowers and the table arrangements arrived in the early morning I would be there to supervise.

Also, since I had agonised over my table placement so much, I wanted to personally place the tiny frames so that, even after my meticulous planning, I was completely sure that everyone would be seated next to someone they either knew or would enjoy getting to know.

I entered the wedding venue on the arm of Max Bryer (who was standing in as 'father of the bride' and giving me away) and Judy Bryer, my matron of honour, to the stirring chords of the aptly named 'Triumphal March' from Verdi's *Aida*. The signing of the registry was accompanied by 'The Arrival of the Queen of Sheba', and when the ceremony was over we walked ecstatically down the aisle as man and wife to Mendelssohn's 'Wedding March'.

Our registrar Alison Cathcart had given us four or five choices for the wedding vows, which we mixed and matched and added some of our own words to tailor them for us.

While the cocktail reception was going on in one room, Brian Aris, our superb and rapid-fire photographer shot us in another. It was great, a few weeks later, to be able to give each guest a memento of our fantastic day.

Because Percy is half-Scottish and he and most of the male members of his family were wearing kilts, we thought a touch of the bagpipes would be appropriate, so we had Jim Motherwell, the queen's personal piper, play us into dinner. So, with a flourish of bagpipes, Mr and Mrs Gibson were ushered into the dining room, which looked absolutely exquisite.

The fourteen tables were set up around the dance floor, in the middle of which stood the cake. Aha, the cake! Isn't that delicious treat synonymous with weddings? Again, the choice was endless. Siobhan, our planner, had shown us brochures and asked us what we wanted taste-wise and frenzied discussions ensued. The cake we finally chose was a gorgeous four-tiered confection made of white chocolate curls enveloping a luscious dark chocolate Suchard filling and trimmed with white roses, jasmine and pale-lilac freesias. It was superb.

Then we had our first dance to our favourite song, 'The Way You Look Tonight'. Soon after the first words an emotional sigh surged from the guests and before we knew it the floor was heaving with all our friends, eager to dance the night away.

The food was also superb. Three weeks previously we had chosen and discussed the menu at Claridge's during what the chef called 'a tasting'. This way we knew *exactly* what we were going to get and how delicious it was. The devil take the healthy-eating regime this night.

Here's what we had:

Ballotine of foie gras with pistachios, salad of French beans with lamb's lettuce vinaigrette. And Brioche.

The vegetarian alternative was Crown of asparagus with avocado and sweet pepper oil.

Noisettes of lamb with glazed artichokes, morels and port mustard. Baby broccoli and gratin of Swedes and potatoes.

The vegetarian alternative was Baked artichoke with wild mushroom ragout under a golden dome of puff pastry.

And assiette of desserts.

Then came the speeches, probably the most emotional and joyous part of the evening after the ceremony. The father of the bride, or the person who gives the bride away, made the first speech, and Max Bryer's was touching.

Then Percy's speech brought tears to everyone's eyes, especially mine, it was so wonderfully moving:

The first time I met Joan she took no notice of me – a good beginning. She came over to where my colleague and I were standing, in the tumult of her book signing, between greeting friends and attending to fans, and was introduced first to my colleague – the stage manager – and we didn't get beyond that. She immediately launched into a delightful story about her own forays into the world of stage management. Then she was off as quickly as she arrived, greeting another friend, attending to another fan. I walked out of that bookstore with the silliest of grins on my face, and I haven't wiped it off since.

Thank you Joan for that silly grin – I've become very accustomed to it. My friends and family will have to forgive me for a moment while I speak words of thanks to Joan's. You here tonight represent, each in some singular way, the human mosaic that makes Joan Collins who she is.

Thank you for the courage that you have, to wake up each day and face life with a spring in your step, a smile in your eyes, but also with the wisdom to realise that when 'life gives you lemons' the only natural recourse is to make lemonade. Life has given you your fair share of lemons, a portion that would make most people bitter and suspicious, but not you, and I think everyone in this room has to be thanked for that, because your family and friends are a constant reminder of what is good about the world.

Indeed, thank you for this endless optimism, for though you speak worldly wise, I can see that in your heart of hearts you believe everyone is basically good, and every decision you make is based on the premise that we are all working together towards a common goal, regardless of the fact that those very decisions can backfire only on yourself, a weight which you shoulder always with elegance and grace, mixed with a healthy dose of fishwife.

Indeed, thank you for that endless generosity, a generosity so built-in that offering to do something comes without an inkling of just how grateful the recipient is, and indeed, years later when told about some little act of kindness, it comes as a pleasant surprise – your life will always be full of pleasant surprises. This generosity makes you the hostess of the world, flitting around to make sure that everyone is happy and at ease, their tumbler always full to the brim.

Indeed, thank you for this boundless energy. Thank you for taking the fastest baths I've ever seen (I've never seen an actress put on make-up as quickly as she does). Thank you for always putting things away if I put something down for the slightest moment, even if it means I have to spend a few panicked minutes wondering 'where the hell did I leave my glasses?' before I realise that, there they are, safely tucked away in your drawer.

Thank you for going and going and going, a whirling dervish leaving a chaotic jumble of joy and merriment in your wake. You'd have better luck catching a ray of sunshine (particularly in London) or a hummingbird. Thank you for being someone you can't and don't ever want to put in a gilded cage, or box away, or put on a pedestal, or make any conclusions about – you're too quick and too full of surprises for that.

Indeed, thank you for this love of life, a contagion that will never be cured – there's no drug more powerful. Thank you for that razor-sharp wit, which produces the eruptions of laughter that resonate in my mind. Plenty of times you've told me you're not smart, but I think you had the theory of relativity sewn up ahead of all of us – that life is about time and space – time is to be spent joyfully and space is to be made comfy. Thank you for that nesting instinct, which makes you enter any room and arrange a pillow here, put a picture there, place a flower yonder, and transform an alien world into the most lived-in, charming and pleasant place.

To my friends and family, thank you for making sure that my eyes were open to see the wonders that were before me, and not to be selfish or to listen to the inner doubts everyone has. Thank you for the ability to realise that here before me stands this woman, fiercely loyal, never down for more than a moment, beautiful, alluring, wise and foolish – tell me, who wouldn't fall in love with you? Everyone in this room has.

I've been aware, but never fully realised, that true happiness can be attained by the act of simply being with another. Joan is my accomplice, my comrade, my confessor, my confidant, my fearless leader and most loyal supporter, my very best friend. This is not something we've said to each other, aside from the simple 'I love you's, always plentiful, but rather expressed in the twinkle of an eye and a smile across a crowded dinner table, the laying of a hand on yours while you're reading, in the rub of a foot against yours during an early morning sleep haze. I believe herein we have the arsenal to battle whatever life has to throw at us and it is my fervent wish, and my pledge tonight, that I can, every day, in some little way, make your life as rich and wondrous as you make mine.

Chris Pennington, Percy's best man, entertained us with his wit and charm after that, and finally I said a few words, although it isn't usual for the bride to speak (well, you know me!).

Percy and I had spent days compiling many of our favourite dance hits from the 1970s and 1980s (which are, after all, the best decades for dance music) and it was well worth it.

The dancing continued until the wee hours. We had a mixture of all ages from eight to eighty, but absolutely everyone really got into the spirit of joyfulness. The two young Fennell sisters, Emerald and Coco, and the three Delevingne girls, Chloe, Poppy and Cara, joined us after dinner and immediately hit the dance floor with an energetic re-enactment of 'Macarena'. In fact, we didn't stop dancing all night. The orchestra interspersed their jazzy Sinatra and show tunes with the disco sounds and we were even lucky enough to have Shirley Bassey sing, *a cappella*, a brilliant version of 'And I Love You So'. The guests gathered excitedly in front of the stage where Shirley was giving her all, unaware that the orchestra had shuffled off the stage, not knowing the tune. After she finished singing beautifully, she looked around, slightly confused, and then Roger Moore leaped forward to gallantly escort her off stage.

'I couldn't hear the band,' she said.

'Neither could we, because they weren't there,' whispered Roger.

We did everything from a Gay Gordon to a Conga, and I can truthfully say I have never had a more wonderful and memorable day.

I want to share our minister's words with you too, because I think they sum up exactly what Percy and I mean to each other.

Love in its many forms is the foundation of all life; between friends, between lovers, parents and children, between sisters and brothers and among all humankind. With a marriage we are therefore present as witnesses, not only to a legal act, but to a deeper truth.

Marriage is a desire by two people to share themselves, their lives and their experiences with each other, and a willingness to accept each other for what and who they are.

Marriage means making a commitment to developing co-operation, friendship, and mutual respect. It calls for honesty, patience, and of course humour! Marriage is where each partner cares for the other and supports them in all that they do.

It demands courage – the courage to be open, the courage to grow and change, and the courage to sort out together the tasks of everyday living.

Marriage requires closeness and distance – closeness for a couple growing together, and enough distance to allow each partner to be an individual. A good partner in such a marriage will be loving, caring, and above all a best friend.

As well as the strong love and respect that Joan and Percy have for each other, they share similar principles and priorities. Their relationship enables them to face life positively and constructively, and they now wish to live with the commitment and understanding that marriage represents.

We attended Liza Minelli and David Gest's wedding in New York, two weeks after ours, and it was lavish indeed and with great attention to detail too. There were twelve hundred guests, in an ancient church in downtown Manhattan, the reception was in another venue an hour away, and the twenty-five bridesmaids and groomsmen and some other guests had to be flown over from various parts of the world. By comparison, ours was a small family affair! Liza had asked me to be one of her bridesmaids, but I quipped, 'Darling, I'm always a bride, never a bridesmaid.'

I always knew that the British press fudged the truth, but my engagement and marriage revealed to me just how they fib with fantastic fanfare, and how frenetically fanciful they can be.

The truth seems not to enter into their concoctions. The *Evening Standard* printed, on its front page, that while lunching at an Italian restaurant on New Year's Eve, I apparently announced that I had been married to Percy that morning! According to other patrons (whose names are conveniently withheld) the happy couple (that's us) 'flashed their wedding rings' (which didn't exist), 'quaffed champagne' (which I don't like), 'ate lobster' (which I'm deathly allergic to) in a '£600 meal' (which is ludicrous for a lunch). Although my PR, Stella Wilson, called them to deny this claptrap, several red tops ran the story the following day, quoting those impeccable sources – two busboys and the restaurant owner, who garnered a lot of publicity for his spaghetti joint.

And why is it that these rags always love printing my age, as if were some sort of suffix to my name? The 'showbiz editor' of the *Daily Mail*, Alison Boshoff, fifty-five, printed the same story, plus various other fabrications the following day, refusing to reveal her 'impeccable sources'. These turned out to be a *New York Post* mention based on a series of fake email messages purporting to be sent by a 'close family friend' but in fact sent by a person (or persons) unknown, who faked email addresses for people in our family who don't even know how to work a computer. Talk about the bad fairies not being invited to the christening. Venomous and spite-filled as these emails were, it didn't prevent the tabloids from printing them without checking the source. Far from checking these apocryphal tales, they were embellished and reused by, among others, the *NY Post* columnist Neil Travis, seventy-one, and Cindy Adams, eighty (at the time).

Then, on 11 February, a full page, yet again in the *Evening Standard*, written by Harriet Arkell, thirty-nine, revealed that we would be spending our honeymoon in a £92-a-night quaint bed-and-breakfast on the outskirts of Auckland. This, too, was immediately repeated as fact by the many sheep masquerading as reporters in our daily press. But it did give us a good laugh.

What didn't make us laugh was when out of the rotting woodwork crawled Glenys Roberts, sixty-five, a hackette for the *Daily Mail*. She had a certain cachet with a group of my friends some thirty-five years ago, when she was married to the popular Mayfair tailor Doug Hayward. This woman had previously done a couple of hatchet jobs on me and people close to me, so I was no longer on speaking terms with her, but in her article she had the unmitigated gall to call herself 'one of my closest friends'. Having intrusively doorstepped some of Percy's and my relations and friends, she wrote two pages of tripe about what a mistake my marriage to Percy would be and how all my friends were horrified. What utter claptrap.

Because I've been an actress since I was sixteen, most of these jibes affected me like the proverbial water off the fowl's back, and, since Percy has broad shoulders, we countered by sticking two metaphorical fingers in the air. We sent legal letters denying their allegations and lies, a fruitless exercise as retractions come in small print, usually on the back page.

But it certainly did affect other people in our lives. Just because I married Percy, why should our relatives be placed in such an untenable position? People talk about freedom of the press with regard to celebrities but what about the freedom of those who are related to or are friends of celebrities? Why should they be exposed to the glare of the spotlight?

During the run-up to our marriage several F-list celebrities whinged to the media about not making the cut. One person, who would go to the opening of a root canal, protested that, as he is yet another of my closest friends, he therefore deserved to be on the guest list. I found the whole thing amusingly bitchy, yet rather pathetic. Get a life, dear.

After our wonderful wedding came the honeymoon, and Malaysian Airlines, which boasts flight attendants as glamorous as any 1950s film star, and airline cuisine that is hard to top, flew us to Kuala Lumpur in twelve hours, without turbulence but with a lot of caviar! We were then transferred to the Pangkor Laut Resort, an idyllic island where we languished hedonistically on the most gorgeous private beach in the middle of the Indian Ocean. Complete with golden sand, emerald sea, our own pool and all mod cons, it was heaven, and I relished every lazy second. 'It's so wonderful, peaceful and quiet,' I murmured as Percy and I strolled hand in hand along the empty golden sands.

'No one around, just gorgeous flat calm sea and clear blue sky,' he answered.

I spotted a jungle gym ahead of us.

'Oh, look! I love doing this at the gym,' I boasted, as we both grabbed the iron bars and swung boldly from side to side – as my bandeau started slipping dangerously low.

'Look out!' called Percy. 'Paps! Pull up your top!'

I dropped onto the sand and stared at the far horizon, where I could see flashbulbs popping from a small boat.

'Damn it! I can see the headline now,' I said. 'Joan flaunts bikini body in front of honeymoon hubby.'

But, luckily, they must have missed the money shot, as the rags only featured a photo of hubby dangling from the handlebars.

14

Flood, Fire and Pestilence

The greatest tragedy in my life occurred when I was asked to do *The Last of Mrs Cheyney* in the West End after its critical and financial success at the Chichester Festival Theatre and I could hardly afford to turn it down. In preparation, I was in Paris, having dress fittings with the fabled couturier Erté, when disaster struck. I was told that my beloved eight-year-old daughter Katyana had been hit by a car and was not expected to live. The horror and the nightmare trip back to London in our friend Roger Whittaker's little plane will never leave me. When I saw my darling girl in hospital, unconscious with shaven head and tubes attached to her tiny body, I became hysterical.

'Keep it inside you,' advised my wise brother Bill, putting his arms around me. 'Don't let Katy feel that you're upset – I'm sure she'll recover.'

I spent six weeks living in a caravan in the hospital car park, staying next to Katy's bed every day and night. When the hospital allowed, I read and talked to her constantly, despite the specialists' advice that my actions were futile and that she would never recover. And thank God my darling strong little Katy did eventually come out of her coma. She had to learn how to do everything again – talk, walk, eat – she was, and still is, a fighter and a survivor.

*

In January 2012, Percy and I had just returned to our Sierra Towers apartment in LA. Katy had been staying there for several weeks, on holiday. She had wanted to spend Christmas visiting her ninety-nine-year-old grandmother, her aunts and several cousins. She also wanted to swim in Sierra Towers' Olympic-sized heated pool.

Katy loved swimming but, unfortunately, the pool temperature kept getting cooler. It was becoming most uncomfortable to swim in. When Percy and I arrived, the front desk informed us that the pool heater was broken and there was no date when they envisaged it would be fixed. Frustrated, and longing to swim, Katy and Percy purchased a wetsuit, as we had seen other guests of Sierra Towers swimming in one.

She put it on in the sauna changing rooms and swam a few laps, but soon became icy cold. She went to go in the sauna but that wasn't working either. She then fainted and fell and hit her head. She was unconscious for some time until her aunt, Judy Kass, phoned her. When Judy heard she had fainted she called security at the apartment building. Katy managed to get dressed but, still barefoot, went out to the landing, where a 6' 3" burly security guard saw her pale and shaking. He asked her if she wanted him to call 911 and to get an ambulance. She had no recollection of saying no. Meanwhile, Percy and I were at a meeting and were not informed.

I had fainted at a *Vanity Fair* party a couple of years previously and when Percy asked if I had wanted an ambulance I too had said no. He, however, insisted on calling one and I was sent to Cedars Sinai Hospital, where they told me I suffered a vasovagal blackout.

My friend Natasha Richardson had also fallen on her head in Switzerland while skiing. Refusing offers of an ambulance, she skied back to her chalet and tragically died a few hours later from the blow.

I was quite aware that if you faint or fall you need to be checked out immediately, or it could be serious.

The security guard escorted a pale and shaky Katy to our apartment on the 25th floor. He made no attempt to hold her up or help her as the rules of the building forbade staff from touching anyone. She kept her balance by hanging onto the walls of the building. When they arrived at the door to our apartment he took her keys and, while he was opening the door, Katy, without support, allegedly fell forward, with disastrous results – her eye socket shattered from hitting the moulding. Now the security guard had to call an ambulance, which took my unconscious daughter to hospital.

The moment we were finally informed, Percy and I raced to ER to find Katy barely conscious, in great pain and with a colossal yellow and black bruise under her left eye. The doctor diagnosed an orbital fracture. She had to have an operation and then she underwent many months of therapy and excessive pain.

The apartment building Sierra Towers absolved itself of any responsibility for Katy's accident, which was shocking. I couldn't believe the total lack of responsibility and compassion. Unable to stay in this overly priced and ostentatious building, we sold it the following year and downsized to a less pretentious address.

When Percy and I returned from LA to our Belgravia flat in 2017, I was horrified to see that the sitting room was a scene of absolute devastation. The entire ceiling above the French windows had collapsed, water was cascading down like a waterfall, and debris and filth were strewn all over my beautiful sofas, furniture and hand-made carpet. Everything was ruined. It had happened the previous day and my brother Bill had luckily discovered it only that morning.

The insurance loss adjustor arrived and tried to minimise the damage. 'It's only your sitting room, and you have perfectly ample other rooms for you to stay here while they make the repairs,' he told us, having to shout above the din of the construction that was being carried out above, below and around us. The entire building was crawling with builders. They were completely renovating the floor above us, and they were joining two further floors above and the roof into a triplex apartment! They were also upgrading the lift and the electrics, no doubt to accommodate the new owners. The place was a war zone, with scaffolding everywhere and workers tramping up and down the stairs and hallways all day long. There was no doubt that these repairs, renovations or restorations had caused the wreckage in our sitting room. So, now we had to have construction inside our flat, while we stayed there? Ha, it would be unbearable!

We hired our own loss assessor, Alex Balcombe, who arrived that afternoon. He immediately told us we could not stay in our flat. 'Health and safety won't allow it. It's totally unreasonable for you to have to stay here.'

'What are we supposed to do?' I wailed.

'Stay at a hotel,' he said. 'Then after you find an apartment to live in for the duration, you will have to move all your furniture and books out of this room and into storage, and all your clothes and bedding too.'

I was so stunned I couldn't speak.

'Then we need to fix the root of the problem.'

'Which is . . .?' asked Percy.

'We think a pipe on one of the floors above you has been badly compromised. In other words, they are completely broken.'

'They *broke*!! How could that happen?'

'This is a very old building and builders' construction crews don't always do the right thing.'

'The insurance men will be coming again later,' he said as he left.

Alex Balcombe had scanned the insurance policy, a book which seemed to be about two thousand pages long. Basically, it said if you cannot stay in your home due to things beyond your control that are not your fault, the insurance company is obliged to put you up in a hotel. We then had to look for a flat to stay in commensurate with the value of our apartment (i.e. very expensive!). But there was a lot of resistance. We spent the first night in our ruined flat while the powers that be decided our fate, but it was untenable.

The next morning we checked into Forest Mere health spa for a few days. While we were there, we heard that a second leak had sprung, this time over our dining room. The walls had cracked, and our beautiful wooden floor looked like the deck of the *Titanic* – after the iceberg. There was no question now that we had to move out.

We stayed at Claridge's for a few days while searching for a rental apartment big enough and with enough closet space for my extensive collection of clothes. The insurance people squawked but we finally found a beautiful unfurnished flat nearby in Chester Square. It was very expensive, but no more than the value of our flat. How the insurance guys squawked!

So, after packing up our possessions (many of which were so utterly destroyed that we had to ditch them), we hired a van and moved into our temporary new home. Furniture, books, pictures, beds, bedding, clothes, jewellery, television sets – everything! It took endless days to move our entire household, during which time it was impossible to do any kind of work. Friends and family came to help pack up cutlery, glasses, plates, saucepans, food and then take them to our new temporary abode.

It was bad enough doing a major house move, but having to leave my beloved flat for just a few months was such a waste of time, effort and money – believe me, the insurance didn't pay for everything. Oh no, they're much too canny. They agreed to pick up the tab for the rental flat for a limited time, after which we were liable to pay.

Our builders, who had to totally reconstruct and rebuild our sitting and dining rooms, promised faithfully that they would have it all done speedily. Ha ha di ha!

Predictably, the workmen dismantled and destroyed my living room and dining room, and then found hidden problems that had to be addressed. I managed to source the same wallpaper, sofa fabric, curtains and carpet and then we waited . . . and waited . . . and waited for the flat to be finished.

Seasons came and went, as did my patience. The time limit had elapsed, and so did the payments from the insurance company, even though the builders were still way off finishing. Three months of paying eye-watering rent ensued and I wasn't working!

Eventually, after months of complaining, we were able to move everything back again, but we were seriously out of pocket, not to mention patience. Alexis Carrington wouldn't have stood for it! She would have bullied and blackmailed the builders and the insurance company until she got what she felt she deserved. It was an absolutely horrible experience and I pity anyone who finds themselves in the same boat. After death and divorce, moving house is the third most stressful thing in a person's life, and to have to do it when you're *not* actually moving house is soul-destroying!

We did manage to throw a rather great spring party at the Chester Square flat though, and many of our friends said they preferred it to *our* flat! But I didn't – I love my flat and I found

Chester Square cold and uncomfortable, despite the great views. It was like living in a glass shoebox.

'Can you smell burning?' I asked Percy.

We were relaxing on our bed one Saturday afternoon in April 2019 after lunching with my granddaughter Miel. We had planned on seeing a movie afterwards, but Miel was tired, so Percy and I decided to head home and watch Jack Nicholson on TV in *As Good as It Gets*.

As we relaxed, smoke suddenly started to seep into our bedroom.

Percy jumped off the bed and sped down the hall, which was filled with black smoke coming from the guest bedroom.

'Call the fire brigade,' he yelled and, arming himself with a portable fire extinguisher, flung himself into the smoke-filled room, barefoot, wearing just a dressing gown. Panicked, I dialled 911 on my mobile phone, but there was no reply because, of course, that's the American emergency number! I managed to punch in 999 and, after telling the operator what was happening, she crisply said, 'Get out of the house right now, and tell your husband to stop what he is doing and get out too.'

'But I need some shoes and my bag,' I stammered.

'You *must* evacuate the building – NOW!'

After screaming for Percy through the by now smoke-filled flat, I stumbled barefoot down the stairs to the foyer and called 999 again.

'When are they coming?' I cried.

'On their way,' replied the operator.

I was truly terrified. My husband was still in our flat, mirroring Steve McQueen in *The Towering Inferno*, and there was no sign of the firefighters. All the neighbours were obviously away for the weekend and there was no one on the street. Suddenly, a nice lady appeared at the front door, holding out a small package.

'It's your caviar,' she smiled sweetly. 'Your husband ordered it yesterday.'

I clung onto her gratefully and said, 'Oh my God, thank you – please stay with me – don't go.'

'Of course,' she glanced fearfully up the stairs where pale smoke was now drifting down.

'PERCY!' I yelled. 'Come down!' I was terrified he had been overcome by the fumes. I clutched my caviar-carrying friend and gulped, 'My husband is up there.'

I was just about to rush back up the stairs to save him when I heard the marvellous sound of fire engines. As the men started to unfold their hoses and other firefighting equipment, the chief jumped out.

'Where's your husband?' he yelled. I gestured up weakly and he bounded up the stairs at the same time as a smoke-blackened Percy came stumbling down. I then blurted out one of the most clichéd lines in films, 'Oh, thank God you're safe.' One of the most clichéd lines, that is, aside from, 'Everything's going to be OK.'

Two young firefighters ushered me into a waiting ambulance and slapped an oxygen mask on my face, not before I immediately called my brother Bill, who lived close by. By now the police had closed off the entire street and festooned it with yellow plastic tape, which fluttered like flags on American Independence Day.

Then I heard a familiar voice yelling, 'Where is she?'

'Sorry, madam, you can't go in, this street is closed.'

'You *better* let me in – that's my sister-in-law in there.'

'Sorry, madam,' the polite voice responded, 'but . . .'

'No buts, that's my effing sister-in-law. I must see her.'

'Let her in please,' I yelled. 'It's Hazel, my brother's wife.'

'OK, OK,' said the fireman, and in swept Hazel, my fabulous sister-in-law, swathed in cashmere, concerned and worried. She has always been the 'be there' person and comforter in our family.

I told Hazel what had happened. 'So now I have no shoes or bag or hairbrush or sunglasses and I'm a wreck!'

'I saw a couple of paps lurking,' Hazel warned. 'Let's get you out of here.'

'They won't let me go home,' I said, as Percy entered the ambulance, reeking of smoke but grinning widely.

'I just had a telling-off from the fire chief,' he laughed. 'He said I should never have attempted to fight the fire with the extinguisher. But . . .' and he smiled even wider, 'he said that I saved the whole building from going up in flames!'

'My hero.' I hugged him. 'You're Superman.'

'Anyway, I can't leave,' Percy said. 'I've got to wait for the inspector apparently. But you can go.'

'Better be careful,' Hazel said, peering out of the window. 'The paps will love seeing you looking like this. Let's go to my place.'

'We'll take you in the ambulance,' chimed a young fireman.

'Great, thank you. You guys are the best.'

Relaxing at Hazel's over cups of tea with the two young firemen, I shuddered to think about what could have happened to the whole building if we had decided to just go to the cinema as planned.

'It was a freak fire,' Percy said later. 'The inspector discovered that a mirror on the window sill in the bathroom had caught the sun and it set fire to the curtains, that's how it started – apparently, it happens a lot.'

'My God,' I said. 'Thank God you had the presence of mind to use the extinguishers.'

'What's so crazy,' said Percy, 'is that the Fire Department don't want people to have them in their houses anymore. They say there's a risk I could have been overcome by smoke and died.

But they are insisting we get monitored smoke alarms in every room.'

'Great idea,' said Hazel, dispensing more tea to the firemen.

Eventually, we were allowed back into our home, and although there was a faint aroma of smoke, we spent the night there. Meanwhile two first responders visited our flat and although we already had two fire alarms, they insisted on putting one in every room.

After all the recent dramas, we decided to take a quiet ten-day family holiday in our villa in the forest near Saint-Tropez: my daughter Tara, her husband Nick Arkle, Tara's daughter Miel and her boyfriend, Tara's son Weston and his friend Theo and our close friend from New York, Jack Rich. We expected to enjoy some restful days away.

Shortly after arriving, a massive mistral kicked off in the area. The hot winds blew mercilessly and brought unbearably hot Saharan aridity. The mistral has such an effect on French people that it's been said that a man who murders his wife during one will not be charged because of 'mistral madness'. I kept a close eye on Percy, and he kept a close eye on me, as did Tara and Nick on each other!

The sizzling temperatures were breaking all known records, so I spent most of the time in the oasis of air conditioning. The villa is high on the hills and we've had several bad fire scares over the years. The previous year, forest fires came within a mile of our villa, so the local *pompier* decided through some marvel of French logic to ensure our safety by putting a large lock on the barrier of the access road from my house to the main road, thereby effectively annulling our escape route had the fire caught in the forest surrounding us! I was, to say the least, not a happy camper for several days until we persuaded the *pompiers* not to lock our barrier.

The mistral winds were now tearing along at eighty miles an hour and, coupled with the 100-degree heat and the smell and sight of smoke, 'I wuz scared, Miz Scarlett.'

It was impossible to sit by the pool because you would not only roast from the sun but the wind would suck up all the moisture from your body. The pool furniture and umbrellas were being buffeted about, often ending up in the pool, and doors and windows kept slamming, frightening the living daylights out of us.

Everyone pretty much stayed inside and the images we had of lazy days frolicking about in the pool were dashed, like cases of rosé falling off a truck. One evening, after an afternoon game of salad bowl, we were celebrating with rosé and delicious lasagne when we noticed several helicopters and planes circling overhead by the sea.

'Those look like fire planes. I'll drive up the hill and take a look,' said Percy.

No sooner had he left than Tara, pointing at a plume just over our hill, said, 'Isn't that smoke over there near us?' Grabbing some binoculars, I ran outside and saw, to my horror, huge columns of smoke and flashes of fire literally half a mile away on another hill.

I immediately thought of the recent fires in Portugal, where people fleeing in cars had been trapped and consumed by flames. We stood rooted to the spot, watching the smokestack become bigger and wider, like the cloud from an A-bomb. Helicopters and fire planes attempted to douse the fiery mass with flame retardant. Then my mobile rang. It was Percy, who said, 'I don't want you to panic . . . but tell everyone to grab their passports and valuables, put on some sensible clothes and get in the cars NOW. I'm on my way back.'

My 'Blitz baby' mentality kicked in, as I recalled the nights of being woken up, jumping feverishly into my siren suit and pixie hat, and stumbling down into the air-raid shelters during the bombings. Although I was too young to be fully aware of how much danger we were in then, I was well aware of the peril we were in now.

Not having a siren suit at hand, I hastily donned combat gear – trackies, baseball cap, an old cardigan the moths had been dining on – and threw a few 'essentials' into a bag. Only later when I unpacked did I realise that, other than a T-shirt, my essentials consisted of three pairs of sunglasses, two paperback books and a fan. A fan! Like I needed one to fan even more flames!

Steve McQueen's quote from *The Towering Inferno* flashed into my consciousness – 'It's outta control and it's coming our way.' I'd never seen our house guests move so quickly with utterly grim fixed expressions, which thinly veiled sheer panic. I felt particularly keenly for my daughter Tara, who had been trapped in bad fires twice in her life before.

Eleven terrified people mobilised to cram themselves into two small cars and escape. As we drove up the hill, we saw massive flames and several fire-trucks and firefighters controlling the dozens of cars that were trying to flee the area.

Our two staff, the two youngest boys and Jack had taken off practically the moment I had hung up. Tara, her daughter, her daughter's boyfriend and Nick came with us. We had decided to meet in the closest village to the south, which was Rama-tuelle, but on the way there we had received a message from Jack and the boys saying, 'It's too smoky, we are now heading to Gassin,' another village in the north. We later heard that thirteen-year-old Theo, in the back of the other car, suggested he call his mother, whereupon Jack, with level-headed New York composure, retorted, 'And say what? That you are in the back of a car running from a raging fire? Call her after you're safe.'

'Looky-loos' lined the narrow roads taking pictures, making navigation on the two-way street difficult, but we persevered.

When we arrived at the gas station, where we had agreed to meet, we saw no sign of the other car. We decided to fill up, hoping the others were just delayed. I went into the shop to buy some water for everyone and met a Dutch man from Gigaro, the town where the fire had started. Wearing shorts and a shirt, he said that the fire had been so close to their house his family didn't even have time to grab anything. 'It is very bad and it's spreading,' he said. The shop owner gave a Gallic shrug and said in French that everything would be OK and it would not be a big problem. I looked askance at him as we both detected the pungent odour of smoke emanating from our neighbour's hair. The shop owner attempted another Gallic shrug and a 'c'est la vie', but it stalled halfway.

Tara in the meantime managed to contact the staff, who had been driving so furiously panicked that they had completely bypassed our gas station! We arranged a new rendezvous point, Sainte-Maxime, across the bay from Saint-Tropez.

We were finally reunited in Sainte-Maxime, outside another bleak gas station, and gazed at the flames leaping up across the bay. I sat in the back of the car quaffing a much-needed bottle of water while everyone got out and huddled together to make onward plans. Then I attempted to join them but when I reached for the door handle, it wouldn't open. I remembered the doors were child-proof so they couldn't be opened from inside. I had given my phone to Percy, so all I could do was bang on the windows with my empty plastic water bottle and yell at the top of my lungs for them to release me. But the group was too fixated on making plans and oblivious to my plight. It's truly astonishing how long six minutes can feel if you're trapped in the darkness of a boiling-hot car with flames nearby.

Finally, my grandson Weston noticed my exertions and came to my rescue. 'What are you doing back there?' he asked with a twinkle.

Percy and Tara were on their phones trying to find places to stay, but the combination of high season and so many other people escaping the inferno frustrated their efforts. I decided to call our friends Warren and Susie Todd, who had a villa in Saint-Tropez. They immediately offered the succour of three guest rooms. By this time, Tara, who speaks perfect French thanks to several years in school in Paris, had managed to find two rooms in a local hotel, but the landlord would only allow two people per room, rendering two of our group homeless. Realising Miel and her boyfriend had to leave the next day, we decided that they should stay close to Nice airport. Fortunately, they had completely packed and taken their cases so Percy set about finding a hotel for them in Nice.

While waiting for a driver to arrive, everyone kept on sneaking glances at their mobiles, checking the latest fire updates on the local news. Miel walked around the group sweetly dispensing hugs and reassuring everyone that 'It will be all right.' Miel's boyfriend kept hugging *her*, while Weston's friend Theo, this being his first trip out of the country, finally got to call his mother.

Tara and family were whisked away to a safe place, and we headed to ours.

The fire continued to rage on, as efforts to contain it were hampered by darkness. Percy drove Jack and me through various checkpoints where gendarmes and *pompiers* remained vigilant and helpful through the night, herding terrified evacuees through chaos to safety. The organisation of the French forces was extraordinary. In all, twelve thousand people were relocated safely without loss of life, while over four thousand brave firefighters and gendarmes, dozens of whom were injured, fought several wildfires over a large area for days.

I don't think there is anything scarier than being trapped in a fire – it's unpredictable, spreads so fast and consumes everything in its wake, like a herd of bison careening down a hill. It brought back the terrifying hours many years ago in Paris with my then husband, Anthony Newley, and our baby daughter Tara. We were trapped in our hotel room with fires above and below us until we were rescued by the *pompiers*.

Tara texted later to say that they were the last people to get a room in the hotel, and there were several homeless families sleeping in the lobby. Many were far less lucky and had less resources than I do, so I feel only grateful. But my deepest gratitude goes to the brave French heroes who, like our own wonderful firefighters and policemen, plunge headlong into danger daily to keep everyone safe.

It was supposed to be a leisurely, picturesque drive through the verdant Provençal countryside and glorious beaches of the South of France as we headed to a wedding in June 2015.

'It will only take two and a half hours to get to Gordes – three at the absolute maximum,' trilled my friend, mother of the bride Stella Wilson. 'You can find the directions online at Amy and Chris's wedding website.' When I suggested to the man of the house that he do this, he was adamant that it wasn't necessary. 'Satnav will tell us how to get there,' Percy pronounced firmly.

We set off at 11.15 in our rented car, with plenty of time to get to our hotel to shower and change before the 5 p.m. wedding. 'On the way, let's show our two house guests how to get to Ikea in Toulon,' I suggested. Percy looked doubtful, saying Toulon was slightly off route, adding perhaps half an hour to the trip.

'Well, I'm sure satnav will show us the way,' I replied breezily, forgetting the advice of our English driver Steve, who calls his satnav 'Edna' and scornfully refers to her as 'bloody useless'.

We bade farewell to our Ikea-bound friends on the outskirts of Toulon an hour later and I relaxed, admiring the magnificent roads and infrastructure – not a bump or pothole to contend with, and the gorgeous scenery. Despite the cost of the tolls, which can be exorbitant, there is something to be said for the quality of the roads that the taxes create – *magnifique*.

After an hour I asked Percy, 'We should be there soon, shouldn't we? Haven't we just passed Avignon? And why exactly are we heading towards that hugely steep mountainous road?'

Grimly he replied, 'The satnav seems to be sending us that way, but yes, we should be there soon,' with a slight quaver in his voice that only a wife of fourteen years can detect. However, his absolute concentration on the satnav and the horribly winding road brooked no argument, so I lay back, tried to relax and listened to a Steely Dan CD for the third time.

An hour later, we reached the top of the mountain. As far as I could see, there were absolutely no signs of life or civilisation whatsoever. I ventured the remark, 'Are we close yet?'

Through clenched teeth came a monosyllabic grunt and, since the winding road was making me feel queasy, I decided to shut up until I saw the sign to Marseille, yet another hour later. 'That should be near, shouldn't it?' I chirped hopefully. The stony silence that met me gave me my answer. Suddenly the view changed and we found ourselves in the shabby outskirts of Marseille, with its grim buildings glaring at us menacingly.

Angry-looking people were milling about and Percy, now furious with 'Edna', hissed, 'She's taking us totally the wrong way. We're way off course.' There were a few more juicy adjectives interspersed in there. To make things even more heated, there was a strike by local taxi drivers demonstrating against Uber.

A friend had told me that upon arriving at Marseille airport, dozens of cabs lined up but refused to take fares, even after our friend offered €500 to take them to the wedding, easily twice the normal fare.

We wound our way through traffic-clogged urban side streets. It was by now way past the three and a half hours allotted for the trip, and not only were we in the seamy backstreets of Marseille, but stories of illegal immigrants breaking into vehicles kept running through my panic-stricken mind like shades of *Bonfires of the Vanities*.

After negotiating several spaghetti junctions, Percy announced victoriously, 'Not far now,' but his tremulous tone gave the game away – not much of a poker player, my husband. I tried to figure out how little time I would need to shower, make-up, do hair and dress in time for the wedding. We passed endless signs but not one said 'Gordes' or anything remotely helpful.

Desperate for a rest room, we found a small garage and shop, but when I enquired '*Où est la toilette?*' he gave another one of those Gallic shrugs the French are so famous for and shook his head, '*ne pas toilette*'.

On we drove – I was now quietly hysterical and Percy quietly furious. Every time we passed a sign, he said, 'Won't be long now' in increasingly strained tones. When we finally went off-road to find a rest stop (the situation was reaching critical mass), he stayed in the car to have a serious chat with 'Edna'.

Which is when he discovered that the previous car lessee had programmed the satnav to avoid all toll roads! Instead of driving the smooth direct motorways, we had been forced into following every winding road in Provence. Tired and weary, we finally arrived by some miracle at the hotel five hours and fifteen minutes later, with half an hour to spare before the wedding.

The hotel, though charming, was newly decorated and freshly

painted, so after barging past the front desk attendant with demands for the key – God knows what the poor chap thought of
us – we found the door to our room firmly glued shut with paint.
The concierge and Percy pushed and shoved and eventually had
to call a handyman, who proceeded to push and shove so hard
they finally managed to pull the handle off the door. All three
then gave an almighty shove and broke into the bedroom.

With fifteen minutes left to prepare for a glamorous wedding,
like maniacal quick-change *artistes* we hit the wedding venue a
minute before the bride walked down the aisle.

The wedding was a magical, romantic and picturesque event,
of the kind that only the South of France can provide: a fairy-
tale setting, overlooking the majestic cliffs created by ancient Ice
Age canyons. The bride, Amy, looked ethereally beautiful; Chris,
the groom, handsome but suitably apprehensive; and Stella,
the mother of the bride, endearingly choked up with emotion
so that our tribulations with 'Edna' soon vanished in a haze of
romance.

Having learned our lesson, the next day it was motorway all
the way and the trip was completed in less than two and a half
hours. 'Edna' in her wicked way still tried to take us 'off-piste',
but we opted instead for our tried-and-true route – no scenery,
several expensive tolls, but clean rest stops and no Gallic shrugs.

No more 'Edna' for me – give me an old-fashioned map every
time – and yes, I can read one!

While touring Hong Kong in the mid-1980s, Judy Bryer and I
were excited about being invited for dinner on a Chinese 'junk',
but when we drove to the harbour we found ourselves in the
middle of a howling gale. I'm not keen on any kind of sailing
unless the water is like glass, and this sea was a shattered chandelier. We gingerly stepped down rickety wooden steps onto

a tiny, old-fashioned, frail-looking boat which was bouncing about on the waves.

'Don't worry,' smiled our Chinese host, 'she is quite safe. We have all the most modern equipment.'

Nervously, we went below deck and were offered a much-needed alcoholic beverage. We sat chatting for a while, hearing excited the babble above us from the people who were getting the boat moving.

Then we were off into the swirling waters of the South China Sea. Glancing out of the tiny porthole, I saw massive waves which gave me more than a touch of fear.

After we had made some small talk with our host, the engine suddenly stopped and all we could hear were even more overly excited voices. 'Are you sure we are safe?' asked Judy anxiously, as our host looked doubtful and dashed above deck.

'I'm going up too,' announced Judy bravely, adjusting the short new wig she had bought that afternoon in the Hong Kong market.

'Are you sure about wearing that?' I asked.

'It's fine,' she said. 'Fastened tighter than a drum,' she added as she climbed the stairs.

'OK, I'll come too,' I said, tying my hair back with a scrunchy and following her.

We clambered onto the upper deck where a scene from hell was revealed. About fifteen sailors were attempting to attach ropes from our junk to several small rowboats and motorboats. Our engine-less boat was being forced towards the entrance of the deadly South China Sea, one of the most dangerous passages in maritime travel. The small boats were attempting to drag the junk back to port, but with little success.

The wind was so fierce that within seconds, Judy's beautiful wig was whisked off her head and blown into the waves. I couldn't help giggling as I patted my tied-back hair and gloated, 'I told you! You shouldn't have worn it.'

By now our hosts were looking terrified, shouting incomprehensible instructions in Chinese to the sailors. As the sailors tried to fasten the ropes, several fell into the sea, bobbing up and clambering into the already overstressed boats that surrounded our junk.

'What the hell is happening? This is a nightmare!' I yelled.

'If we don't get our engines working soon, we'll be swept out to sea, and that won't be pretty,' gasped our host.

'Can't you send out a Mayday signal?' I asked. He looked at me incredulously then turned to scream at the sailors even more loudly.

'I've never been so scared in my life,' wailed Judy, hanging onto the flimsy railing.

'Me neither,' I said as the boat pitched back and forth. The storm raged, and we hung onto the railings as the hurricane seemed totally out of control. All we could do was pray, terrified we'd be swept overboard. It was like being in a disaster movie. 'I'm never getting in a boat again!' I said.

After an eternity, the sailors managed to get the engines working and the boat limped back to harbour. On trembling legs, we climbed the rickety steps up to the quay.

'I need a drink!' I gasped.

'I need six!' said Judy.

That was not the only time travelling has not quite gone to plan for me . . .

In the year before everyone owned a mobile, my PR Stella Wilson rang to ask if I would like to open a new boutique hotel on one of the beautiful Greek islands.

'Oh, what fun! Let's ask Biggins too,' I said.

Accordingly, one fresh June morning, the three of us arrived in Athens and were whisked by boat to the Island of Corfu. We arrived in a tiny ancient seaside village on the outskirts of Corfu and were shown to our quarters. There we were presented with three prefabricated Nissen-type beach huts, which were simply furnished just like army barracks: one single bed and a chest of drawers in each hut, and in my connecting room, a small fridge. When we opened it, the stench of decaying meat from an old sandwich and a shrivelled half-peeled orange hit us like a dead wet squirrel.

Our host offered to show us around the hotel grounds, which took about four minutes. Then he proudly pointed to a dirt road and a sign scratched onto a piece of driftwood which said 'Joan Collins Boulevard'. We were now in hysterics as Biggins was on top form, cracking sarcastic jokes.

The following day, we were invited to the beach area. This had been cleverly advertised as having 'golden sands, azure, calm seas and a myriad of entertainments, a tasty beach buffet, jet skiing, water skiing and boating'.

Our buggy driver, who looked about thirteen, dumped us on a stretch of the not-so-golden sand, threw three small towels at us emblazoned with the logo 'Thompson Hotels' and zoomed off with a cheery wave. Our cries of 'Where is the tasty beach buffet?', 'Where are the boats?', 'Where are the deckchairs?' scattered in the wind of his sandy wake.

'*Où est la toilette?*' I whimpered, as he disappeared.

'We're in Greece, not France,' Christopher Biggins chided.

We were alone, stranded, with not even a bottle of water to slake our thirst.

'I'm sure he'll come back soon with water,' said the ever-optimistic Stella.

'We could stay here for days,' said the pessimistic Biggins.

'Then, in about a week, they will find our mouldering skeletons.'

He looked thoughtful. 'I wonder who'll get top billing when the tabloids find out?' he mused.

'I will, of course,' I replied crisply.

'Just let's relax and enjoy the day,' pleaded Stella.

So, we did. For hours and hours and hours, until our tongues hung out from thirst. I seriously considered doing what one of the mutinous sailors did in *Mutiny on the Bounty*.

'I think I'll drink some seawater,' I joked gaily.

'Don't you dare!' screamed Biggins, as he splashed seawater over my sunburnt face.

'Just kidding, sea water is polluted anyway. Get it off me!'

'And fish fuck in it,' laughed Biggins.

'Oh, please – that old turkey,' I groaned. 'Get some new material, Biggins.'

'If only we had one of those new porto-phones,' I said.

'Oh, they'll never catch on,' scoffed Biggins.

After what seemed like days, the spotty youth returned in the buggy and threw three tiny bottles of Evian water at us. 'Sorry, I forgot to give you these. Do you want to get back to base now?'

'Does Dolly Parton sleep on her back?' I joked grimly.

'I don't know, does she?' asked the youth, as we clambered into the buggy.

That night, amidst great fanfare (for a village), I opened 'Joan Collins Boulevard' and the accompanying hotel, and the next morning we left, never to return, but with some amusing memories to share.

Another incident occurred in Memphis, when I was on tour with my book, where I was honoured with the title of 'Honorary Duckmaster' at the famous Peabody Hotel. For the past seventy years, this fine establishment has been holding a daily ceremony whereby the five cute ducks that reside there are brought down from their penthouse suite to the decorative pond in the hotel lobby. When Percy and I got into the elevator from our tenth-floor suite, the terrified ducks were huddled into a corner squawking nervously. 'We don't usually stop to pick up the duck-master,' said the head duckmaster, 'so the ducks are a bit scared.' They certainly were. I suddenly realised the entire floor of the lift was covered in the evidence of their fear. Unfortunately, their agitated flapping meant my white trousers were liberally splat-tered as well. Nevertheless, it was quite a spectacle to walk the red carpet behind the little waddlers while hundreds of tourists gaped at and photographed not only the event, but no doubt my newly patterned pants . . .

I broke my toe in Minneapolis in 2000. This is far from the glamorous image of leaving my heart in San Francisco and in-finitely more painful.

I stubbed it on a faux Chippendale dining room table leg during a breakfast meeting at the hotel. It was a hot September morning and the traffic on the motorway was gently buzzing outside when my toe brushed against the raw metal end-claw of the table leg which was sticking out menacingly, and my howl of pain pierced through the almost bucolic setting. After X-rays at the local hospital, the doctor said, 'Yup, it's a severe fracture and the metatarsal [or something like that] is dislocated.'

'What can I do?' I wailed.

'There's nothing you can do with toes except wait. Only time heals toes.'

Hobbling in sandals back to New York and various meetings, I soon realised as autumn cast its gentle glow that I could not cram my foot into any of my stilettos, flats, boots or even sneakers. My right foot had swollen to two sizes bigger than the other. Being somewhat of an Imelda Marcos, I locked myself in my closet for a marathon shoe-fitting session which ended up making me feel like one of Cinderella's ugly sisters as I tried cramming into pair after endless pair. Eventually, I went to Bloomies for a restock and re-fit.

After two weeks of considerable pain every time I put any weight on my foot, Percy insisted on whisking me off to the Number 1 foot man in New York, Dr Rock Positano. Anyone with a name like that is bound to rise high in his field and Dr Rock was no disappointment. After examining the toe, he told me the doctor in Minneapolis was wrong and should have insisted I keep my foot bandaged all the time and iced twice a day – so much for middle-American medical advice. Needless to say, with the bandage on, I now needed shoes *three* sizes bigger and so another shopping rampage was afoot.

Six weeks later, I was still hobbling around bravely, gritting my teeth, and remembering Grandma's words: 'You must suffer to be beautiful.'

So, wearing on one foot a size 5 shoe and on the other a size 8, over the bandages, I ventured forth to Harry's Bar for dinner with my friend and brilliant designer Valentino.

Va Va, as we call him, must have eyes in the back of his head. As soon as he saw me, without missing a beat, he said, 'My dear, what happened to your foot?'

The man must have a sixth sense as he never even glanced at my feet.

In 2022 when we arrived at our Provençal villa, where we holiday every year, we were greeted by the sight of our front gate hanging off its hinges. Our concierge gave his bloody Gallic shrug again and said, 'the people' were coming to fix it, but they were 'very, very, very busy'. Everyone is very, very, very busy in France during the summer. Either very, very, very busy or on holiday.

The next day, the couple who were going to work for us for three months, who the agency had thoroughly vetted and we had interviewed twice, quit! The husband told Percy he had a heart condition and couldn't do the job, and his partner could neither cook nor drive!

'Why didn't you tell us?' we asked at lunchtime, surrounded by four house guests.

'I told the employment agency that I had potential heart problems,' the man replied. 'They should have told you, I'm sorry.'

We were stumped. This was the first proper holiday with invited guests since COVID. This was a disaster.

We muddled through, all guests chipping in with cooking and washing up in 95-degree heat. It was almost too hot to lie in the sun under an umbrella.

Two days later, our rental car broke down. Percy exchanged it, got charged a premium due to the seasonal price rises, but two days later that one broke down as well. When we exchanged it again, the prices had skyrocketed so much that it became cheaper to buy a car!

After the front gate was finally fixed, rats suddenly infested the guest room that my daughter Katy was staying in. Luckily, in came the very, very, very busy exterminators who managed to get rid of the little blighters.

A month later, the employment agency found another couple to work for us but, within ten days, one of them was whisked off to hospital with gallstones and was unable to work for three weeks! As this was the time when our annual poker group arrived, we now had eight house guests and only half of a working couple.

Then disaster struck me.

It was just a painful twinge in my right leg as I followed Tonya the Trainer's exercise routine on Zoom in my bedroom. Then I screamed from the pain and collapsed in agony. I tried to play poker with the gang, but each day the pain in my thigh became more and more intense.

Percy attempted to find a good doctor in Saint-Tropez, but they were all away. After multiple phone calls and practically begging, we managed to get an appointment for 3 p.m. that afternoon at the Princess Grace Hospital in Monaco. It was not an easy task to get from our village in Provence to Monaco, some ninety miles and a good three hours away by car, but we had to be at the hospital by three o'clock or the two specialists couldn't see us. It was a weekend after all.

There are some advantages to being Joan Collins and we took full advantage of them in this crisis. A helicopter was summoned and off we went, me screaming with every step in mounting agony. We arrived on the dot at the famous hospital to be met by the specialist and a wheelchair, into which I was plonked.

After an MRI and several agonising injections into my back, I was told it was probably a pinched nerve or slipped disc and I would have to stay overnight. An IV was attached to my arm, filled with glorious painkillers, and I finally fell into a peaceful sleep in the hospital bed.

Because no one was available over the weekend to order my discharge, I ended up spending two nights at the hospital in a beautiful haze. I was so drugged up I barely noticed the mediocre hospital food. One advantage to this was that I lost a few pounds, although I don't recommend that diet.

On Monday morning, after the doctor's report, I was told to go home, stay in bed, not move, and take even more pills, almost twenty a day!

'How long do you think this pain will last?' I asked the doctor.

'At least two weeks to two months,' he announced in his smooth French accent.

'WHAT?!' I almost fainted. I had house guests practically all summer; it was our much-anticipated holiday since the previous year we had both caught COVID and had to cancel our guests.

'You will just have to live with the pain, I'm afraid,' he concluded. Was that a faint smile I saw as he requested a photo with me?

For ten miserable days, I lay in bed convulsed with pain, even though I was taking tons of painkillers. Then I decided I *had* to get out of bed and try to be as normal as possible. Bravely, I attempted to walk, though every step was agony, and I screamed like a Hammer horror heroine. Friends from everywhere sent messages of love and support, but neither those, nor indeed the painkillers, helped to relieve my agony.

'Be patient,' said another doctor.

'Not my strong suit,' I replied. 'Gimme more drugs.'

Percy and his cousin Tommy gingerly carried me every morning into the pool, where floating on the water provided some relief and I tried some gentle exercises – but oh my God, the pain was searing.

After a week Percy packed me into a wheelchair, and we drove to a local restaurant for dinner. Having told the restaurant I was temporarily disabled, we found there was no wheelchair access at all.

We tried another restaurant, but it was the same thing – it seemed there was no access for wheelchair users anywhere in Provence, not even a tiny ramp. I started to realise the frustration and anger that long-term wheelchair users must experience, and my heart goes out to them, as in the US and UK there are accessibility ramps almost everywhere.

After I had my second MRI at the Princess Grace, I then had another series of shots in my back which hurt so much I fainted.

But it didn't stop a junior doctor from saying, 'And now can I have a selfie, please?' Percy almost hit him.

The next morning, we drove back to Destino. Helped by Katy and Rene Horsch, the man with the muscles, I kept on doing the pool exercises – and boy did his muscles come in handy when he and Percy pulled me out of the pool!

On Wednesday, 3 August, four weeks to the day since my injury, I was walking, swimming and exercising in the pool, and feeling much better. The nasty side to this is that some so-called 'friend' gave an interview to a US tabloid insinuating I was on my last legs and not expected to live. Well, them's the breaks and fingers crossed I will be fine. But I was lucky. Thanks to my great team of doctors and physiotherapists in London and the wonderful hospital staff, and Percy and all my friends, I was able to make a full comeback. Sadly, not everyone is so lucky.

And so, we said goodbye and farewell to the long hot summer of 2022 which, despite the searingly hot and dry weather, was for us a total washout!

15

Rules For Life

On 19 March 2020, when rumours of lockdown abounded, I went to dinner at 5 Hertford Street with our friend, the journalist Andrew Pierce. We had been booking restaurants all week to enjoy our last few days of freedom, only to have plans cancelled as they had all decided to close. Thankfully, Robin Birley kept 5 Hertford open. Little did we know then that Boris would announce total shutdown that evening!

The restaurant was eerily empty. There were only three of us in the entire building – positively apocalyptic. We all got quite drunk, as Robin kept yelling, 'It's just a flu! Don't worry!'

I had been really looking forward to that springtime in London, as I am quite a social animal and there were many events planned. Percy and I enjoy going out for lunch, dinner, movies or the theatre three or four times a week. But we also love staying at home and enjoying each other's company, which after twenty years of marriage is quite a feat!

But now COVID obliged us to stay at home, with no chance of parole. It was tough, particularly as the governmental guidelines were so nebulous. They seemed to indicate we should stay at home, but it was apparently not mandatory, whereas my friends in France and America were in total lockdown that sounded incredibly daunting. But after all, 'health is wealth' and that's all that matters. More than money or success, health can't be bought or traded, and I'm lucky. As my GP told me last month I was 'stunningly healthy'.

The thought of living in total isolation (except for my husband) was almost worse than actually getting the virus, which, according to lore, if you're healthy means that even if we got it, it would likely not have been fatal.

It was horribly fascinating to binge-watch the nightly news as each ghastly statistic (and each country's draconian method of dealing with them) unfolded. I sat in a dreamlike state as if watching the worst disaster movie. I was overwhelmed by the sorrow of the poor souls who succumbed, and every throat tickle carried thoughts of self-isolation. Crime-scene tape would enfold my bedroom and a masked attendant (likely my husband) breathing Darth Vader sighs as he dropped supplies from a safe distance. It was so much to take in. We heard the horrible numbers of those who died every day, hoping that it wouldn't visit us.

I firmly believe that the best antidote to diseases of the mind – meaning fear, resentment and anything that wears you down – is to keep busy. If you look at your life, there is always plenty to do. Tackle that shed or dusty attic or drawer, write the great British novel that lives inside many of you, clean up that email inbox. I grew up without TV, internet or video games, and during a time when parents were not geared to cater to their kids' every whim. I learned from an early age how to amuse myself.

So, during this early interim COVID period, when people didn't yet know what their lockdown future held, I came up with a few golden rules for my husband's and my self-imposed seclusion to follow. Things changed as the weeks turned into months, but these stayed constant throughout:

1) SLEEP: The best and most precious remedy to life's ills is sleep. (Unless your partner snores.) Fortunately, we have a spare bedroom, so Percy can banish himself to help us both get our golden slumbers and wake up refreshed and optimistic.

2) READ: My husband decided that one of his projects for the duration was to clear out the basement of the great mass of books that I've stored over the years. 'We'll give them to charity,' he said. The only problem with this was that I rediscovered many books I wanted to read again. So, while he was casually tossing them in boxes, I was quietly taking them away, and I had the added delight of watching his flummoxed face as the boxes never seemed to fill up . . .

3) PLAY GAMES: I love playing games (as evidenced above, but also more traditional games) such as poker, gin rummy and Scrabble. The only issue with this is that if one partner is more adept (me) it can lead to bickering. My alarm bell rings when Percy starts taking longer between turns at Scrabble and sighing deeply. This indicates it might be time to call a pause and go watch TV. Once, I beat him three times straight at Scrabble! He wasn't a happy puppy. But then he came back and beat me three times, so we're very evenly matched in our Scrabble abilities.

4) WATCH TV: There are a myriad of great (and a myriad of ghastly) offerings now on TV and every possible viewing platform. BritBox offers some fabulous British vintage fare to watch: *Upstairs, Downstairs* – much better than today's period pieces; *Fawlty Towers* – utterly brilliant yet politically incorrect! Any films with Barbara Stanwyck or Robert de Niro seem to be on there too. I

even found a box set of *Dynasty*, which was quite amusing actually. It definitely stood the test of time, and I was fascinated watching it. I hadn't seen many of the episodes and I didn't recognise half the dialogue or the clothes I wore. If I get bored, I'll bring out another box set of *Dynasty*.

5) KEEP AN EYE ON THE INTERNET: Streaming, of course, requires something called the internet. My husband, the prophet of doom, remarked early during the pandemic that he doubted this internet thingy would be able to hold out much longer with everyone putting a strain on it. A few days later, he burst into the room exclaiming, 'See? I was right. The internet is dead!!' 'What can I do? Can I help?' I replied (more to be supportive than to actually help). He grunted and left the room. A few minutes later, on the way to the kitchen I noticed something unusual. 'Darling,' I said, in my most placatory tone, 'isn't that white box thingy supposed to be plugged in?' A look of panic crossed his eyes. Minutes later the internet was back up, no doubt due to his talented technical exertions and my observance.

6) ECONOMISE: My husband and I also share another life experience: rationing. I went through the war and subsequent shortages, and Percy lived in Peru, in (what was then called) a Third World country through various coups, recessions and economic shocks, so we've learned how to economise. Tin foil is washed if dirty and neatly folded for re-use, loo rolls and soap are sparingly used, boxes saved for books or whatever else needs to be stored. We both even remember saving string and paper. Such economies, particularly figuring out novel ways of filling the fridge and cupboards, kept us busy for hours.

7) EXERCISE: Another great cure for all ills, exercise is key, but can also be a source of resentment. My husband has been on a health kick for the last few years, so he will wake up early for a run or a workout and come home flushed with virtuous accomplishment, while I lie in bed reading all the papers, sipping several cups of coffee. Percy's smug face seems to say, 'So, when are you getting moving?' I contemplate throwing the contents of my cup at him. But then I think better of it – what a waste of coffee.

8) CHAT TO ALL MY FRIENDS AND FAMILY: Nothing is more important (particularly when my 'hubby' seesaws between doom-mongering and virtuousness) than being in touch with other people. I love getting newsy emails from friends and family, particularly when they convey humorous observations of this new world. 'It's amazing,' an American friend remarked to me, 'judging from the empty supermarket shelves in Hollywood, how few gluten allergies there seem to be now.'

9) COOK: With new restrictions come new ideas – every closed door opens a window, or some such rubbish. 'When life gives you lemons, make lemonade!' I like to say. My husband and I found novel ways of using beans, pulses and other items, which, frankly, I never knew we had in the cupboards. But beware not finishing everything on the plate. 'That's at least a hundred grams of pasta you've left on your plate,' he scolded once, 'and the supermarket shelves are empty.' I gently pointed out that if he hadn't served me enough to feed a rugby squad, there might not be so much left over.

10) WRITE: There is nothing I enjoy more than observing our foibles and fancies and putting them down on paper, as I have done here!

*

I was asked to make a toast to the WWII veterans. It was a beautiful day at the beginning of May 2020, the seventy-fifth anniversary of VE Day. It was a day that stands out for me. Percy decked our terrace with Union Jack flags and bunting and at 3 p.m. I went onto the balcony. While several journalists, photographers and TV cameras hovered on the street below, I made a short toast to the heroes and heroines of the Second World War, Percy popped the champagne, and I raised my glass and gave the peace sign. The photographers yelled, 'Joan! Joan! Go here, Go there!' Little me obeyed while Christopher Biggins, Charles and Pandora Delevingne, my brother Bill, sister-in-law Hazel and Alex Silver all stood in the street cheering. We had a wonderful street party – keeping our distance, of course!

It is hard to commemorate or celebrate a day when it is only you with one other person. But Percy, of course, made my lockdown birthday fabulous. He came into my bedroom carrying chocolate cake complete with candles and surrounded by many presents. All day long the doorbell rang and flowers and cards arrived. Percy had compiled a video in which so many friends and loved ones had wished me a Happy Birthday. It was extremely moving. Robin Birley had sent us a divine packed dinner from Oswald's, including my favourite dessert: Tarte Tropezienne. After dinner, we watched the video again, and BBC2 showed two programmes about my life. A wonderful day, in spite of the circumstances around us.

But, COVID or no COVID, I had to keep working because the bills didn't give a hoot about the pandemic. And for me, today's work is where I can find it. That means I have to travel to faraway places and quarantine when returning. So, I often have to stay in while my friends are out shopping and going to restaurants.

One day during quarantine, the phone rang. 'Oh, no! Not again!' I wailed as a strange, muffled voice announced, 'This is your COVID Quarantine Officer. I'm at the door.'

Percy and I were in our attic sorting through stuff and we scrambled hastily down the steps. I picked up the intercom video, and saw a young man wearing a Metallica T-shirt and a hoodie. He asked my husband if he was who he was, demanded to see his passport, flicked through his iPhone and left. We complied meekly, not once challenging him to show *his* credentials and smiling nervously for fear of incurring his wrath.

An hour later the phone rang and we didn't get to it in time but feared a message from a dreaded COVID Nazi.

'I hope they don't think we've gone out?' I said fearfully, having heard about a friend who was fined £1,000 for popping out to walk their dog at 6 a.m. Her husband was fined £10,000 for saying she was in bed! At 4 p.m. another call came. This time a schoolmasterish voice demanded my year of birth (something that rankles at the best of times).

All this is before worrying about being 'grassed up' by a neighbour. Fortunately we live in an area of London populated (or rather un-populated) by oligarchs who have parked their money in London real estate before their governments rip it off their cold dead fingers. During the 'Clap for the NHS', my husband and I would go outside with our pots and pans only to be greeted by one dog barking indignantly about being woken from its nap. I hope it was being fed.

'Behave!' 'Follow the rules!' 'Obey!' 'Stick to the guidelines!' These words strike anarchy into my heart. I'm not a robot, I'm a freedom-loving social being, but nevertheless I obeyed. 'Stay at home, or you'll die,' 'Keep away from other people or you'll be fined,' 'It's going to get tougher and tougher,' screeched the PM as Messrs Doom and Gloom nodded in agreement. There was no question in my mind that the only way out of this catastrophe was to get vaccinated. I spent weeks of envious anxiety, reading daily reports of various famous names getting vaccinated: Sir Ian McKellen, Dame Joan Bakewell, Dame Esther Rantzen – why not me?

I posted a photo on social media of Alexis behind bars with the caption 'What it feels like, waiting to be called up for my vaccine!' Checking the feed the next day, a message from someone called Raj Gill appeared. He said he ran an NHS surgery and that they had run out of people in my age category for the vaccine, so would I like to come into his surgery. Percy swallowed his doubts about this being a fake and called him. 'You have to get here before 5 p.m. – I'll try to keep a shot for her,' Raj told him. I put on sweatpants and a baseball cap and we bundled into a taxi.

Ever since the beginning of the ghastly plague, I had hoped for a vaccine. So, when this opportunity came up, I didn't give it another thought. As a little girl, I was first in the queue at my school to receive the mandatory DPT vaccine. My needle-phobic mother had a fit when I told her, so sadly I too developed an abnormal fear of needles for many years. However, having read more and more about the preventative properties of vaccines, I now dutifully take the flu shot every October, the pneumonia shot when advised and, because I've seen first-hand the crippling pain it can inflict on people, I also take the shingles shot.

In the GP surgery, Ammara Hughes chatted to me gaily as Raj Gill, my social media knight in shining armour, bustled about. Before I knew it, I felt a small scratch in my arm and Raj announced: 'It's done!'

'Really?' I exclaimed, greatly surprised. 'It was certainly seamless and painless!'

'Of course,' he smiled.

Getting the vaccine meant that two weeks later we could join Piers Morgan, Celia Walden, Amanda Holden and her husband Chris Hughes at the River Café for dinner. When we arrived we found that they had already sat down outside! It was utterly freezing, and even though I was wearing a heavy fur coat and boots, it was frigid. Amanda had her back against the wall, so she was protected from the wind. Percy and I were not, and even though there was a big heater close to my face, I was frozen. I was also shoulder to shoulder with Piers, who was laughing and chatting inches away from my face. 'This is the man who preaches on TV all the time to keep the two-metre "Social Distance"?' I whispered to Percy. I'm in the so-called 'vulnerable' category (that horrid ageist term); I bet he wouldn't have put his parents in that position. When we got home, Percy's hands and feet were frozen stiff. He sent Piers a thank you for 'as lovely a dinner as anyone could have in the Gulag'!

We attended Rupert Murdoch's ninetieth birthday at his house near Henley, once the home of Alfred, Lord Tennyson. I sat next to him and on my left side sat an awful man, described by some as 'an aristocrat'. He kept punching me on the arm where I'd had my second vaccine, to punctuate his unfunny quips.

'That hurts.' I said. 'Please don't hit me, I just had my booster.'

'What's a booster?' he leered.

Honestly, the so-called upper classes can be so removed from real life.

Rishi Sunak, the then-Chancellor, and his pretty wife were at my table with Piers and Celia, Alan Yentob, Jerry Hall and Michael Gove, looking happily (almost) divorced. All in all, a very interesting group of politicos and celebs. I was the only actress there (or actor, as one is supposed to say these days!).

16

Not Glowing Enough

In early July 2020, we lunched at Château de la Messardière in Saint-Tropez to meet Spanish producer José Luis Moreno and his two sidekicks to discuss me being in *Glow & Darkness*. This was a new TV series he was creating about the life of St Francis of Assisi. I struggled to see how the subject could appeal to the masses, but he promised epic battles and steamy love scenes. Moreno was incredibly charming and flattering; his team had brought three amazing thirteenth-century gowns to show me, plus a book of colour drawings of costumes, jewels, crowns, rings, etc. and one showing pictures of the cast. This included Jane Seymour (who apparently was going to play a twenty-five-year-old); Denise Richards (ex-Mrs Charlie Sheen); Mira Sorvino; Geraldine Chaplin; and Steven Berkoff. It was a fun lunch and I felt enthusiastic about the project. He said I was to play a forty-year-old but it wouldn't be a problem as the lighting and CGI would take care of it. I was dubious, but what the hell, work is work. He also gifted Percy a beautiful briefcase and a Montblanc pen set.

September brought an autumn glow, and chill, to our days in France. I had a long phone meeting with Moreno, who said not to worry about looking younger. His digital group had studied my face in pictures and said no problem in taking off thirty or forty years!

So, in mid-October, I commenced principal photography on *Glow & Darkness* in Spain. They flew us by private plane to Madrid and we arrived at a horrible, dirty-looking hotel – the bellman looked like 'Igor' in a stained shirt that was half untucked, the carpet was soiled and the soap was the size of a quarter. 'I can't stay here,' I announced, so Percy and I schlepped around Madrid trying to find better quarters. We finally found the Grand Palace, built by order of King Alfonso XIII in 1912, where liveried staff jumped at your briefest glance. A model of Victorian luxury, it was much more appropriate, given that I was playing a queen.

Although we were exhausted from travelling and having to move hotels, Moreno said we had to drive for an hour and a quarter to have dinner at his house. He insisted that we watch an hour of trailers of the show. (It was overly dramatic and blood-thirsty, but the production value was high, and blood and sex is what people want, I guess.)

It was beginning to dawn on me that José Luis seemed somewhat of a martinet, and an overly sensitive one at that. He reportedly didn't allow Jane Seymour, who was meant to join us for dinner, to leave her hotel until we finished watching the trailers. This meant dinner was now delayed since we had to wait for her to drive an hour and a half. At 10 p.m. we finally sat down for dinner, and there were about twenty different courses. I had to be up and running at 6 a.m. the next day for fittings and press, so by 11 p.m., thinking of the long drive back, Percy told José Luis that I needed to leave. Going down in his private lift, he boasted, 'I'm going to take care of you, Joan. I will treat you like a princess.'

I snapped. 'I've been around long enough, José. I don't need to be taken care of. Percy does that.' Moreno looked furious.

The next day, Percy got a half-hour bollocking from José Luis in Spanish. He was 'hurt and offended' by my dismissal of him 'wanting to take care of me'! I realised I was going to have to walk carefully on a few eggshells during this shoot.

On the first day I was nervous. I couldn't learn the new dialogue, which I'd only just been given. It was a mixture of cod Shakespeare which was directly translated from ancient texts by an Irish poet and ye olde English. I finally admitted defeat and, for the first time in my life, asked for 'idiot boards', which are cue cards on large boards on which the dialogue is written. I was devastated at the time, but it was the sensible solution as the speeches were extremely confusing and hard to learn.

After a sleepless night with disturbing dreams of thirteenth-century battles combined with massive swirling garlicky dishes of food, the morning of my first day of playing Adelaide of Savoy, twelfth-century queen of France and second wife of King Louis VI, dawned.

The cue cards had been written on flimsy bits of A4 paper stuck to trees and posts which flapped around in the wind and were so small that I couldn't read them. I was horribly embarrassed. I'm a pro, but I felt like a dumb rookie. Jane sympathised, telling me she couldn't learn them either and had been working with the script much longer than I had. Eventually I managed to muddle through my scene with Jane. As Eleanor of Aquitaine, she came galloping up to me on a white stallion, bareback! She is a very brave lady and managed to control the horse while we spoke our lines – with dignity, I hope.

The second day of the shoot was one of the toughest, because there were so many scenes that day to shoot, and the dialogue was still so hard to learn. Despite the massive cue cards that Percy held up for me, the lines were so convoluted and repetitive and didn't make sense that I still fluffed them, which embarrassed me further. Steven Berkoff had warned me about this when we had dined recently in London. 'It was an absolute nightmare, darling,' he said.

Everyone on the shoot was overworked and overwhelmed, including the wardrobe department. Nobody's dresses fitted properly and the styles were a mixture of eleventh-century Spanish, sixteenth-century Elizabethan, and a touch of eighteenth-century France! Critics of fashion will slaughter this series, I thought.

My final scene was a very dramatic crying scene, but at the end of shooting my role, the crew whooped and applauded: which brought tears to my eyes. I organised champagne for all the crew and made a farewell speech, wishing them well.

But then we had to stay for the press conference held at a hotel. Many journalists were in attendance, but they only asked me two questions: 'How did you like Madrid?' and 'How did you like playing the role?' I answered crisply in two minutes, and 'Herr Direktor' then translated my remarks for fifteen minutes!

The final fitting end to the production was learning, after a month had passed, that I still hadn't been paid. Jane called to tell me Denise Richards had been fired and told to get out of her hotel, as had many other actors. Jane then gave an interview to *The Times*, mentioning my age and arguing that if I could play forty, then she could easily play twenty-five! This became a cause célèbre in the press, even though Jane and I were friends. *Glow & Darkness* was one of my least favourite work experiences, and as of today it has *still* not been released! And I don't think it will be . . .

17

That's What Friends Are For

The past few years have shown us all the immense power of friendship. As soon as we got the COVID all-clear, Percy (who is also an American citizen) and I decided to take advantage of the fact that US citizens could fly to the USA with their spouses. The flight was practically empty, only seventeen people on board, and LA was open for business. Hurrah! It was such a relief to be able to go out again and socialise with friends.

Soon after we arrived, Michael Feinstein hosted a party for Liza Minelli's birthday, and Liza and I sang together with Michael at the piano. I ended up dancing with my doctor, Lawrence Piro, and everyone joined in. It was fabulous to see Liza on good form and singing all her hits, and fabulous to be living the good life again.

Liza hasn't had a lot of luck in love. When we attended her last wedding in New York in 2002, I wondered if it wasn't a bad omen to have ten bridesmaids dressed in funereal black. Many of the guests (some of whom had never met either bride or groom) were taking bets on how long these nuptials would last. They were spurred on by that ghastly X-rated kiss, which has since firmly planted an image in my head of David Gest as a catfish stuck against the side of a fish tank. Then Gest, who someone at the wedding described as looking like 'a boiled egg with sunglasses,' sued poor Liza for $7 million because, apparently, little Liza had slapped him so severely that he became distressed and brain-damaged! At least she refused to give him any of her Judy Garland Warhols. They look fabulous grouped on the walls of her charming apartment where she entertains her friends, and enjoys singing songs with Michael at the piano. I've often been asked to join in, and I don't mind admitting that singing a duet with the iconic Liza Minelli is one of the highlights of my life.

It was around this time that I caught up once again with my oldest friend, Evie Bricusse. Her husband Leslie, lyricist of so many enduring shows and songs, was very ill in France. I was extremely upset, as I didn't think he was going to make it. Cancer is a brute. I've lost so many friends and also my mother and lovely sister to this terrible illness.

Years ago I had travelled to Acapulco once again to stay with Leslie and Evie in their gorgeous house overlooking the bay and to hang out with several mutual great mates. Those were the halcyon days of the 1970s, full of promise.

Every night we would sip margaritas on the terrace and watch the amazing sunset with our starry friends. George Hamilton, Roger Moore, Neile and Steve McQueen and many others came to stay at the Bricusses'. I will never forget the sight of Sacha sitting on the back of Steve's motorcycle as he zoomed off into the hills, my ecstatic son holding on tightly to his hero as Steve yelled to me, the worried mother, 'Don't worry, honey – I know what I'm doing.' One day, he motorbiked up to the house with a tray of cherries jubilee perched on his head!

Leslie and Evie had a wonderful houseman called Rodrigo who did everything, including taking Evie and me to the local markets, where we stocked up on ponchos and beautifully embroidered tops and dresses. One Easter Sunday, Rodrigo proudly presented my children Tara and Sacha, Roger Moore's son Geoffrey and daughter Deborah, and Leslie and Evie's son Adam each with a tiny newborn chick! The kids were thrilled, us adults were shocked. Each chick had its feathers painted in vibrant neon colours, and the children were in heaven playing with the poor little creatures.

'Is this animal cruelty?' I whispered to Tony Newley, my then husband.

We had a lovely Easter brunch watching the tiny chicks waddling about. Sadly, when we returned after a long day at the beach, most of the little darlings had died and we had to comfort our desperately upset children, who were sobbing in grief.

When Leslie died in 2021, Evie came back to London. She sadly recounted how Leslie died in her arms after his long cancer battle. His last words to her were, 'Go on living for both of us now, and I'll prepare heaven for you.' We cried and laughed, reminiscing. Evie has been one of my best friends for sixty years, so I will do my best to support her.

I gave a speech at Leslie's memorial service in London but I couldn't stop sobbing. I want to share it here.

Once upon a time in trendy 1960s London, there was a fabulous glamorous restaurant in Mayfair where anyone who was anyone would go for lunch, drinks, or supper. It was called the White Elephant. It was mainly frequented by a showbiz crowd with many stars of the moment. At lunch one day, I noticed two young men huddled together in a corner laughing with each other hysterically. As I passed the table with my agent, Peter Charlesworth, he introduced me to Anthony Newley and Leslie Bricusse, saying that 'these two guys are the toast of the town'. We exchanged a few words and Peter explained that Tony, who was also his client, was the hottest young man in the West End right now, thanks to *Stop the World: I Want to Get Off*, co-written by Leslie Bricusse. It was, without a doubt, the hottest show in town.

Intrigued, I went to see it. It was so modern and original, and I was very impressed. I started dating Tony and we became joined at the hip with Leslie and his gorgeous wife Evie. We went everywhere together, sharing the same sense of, sometimes childlike, humour and finding the slightest things hysterically funny. One Christmas, at the Bricusse house in Stanmore, we bought each other dozens of useless and sometimes rude presents, Evie cooked a four-course dinner, we wore silly paper hats and told bad jokes. Tony was telling a very interesting anecdote, wearing a pointy paper hat; when he leaned forward the pointy hat caught fire from a candle and started burning. We were laughing so hysterically that no one could speak and just pointed at his head.

Tony of course thought we were laughing at his story. Finally, as the flames got closer and closer to his singeing hair, I managed to throw a glass of wine over him, which made Leslie laugh even more.

Soon after, with Tony still performing to sold-out houses, Leslie suggested a Jamaican holiday. He, Evie and I went to Jamaica; we didn't take into account that it was right next door to Cuba, which is where the Third World War was probably going to start shortly. The Soviets were pointing nuclear weapons at the USA. The entire world, and Leslie, were terrified, but Evie and I weren't bothered about it. We just couldn't take it seriously and would loll around on the sand drinking rum punches while Leslie watched the news on the tiny hotel TV, trying to book a flight home and getting more and more upset, telling us that we were trapped and would die in the coming Armageddon. Anyway, we survived to have more adventures.

Shortly afterwards I took the three of them to LA, then Las Vegas, where we formed a mutual admiration society with Sammy Davis Jr, and, as Evie says, 'Joanie introduced us to everyone.' Leslie religiously kept up with everyone's birthday and woe betide if anyone tried to chop off a year or two. Although they socialised like crazy, Leslie's work ethic was admirable: he wrote every day, sometimes with Tony, and turned out *Victor/Victoria* among many other shows. And to his friends or enemies, he sent beautiful handwritten erudite missives of heartfelt congratulations, or sometimes fulminating anger and insults. We used to call him 'Les the Letter'.

He always kept up with trends and he was the first man I ever saw wearing a handbag, or a man bag as he called it.

Leslie was very competitive, and we used to play Scrabble a lot. He would often beat me but, as I got better and learned more small words like xi and zo and xu (which he said I couldn't use but they were in the Scrabble rules), I would beat him all the time, so he quit playing with me!

Leslie's handwriting was impeccable, no matter how fierce a hangover he had. Although hangovers were a rare occurrence because Leslie's knowledge of and capacity for wine was peerless. Few people were allowed to order any wines if he was hosting a dinner or a lunch.

He had a wine cellar that was unparalleled, which I think Adam (his son) often took advantage of. He also collected first editions of books and would love to have them signed by the author. Another thing he collected, as we found out when we spent a lot of time with him in Acapulco, was a vast array of safari suits, all in pastel colours from peachy pink to powder blue, which he had specially made by an Acapulco tailor. Leslie also collected names. No story or anecdote was complete unless he dropped Sammy, Frank or Liza into it, and decades later, Julie, Mike and Rog.

But most of all, Leslie collected friends – a vast array of wonderful, talented and special friends, many of whom are here to celebrate his enduring memory.

Leslie's favourite motto was to live each day like a small lifetime, where you achieve something, you learn something, and you enjoy something. A motto I have tried to follow.

Farewell, my friend, you will be missed.

18

What a Swell Party That Was

I've always loved parties. Parties often mean adventures – whether talking to someone completely new, or catching up with old friends; you never know where a conversation might end up. I love throwing them too and everyone who attends says they are fabulous.

Percy and I played poker at Julian Clary's recently. We love playing and we are very good at it. Julian is witty and droll, very different from his drag act. His three dogs were behaving a touch erratically that night and he was concerned, issuing instructions to his husband, Ian Mackley, to take care of them.

'You treat them like your children,' I said.

'Yes, they are. And we hire dog-sitters when we go out for long periods.'

'You are kidding me!' I said.

'Of course not. The doggies miss us, and they feel abandoned when we leave,' Julian replied.

'Oh really?' I was quite speechless!

I've been lucky to be invited to many intimate dinner parties. Gabrielle and David Peacock recently hosted a dinner for Princess Beatrice and her husband, Edoardo Mapelli Mozzi. Their Provençal villa, which is just above ours, is enormous, beautiful and airy. James and Sofia Blunt and Celia and Piers

Morgan were also there, and it was a boozy, fun, dinner. Princess Beatrice was interestingly talking about how great the Queen and Fergie were when she was planning her wedding. Piers badgered her to talk about Meghan and Harry, but she deftly and diplomatically swatted him away. I was impressed with her graciousness.

When, I attended a super-stylish dinner at Lord and Lady Bamford's new house in Belgravia. Carole had just decorated it in her inimitable, superb style and the atmosphere was comfortable and elegant. Many mates were present: Biggins, Theo and Louise, Debbie and Bolo Bismarck, Richard E. Grant and my old friend Rupert Everett.

'I didn't know you knew the Bamfords,' I asked Rupert.

'I don't. She called me out of the blue,' he replied. 'This party's for you. Didn't you know?'

'No, I didn't' I laughed.

Great food and great conversation. Carole really does it better than anyone. The twenty-first birthday party she threw for her daughter Alice was unforgettable. The theme was 1920s Gatsby and everyone went to town with their stunning outfits. My daughter Katy looked fabulous in her beaded flapper outfit, and we all Charlestoned the night away..

I always love seated dinners with close friends. A few years ago, we were invited to Italy for a surprise dinner by a good friend, famed for his excellent soirées. At the airport lounge, waiting for his private plane, were Elizabeth Hurley and another actor friend. They came running over and, in hushed whispers, pointed to a flashy creature with a huge embonpoint looking sulky in a corner. She was a well-known reality star.

'How did she get invited?' whispered Elizabeth.

'No idea,' I replied. 'Well, she won't know too many people

here,' I added, glancing around the lounge filled with politicos and intellectuals.

When we arrived at the Italian villa, I asked the lady in question how she knew the host.

'I never met 'im in me life,' she squawked.

The woman with her said, 'I'm her agent and we got a call to come yesterday.' Percy and I exchanged quizzical glances.

At dinner that evening, I sat opposite Boris Johnson, who was seated next to the buxom reality star. She was so inordinately proud of her massive new chest that she asked the gentleman on the other side of her: 'Would you like to see my new boobs?'

He looked frightfully embarrassed but was too taken aback by the question to reply, whereupon the lady forced the point by whipping her off-the-shoulder top down and revealing her prizes. The entire table, except for Boris Johnson, who hadn't noticed, fell into a fit of muffled giggling. So, I boldly asked the reality star to reveal her assets to Boris, who was in deep conversation and had missed her party trick. She obediently obliged. Boris merely glanced at them, frowned disinterestedly, and returned to his conversation with his dinner partner. Maybe he wasn't quite the swordsman the media like to paint.

I love Italy. When asked to appear on an Italian talk show in 2001, I was delighted to attend. In the green room, I caught up with Lionel Richie (big fan!) and my old pal Bill Wyman from the Rolling Stones.

'Did you know,' said Bill, 'that we're supposed to perform on the show and do something no one's ever seen before?'

'Oh, dear,' I said, 'my agent didn't tell me that. What are you going to do, Bill?'

'Ah, it's a surprise,' he replied. 'What about you?'

I thought for a second and then said, 'What about this?'

Lifting up my big full skirt, a gift from Alexander McQueen, I then went into a full-on 100 per cent split. 'My grandmother taught me to do this,' I laughed. 'Will it do?'

'You bet,' replied Bill, and Lionel looked impressed. 'It'll bring the house down,' Bill added.

Onto the stage I tripped to loud applause and, when the MC asked me to do something that would surprise everyone, I certainly did when I performed a perfect split. I was thrilled that the audience cheered but, because I hadn't warmed up beforehand, my inner thighs were in agony for days! Thank God for ice packs.

When my great and dear friend Charles Delevingne turned seventy, Susan Sangster threw a fabulous lunch party for him and thirty-two of his closest female friends and family. It was an extremely jolly affair. The champagne flowed and silver individual pots of caviar glowed. Susan had put together an eclectic group of gals, and a marvellous scrapbook of pictures she had gathered from all of us – some funny and cute, some very embarrassing were screened.

I made a speech recalling the first time I met Charles decades ago. I was renting my house in South Street and the real estate company sent their brightest star to negotiate. I was at the top of the stairway when I buzzed the front door open and there stood twenty-three-year-old Charles, complete with bowler hat, furled umbrella and old school tie, with sunlight streaming in behind him, like some sort of new Messiah.

'How do you do? I'm Charles Delevingne,' he said smoothly, in perfect received English pronunciation.

'Of course, you are,' I replied, unable to think of a wittier rejoinder. I was so impressed by his charm and charisma that I almost fell down the stairs.

Then Dame Vivien Duffield stood up to speak and made a witty speech extolling Charles's charm. After that, Cara, his youngest daughter – and my goddaughter – made a beautiful and tender speech which brought tears to some of our eyes. Finally, Pandora, his lovely wife of thirty-seven years, told him that he had been the best husband in the world – high praise indeed! As Charles is one of the most popular men in London, with both sexes, this was a fitting tribute lunch. Charles told us in his speech that the following day he was being given a similar lunch, this time with men only.

'Thirty-two women today, and tomorrow only sixteen men, which just shows that I like women twice as much as I do men!' he joked.

In 1982 when *Dynasty* was at its peak, two great friends, Sandra and Baron Enrico (Ricky) di Portanova, opened their spectacular mansion, Arabesque. This was a white marble palace with two swimming pools, a cascading waterfall, a private beach and the most gorgeous tropical flowers and plants everywhere.

Ricky and Sandra reigned as the uncrowned and undisputed king and queen of Acapulco all through the 1980s and 1990s. Their incredible villa was one of the most fantastic homes I've ever stayed in and glamorous Sandra was one of the wittiest women I knew. When Ricky was deciding whether or not to invest in a new private jet, she quipped, 'Darling, you can't afford a G2 and me too!'

They threw parties practically every night that were legendary, as was her amazing collection of exotic and extraordinary table decorations. I stayed with the Portanovas in Houston and at their home in Acapulco at least thirty times, and I practically never saw the same table settings twice. Gold vases, silver candlesticks, shells, coral, flowers, fruit, glittering ornaments, even sand and precious stones – Sandra collected everything and used them all in stylish and inventive tableaux that were a feast for the eyes as well as the palate. She called them her tablescapes.

Incredibly popular, their villa was always hosting the rich and famous, from Henry Kissinger and Placido Domingo to Tom Hanks, Sylvester Stallone, Barbara Walters and Tony Curtis.

I first saw the Portanovas lunching at Harry's Bar in London in the late 1970s. It was April and a young, titled woman came to their table to try and book them for lunch or dinner 'anytime'. 'Darling, we're not free until October,' said Sandra dismissively. I was most amused and shortly afterwards we became great friends. Sandra was tireless in entertaining brilliantly, always wearing a flamboyant and low-cut couture gown. Whenever I went to stay at Arabesque I always packed glamorous gowns and beautiful caftans for pool lounging, because everyone was always supposed to be dressed to the nines. In true 1980s style, Sandra wore an amazing collection of what she called 'beach jewellery', keeping the diamonds and emeralds for night-time. Tony Curtis loved wearing his 'gong' bestowed by some king or royal of a little-known country.

Despite his title and name, Ricky was British, but he spoke and looked like a 1930s movie star. He constantly smoked enormous cigars, drank quite a lot and was madly in love with Sandra – as was she with him. They were larger than life, but sadly their lives were not long enough.

Sandra died in 2000, rumoured to have been murdered, and Ricky passed away two weeks later, they say of a broken heart. I, and so many of their friends, will always miss them and their amazing lifestyle and *joie de vivre*. Acapulco was never the same again. Shortly afterwards, when the drug cartels came into power, the Bricusses sold their hacienda, and we heard that his houseman, kindly Rodrigo, had been murdered a few weeks later. Sadly, I've never gone back to that enchanted place called Acapulco but I still miss it.

*

Backstage at the 2020 Pride of Britain awards at the Grosvenor House in Park Lane, I passed a haughty Sharon Stone, swathed in a witch-like floor-length black cape. We studiously ignored each other as I went to sit with Susanna Reid and Ben Shephard from *Good Morning Britain*.

I had last seen Sharon at a chic dinner party that Veronique Peck, Gregory Peck's widow, hosted at her elegant house in Bel Air. In early 2003, everyone dressed properly, as befits a seated dinner, but Sharon arrived in jeans and a T-shirt.

'Oh, you're so dressed up!' she sneered at me.

'So is everyone else,' I retorted.

She was seated next to Leslie Bricusse and flirted with him outrageously for the entire dinner, telling him how she loved his work and would adore to do a musical with him.

Leslie's signature spectacles fogged up and he never once acknowledged his dinner companion on the other side, so smitten was he with 'La Sharon'. His wife Evie was none too pleased. 'How's your neck, Leslie?' she enquired with steely sweetness. 'No crick from talking to *Sharon* the entire time?' I had never seen Leslie blush before.

My co-presenter at the Pride of Britain was a beautiful, serene woman, Dame Sarah Storey, Paralympic champion, who coped brilliantly, having been born without a functioning left hand.

We presented the ITV Fund Raiser Award to Mark Ormrod. Wounded in Afghanistan, he had lost both legs and one arm and after many horrendous operations he was living a full life with his lovely wife, Becky.

'Are you in pain?' I asked.

'All the time,' he grinned, 'but I'm better off than most.'

What an amazing man – a lesson to us all.

*

I was honoured to receive the *Harper's Bazaar* Icon of the Year
Award. A fashionable crowd converged at Claridge's. Claire Foy
was also receiving an award, looking delicate with amazing skin.
There were a million gorgeous models, all of whom were at least
six-foot tall, wearing stupendously high heels and short skirts.

I was seated next to the new designer Harris Reed – 6' 4",
with long red hair and a brocade trouser suit, open to the waist.
They (correct pronoun – I asked them) were vociferous in their
admiration of *moi*. They are only twenty-four, but already a big
mover and shaker in the fashion world!

Two days later I received three pretty gold necklace from
them, which I love wearing.

It's always huge fun throwing a party for yourself and my book
launch a few years ago for *Passion for Life* had all the ingredients
of a *mahvellous party*, as dear Noël sang. Guest lists of PR events
tend to be organised with surgical precision by a press agency
motivated by column inches, and therefore end up peopled by
the usual suspects, but I really wanted this party to be unique, so
I personally invited my friends, some of whom just happened to
be very famous!

The venue was No. 41, a glamorous nightclub next door to the
Westbury Hotel, enhanced by a fleur-de-lis carpet and decorated
with Titian-style baroque paintings, burgundy velvet banquettes
and a magnificent, mirrored bar. One hundred and twenty souls
were invited, and I thought that, as often happens, many of the
celebrities wouldn't show – but I was so wrong.

Shortly after the designated hour, Tom Ford, the epitome
of masculine glamour and style, arrived, closely followed by
A.A. Gill and Tim Jeffries, no slouches in the dandy department themselves. Then within what seemed the blink of an eye,

bestselling authors Jeffrey Archer, Lynda La Plante, Peter James, and William Boyd turned up, closely followed by socialites Tara Palmer Tomkinson, Tamara Beckwith and Amanda Eliasch. Hairstylists to the stars Nicky Clarke and Charles Worthington threatened scissors at dawn. Friends and family mingled, everyone having a glorious time.

'It looks like everyone who accepted is here,' I whispered to Percy.

'Not quite,' he said, as Graham Norton, Julian Clary, Elaine Paige, Esther Rantzen and Gloria Hunniford all seemed to arrive at once.

I chatted to artists Tracey Emin and David Downton, accepting compliments on my book and signing many copies, as the proceeds went to my children's charity, the Shooting Star/ Children's Hospice, and my guests are a philanthropic lot. Evie Bricusse, no slouch to partying herself, gasped, 'Every time I turn around, I see another household name!' And it was true – names were coming in faster than I could drop them.

Towards the end, when I thought it was a 'wrap', in swept Signor Valentino Garavani accompanied by Giancarlo Giametti and the fabulous photographer Mario Testino – like a second-wave assault on Normandy. I have never seen so many *bien connu* lionise someone as they did Valentino, who took it all in his immaculate stride. I didn't want the festivities to end, and I stayed on a high for weeks thinking about it. To paraphrase Frank and Bing, what a swell party that was.

One of the great party-givers, the late Prince Azim, the second-born son of the Sultan of Brunei, threw a lavish birthday event for his two sisters and himself at a magnificent hotel deep in the heart of Leicestershire. No ordinary group of guests this.

As Percy and I, with my daughter Tara and her fiancé, drove

up, standing in the doorway, smoking and deep in conversation, were Faye Dunaway, Ursula Andress and Jerry Hall, a trio of vintage beauties still well in season. 'Wait 'til you see who else is here,' whispered Jerry, as legendary Sophia Loren, in all her red-frocked splendour, swept into the anteroom to greet the royal family of Brunei. Then Mariah Carey sailed gracefully into the room, with just a simple entourage of three or four in tow. Jaws dropped at her skin-tight gown, seemingly sprayed on à la Marilyn Monroe.

After greeting Prince Azim's sisters and mother, I remarked fatuously to one of the sisters, 'Ooh, is that real?' about the playing card-sized rock adorning her finger. She attempted to remove it and gift it to me, but I refused – silly me!

We adjourned for dinner and all of 'the girls' surrounded the young prince, who seemed especially entranced by Mariah Carey. I had read and heard much about this allegedly difficult and impossibly demanding diva. To my surprise, she turned out to be utterly charming, delightful and amusing, with absolutely no hint of 'diva-dom' at all. I spoke to her at length and not only was she intelligent and captivating, but she possessed a good sense of humour. How sad that the media have chosen her as one of their 'Aunt Sallies' to throw barbs at and constantly malign.

I know of several actresses who receive nothing but plaudits from the press, yet are actually closet bitches. It seems once you've been put in a box that's either good girl or bad girl, that's where you'll always stay.

Takes one to know one!

One of my least favourite things about social interaction is how some 'friends', who were introduced by me to one of my more interesting pals, will call me for their contact details and invite only them to supper, without including us!

In every book of etiquette, it is one of the rudest things you can do. I used to be close friends with a most brilliant and famous name in fashion and design. A few years ago, he called me in person (which he rarely did anyway) and asked me if I knew a famous footballer and his fashionable wife. I told him I'd met them a few times and could give him their PR's number.

Before I knew it, they were bosom buddies with the Beckhams and taking trips on his yacht, without me!

What's annoying about this is that none of my friends have ever introduced me to anyone I would remotely want to steal from them . . .!

I was looking forward to celebrating the January birthday of one of my friends, which is a tradition between us.

After drinks at our apartment, we met my friend, her daughter, son-in-law and two of her friends at the Arts Club, a private members' club in Chelsea. It is so posh you're not allowed to take pictures, or use any kind of phone. They pride themselves on their exclusivity and perfectly correct manners – absolutely no drunkenness or rowdiness allowed.

So, off Percy and I went, looking forward to an enjoyable evening with friends. As soon as we sat down on a crowded banquette, a woman came to our table to tell me, 'I love your outfit.'

'Thank you,' was all I said, having not even had time to say hello to our group.

We noticed she was holding a glass and swaying drunkenly, so we didn't continue the conversation. Several angst-filled seconds passed before she blurted out, 'Yes, I really like you. Do you like me?'

'Sorry . . . erm, but we don't know you,' said Percy. 'We're just having a birthday celebration for our friend here so, hope you understand, we'd like some privacy.'

'But I just want to sit down and talk to you,' the woman slurred.

We continued this boring badinage until finally Percy said, this time more firmly, 'I'm sorry, but I've told you this is a private celebration. We don't know who you are. Please leave us.'

Her face turned bright red. 'Fuck you!' she yelled at Percy and flounced off. Or rather, flounced off as best she could in her drunken state.

'So much for an exclusive and private club,' I laughed.

Suddenly, I was hit in the chest by a rock-hard object that was hurled from a table across the room. It hit me with such force that tears came to my eyes, and I was in shock. Percy picked it up and it turned out to be a stale bread roll. We looked in the direction whence it came and saw that same woman grinning menacingly at us. She had thrown it at me in a drunken fury and boy, did it hurt. It really hurt.

Unable to stay any longer in case a mortar barrage of stale bread rolls would ensue, Percy and I walked out to the lobby, where I sat dabbing my eyes while Percy went outside to find a cab.

Was I being over-sensitive to be rather upset that neither my friend nor any of her guests came to check up on me? In retrospect, I think not. Had that missile hit me in the nose or teeth, the force of it would most certainly have broken them, and this was only a month before our big anniversary celebration. Percy would have certainly attracted askance glances had I shown up with a black eye or a broken nose . . . However, I shall never set foot in that so-called 'exclusive' club again. They even refused to tell me who dunnit!

20

Saint-Tropez Silly Season

Saint-Tropez is the party capital of the world in the last two weeks of July. There are always two or three parties a night in the port city or its environs – Ramatuelle, Gassin, Sainte-Maxime – not to mention the cocktail parties and charity balls in Monaco, Nice and Cannes.

For several years, Leonardo DiCaprio hosted his annual charity ball and auction in a vineyard outside Gassin, at which any billionaire worth his salt competed to buy an overpriced multimillion-dollar art installation, a small island no one had heard about, or dinner with Leo himself, or Brad or George. Sometimes, the auction prize would even include a weekend at some superstar's Lake Como villa . . .

I attended some of these events over the past few years, but I must admit most were staggeringly boring. There is a predictable sameness to all of them.

Usually starting at 9 p.m., which is still hot and brilliantly sunny in July and early August, there is a considerable amount of milling around and socialising outside the venue for at least an hour and a half, where you try to avoid the people you have been avoiding all summer while trying to chat with the people you actually want to see. Geographically, this is very tricky.

Although the organisers attempt to have everyone sitting at

their €10,000 per seat table by 9.30 p.m., they never succeed until about 11 p.m., because, after all, the people who've spent three hours socialising at lunch with each other at the beach restaurants or on their boats now *must* catch up on what has happened in the interim.

Because the auction doesn't begin until the first course is over, there is another interminable wait while the waiters serve, and the minglers mingle even more. The first course consists invariably of a very tired-looking lobster or shrimp on a bed of wilted rocket. All of which has been exposed to the heat for several hours. I wouldn't touch it with a ten-foot bargepole, even if I wasn't allergic to shellfish.

By the time the auction starts, everyone is usually so drunk that they pay far more than the prize is worth. But it is all for a commendable cause (save the tigers, save the icebergs, save the world) . . . and good for bragging rights at the next day's super-yacht lunch.

I'm sad to say, many iconic and remarkable Pampelonne and Saint-Tropez beaches have been closed by the mayor because of the unavoidable soil erosion.

Oh, how I miss the joyful camaraderie and pure fun of rosé-fuelled Saint-Tropez beach days, which seem decades ago now, like the famous Voile Rouge, where often Jack Nicholson would jump from his tender and climb up the sand to hold court at a table including the photographer Willy Rizzo and his actress wife Elsa Martinelli.

Every year, Charles and Pandora Delevingne would host a birthday party for their youngest daughter, my goddaughter Cara. Amid screams of excitement, a bottle of champagne would be hacked open with a scimitar and sprayed all over our group and the surrounding tables. Not to be outdone, Philip Green would order champagne by the *case* and deliberately spew it over everyone in the restaurant, while the amiable owner Paul strutted around chatting to his patrons in nothing but a tiny posing pouch, a cowboy hat and with a huge cigar clenched between his teeth. He must have been the inspiration for Borat's famous mankini. The fabulous DJ Luigi Davenia would play a selection of everyone's favourite 80s dance hits at maximum volume and, after the first course, most people would start dancing, while the young jumped on tables to gyrate wildly.

Bagatelle Beach took over the frivolity when La Voile Rouge was forced to close and the same raucous celebratory atmosphere was maintained until its own COVID closure. Club 55 is still a timeless classic and the owner Patrice made sure everyone stuck to the COVID rules – when they re-opened, all waitstaff had to wear masks, as did the patrons.

In the 1980s, Cher used to drop by our table, her skimpy outfits festooned with dozens of necklaces and bracelets, as was the fashion then. Roger Moore would always stand up when people came to ask for his autograph, much to the annoyance of his wife Luisa. At a lunch given by Hollywood producer Mike Medavoy, Johnny Depp, at the height of his Cap'n Jack Sparrow fame, worked a long queue of avid child fans who he thrilled by posing for pictures with them all through his lunch.

Elton John's lavish AIDS charity ball was held at socialite Johnny Pigozzi's house in Cannes in July 2019. It was full of interesting people – Chris Martin, Pete Townshend, Taron Egerton and, of course, Elton's husband David Furnish. The house has amazing memories for me. In the late 1980s, I shot my miniseries *Sins* there. I had cast the fabulous and legendary Gene Kelly to play my older husband. The whole experience was other-worldly. Firstly, playing scenes with such an icon, who had been one of my favourite childhood movie stars, was beyond thrilling. Then the gorgeousness of the lush gardens, which gently sloped down onto a golden beach and a superb view of the glittering Mediterranean Sea, was breathtaking.

I told Gene I was hoping to buy a house near Saint-Tropez, and he told me that he had visited there in the 1950s, when it was just a simple fishing village. 'It was on the cusp of becoming famous because of a nubile young starlet called Brigitte Bardot, who was filming *And God Created Woman* on the golden beaches of Pampelonne,' he told me.

Bardot, with her signature 'just got out of bed' coiffure, stunning bikini body and sexual allure, soon became the poster girl of Saint-Tropez, and even now the village is still plastered with photos and posters of her gorgeousness. She is on the cover of most books about the village and there is even a Brigitte Bardot shop which sells her memorabilia.

I was staying at the Hotel de la Ville in Rome in the 1950s, a popular watering hole for French and Italian actors and directors. On my second day, while enjoying a drink on the terrace with Christian Marquand and Dewey Martin, one of the stars of *Land of the Pharaohs*, a vision appeared.

'Who is that?' breathed Dewey in awe, as the most gorgeous girl I had ever seen walked to the bar.

'*Ah, elle s'appelle Brigitte Bardot, une nouvelle femme vedette du cinéma, et une amie de moi,*' said Christian. '*Bonsoir, Roger.*'

Bardot's escort, Roger Vadim, was a young, intense man with a shock of black hair and sharp features. He shook hands with Christian hurriedly, gave me the once-over and hastened to the bar where Bardot, to whom he was then married, was getting more than admiring glances from every man in the place.

She was about my age and was indeed delicious: an enviable, petite beauty wearing her soon-to-be-famous pink-and-white tight-waisted gingham peasant dress with the extremely low neckline, her masses of blonde hair looking as if she had just tumbled out of bed, with the innocent eyes and those lips that every man desired.

Every woman wanted to look like her. I even whipped over to a dressmaker the very next day to have the pink-and-white gingham dress copied!

Although we never met again, I remained a fan of Bardot's. Not particularly for her acting – although I thought she had a lot more talent than her sexuality allowed her to show – but for her free and honest approach to love, men and sex. I was also interested through the years to see her ever-changing parade of lovers and husbands, and I admired her self-admitted freedom from sexual taboos.

When the Saint-Tropez silly season is back in full swing, the massive gin palaces pull into the tiny port and hundreds of wannabe social mountaineers wearing over-the-top gear land in private planes or debark boats – not to mention a liberal smattering of Eastern European hookers and a large dose of Eurotrash who probably hitchhike.

One night, we arrived at one of the de-rigueur parties early to avoid the crush of queuing cars. In previous years we'd been stuck for over an hour in these queues and wished to avoid the same fate. We were greeted by the security mafia, a phalanx of six stone-faced guards who wouldn't have looked out of place at the gates of Alcatraz. '*Carte d'identité*,' a moustachioed virago demanded of me. I looked puzzled, as she was holding my invitation with my name, along with a list of my guests, clearly printed on it. An altercation ensued between us and the guards, observed from inside the gates with some amusement by the local photographer, who threw me sympathetic Gallic shrugs and rolled his eyes at the obdurates. He eventually came to vouch that we would check all heavy artillery at the door and we were ushered into Eurotrash heaven as a despairing line formed behind us, none of whom probably possessed an identity card.

I sauntered into the spacious hallway of a billionaire's palatial villa in le Cap des Salins, one of the most prestigious addresses in Saint-Tropez. The host, to my surprise, was there *en déshabillé*, yelling vociferously that we were too early. So vociferously, in fact, that his hairpiece was flapping up and down equally indignantly. We tried our best to make apologies in French but obviously failed, since he stomped back into his quarters, mumbling along the way.

Maximum effect had certainly been achieved on this villa. It was a blinding vision of shining, whiter-than-white marble floors with zebra-skin walls slotted between black mirrors, and fat black candles clustered on every surface.

It was a warm night and a full moon glimmered on the calm Mediterranean. Long tables were set out on the terrace, thick with candles, orchids, Tiffany glassware and gold cutlery. The sound of cicadas competed with the sound of South American sambas from Luigi, the famous disc jockey, and the lights of Saint-Tropez twinkled across the water below.

The setting was beautiful, and we took a table at the balcony to survey the scene. On each table were two bottles of warm wine, marked in clear block letters on white labels. One read 'Chardonnay' and the other was similarly emblazoned 'Syrah' – no other identifying marks to be found. They tasted so suspiciously of paint stripper that we all quickly switched to vodka.

The host, now put together, was standing on the edge of the black onyx pool, a Havana cigar clenched between moustachioed lips, his slick, dyed-jet-black hairpiece gleaming like a patent-leather helmet. Clutching at his legs, one on each, were his adopted twins, a pair of gorgeous three-year-old infants, dressed in the latest blue denim diamanté-studded Saint-Tropez baby gear. One young ingénue, wearing a chiffon dress, tried to engage our host in conversation, but unfortunately caught her dress in one of the candles surrounding the pool. Her dress went up in flames impressively quickly and her date, without other recourse (and rather quick-wittedly, I thought), pushed her into the pool, amid shrieks of laughter.

It's remarkable that this caused only a minor stir and the majority of the oblivious guests sat down on the moonlit terrace to a dinner of – *quelle surprise* – an exhausted-looking lobster on a bed of wilted rocket. The main course was at least edible, but whether it was tough veal or very dark chicken meat remains a mystery.

During the second course, a young magician entertained the guests at the table, because God forbid they'd have to rely on conversation. Brilliant bon mots at these parties usually consisted of celebrity gossip, scintillating questions such as 'When did you get here?' 'How long are you staying?' and comments about the weather. The conjurer took control of the table, asking people to choose a card, which would magically appear, half covered in saliva from under his tongue. After masticating several cards and regurgitating them in this fashion, which was met with limited applause, he started doing things with balloons.

'*Regardez*,' he beamed proudly as he blew up a red balloon into a long sausage shape and swallowed the entire thing as the guests watched in shock and amazement.

The magician finally retrieved the balloon from the depths of his throat and presented it to a guest with a tiny bow. With her fan, she swatted it over to another guest with an offended squawk. The balloon burst in his face.

For his finale, the magician let off a series of tiny firecrackers behind several of the ladies' ears, which caused them all to shriek and hold onto their hairpieces.

'I've had enough!' I said to Percy. 'Isn't it time for dessert?'

After admiring various quaint costumes and being told that Mary J. Blige or Puff Daddy would be arriving soon, we watched the superb fireworks display, danced a bit, and legged it home.

The next day, while we were lunching at the latest *plage à la mode,* Puff Daddy or P. Diddy or Sean Puffy Combs (what does his ID card say?) strode off his tender and onto the packed beach fetchingly (if unseasonally for 90-degree weather) clad in a black satin shirt and matching trousers. Flanked by several minders, one of whom held a large umbrella over him, he graciously paused for a few autographs and photo ops for admiring fans while mere mortals gaped.

The cult of celebrity reigns supreme in this neck of the woods, and the paps lie in wait everywhere, hidden like crocs at the riverbank. I made the mistake of taking a dip in the murky waters of the Med and in a thrice I was 'papped' as snappers appeared, popping out of the sand like prairie dogs. '*Mea culpa,*' I sighed resignedly the following weekend, when some less than flattering pictures of myself, accompanied by fairly rude captions, appeared in some of the Sunday tabloids.

The shiny new vodka palaces lie scattered across the bay of Saint-Tropez like the discarded toys of a spoiled child. Each year they seem to grow bigger, as do the gorgeous girls who cluster on deck and throng the boutiques and clubs. Many of these boats are owned by Russian billionaires – how did they become so rich so fast? – and it seems that for each ugly, stocky oligarch three or four dazzlers hang on each arm. What did the Russian government feed their pregnant women and toddlers two decades ago that make them sprout into gorgeous, skinny beanstalks? And why is it only the girls who seem to have inherited that giant gene? All the men seem ordinary, both in looks and height; maybe their massive wealth makes up for their massive bellies.

Watching some of these men dance is pretty hysterical. They say you can tell how a man makes love by the way he dances. If that's the case, then most of the Saint-Tropez partygoers must be pretty sorry in the sack.

At Cave du Roi, the local dive where a jeroboam of Cristal can set you back ten thousand euros, I stood with two girlfriends, primping in the powder room, our mouths agape at the height of these gorgeous giraffes. None of them were under six foot as they sauntered about in barely there minidresses and five-inch stilettos, idly tossing waist-length extensions. Either the government gave them hair-growth supplements in infancy or Russia is making the most realistic extensions since Lady Godiva! Feeling like the dwarves from *Snow White*, we sat in the club becoming more hysterical as each Amazonian tottered past: truly a scene from *Attack of the 50 Foot Woman*.

The Riviera weather, however, can be unpredictable, and recently people have been packing up and hot-footing it to calmer climes. At one smart party in Saint-Tropez, the wind was so fierce that everyone's hair was standing on end, including that of a be-wigged gentleman whose girlfriend rested her hand casually on top of it for safety. The following Thursday, at a soirée by the Byblos, pool umbrellas were swept across the terrace like missiles and I was nearly decapitated by a flying menu. Definitely time to go home, but I still love my home here.

21

This England

I've always considered myself a working actress and, along with about 98 per cent of my fellow thespians, spend a great deal of time 'resting' involuntarily. It therefore irks when the media refer to actors disparagingly as 'luvvies' and represent us as parasites and 'celebs' who only love swanning around and dressing up.

During the play *Full Circle* in 2004 (a sweet 1950s drawing-room comedy), I worked with the nicest, most hardworking and dedicated group of actors you could find, and that is how I've found most thespians to be. Because most actors love working in this vastly overcrowded profession, they often get paid far too little (the Equity minimum is just over £500 a week) for rehearsing six days a week, eight hours a day, and often spending extra hours going to fittings and learning lines. I know it is a lot compared to a pensioner's £203 per week, but I believe it's on the low average means of the nation, and certainly a complete joke when compared to my accountant's fee of £650 an hour!

But the big stars – such as Tom Cruise and George Clooney – still command millions.

I saw England from every angle in the three-month tour of *Full Circle*, and it surprised me how gorgeous the English country-side still is, and how hideous the infrastructure of some of our cities can be. In France and Italy, most towns have some sort of cohesion in their one-way systems and in the architecture of their civic and municipal buildings. By contrast, some English town centres seem to have fallen victim to saboteurs bent on uglifying them. One regularly finds a twenty-first-century monstrosity built out of giant glass eggshells sitting next to a classic sixteenth-century steepled church, which is in turn adjacent to a concrete bunker. I thought town councils in England were particular about the way their towns looked, but after eleven weeks on tour witnessing the lunacy with which town planners have embraced every faint architectural breeze that has wafted through the last four decades, I'm no longer sure about that.

There is little beauty to be seen other than in the countryside, and each high street seems identical to the one in the last town we hit, with their KFCs, McDonald's and Gap everywhere. There are so few unique, individual shops that specialise in one-of-a-kind clothing that you won't see everyone wearing, and almost bygone are the days of butchers and fishmongers, plus the shops that used to sell interesting *tchotchkes*. Replacing them are huge malls and complexes, offering us mass-produced 'made in Taiwan' tat.

What *is* individual, however, is every British hotel room. I discovered that each has its own unique kind of light switch, climate controls, TV remote, telephone system and bathroom works. Every shower and faucet offers new mysteries and challenges which I, invariably, am incapable of surmounting. Taps don't even have H and C on them anymore, so you have to guess while either scalding yourself or risking frostbite. Adding further frustration to the British hostelry experience is the lack of bathroom cabinets or drawers in which to put things away, and since you may already know I do not travel lightly, our suite often resembles an Oxfam shop by the time I've unpacked. I presume the reason for this is that, in the past, guests would leave things behind in drawers and hotels would have to send them on. May I suggest that hotels simply put signs up saying they are not responsible for items left behind and open an Oxfam shop in an unused room to dispose of them?

I hadn't been on a bus since I was eighteen, but in the suburbs of Birmingham while touring with *Full Circle*, I had no choice. I'd gone to an afternoon movie with Nickolas Grace, and when we came out the temperature had dropped to below freezing (in April). Gamely braving the frigid air, we searched for a passing taxi while trudging the three miles back to our hotel. 'Niko, I don't even do walking in the summer,' I huffed, the wind so cold that my teeth ached. 'Right, let's grab a bus, then,' said he.

'A bus!' Edith Evans would have been proud of my incredulous inflection, but before I could protest Niko hauled me onto a passing double-decker and dragged me to the upper regions. My trench coat dragged on the stairs as I stumbled up the narrow corkscrew. A few passengers glanced at me, but red-nosed and baseball-capped I bore scant resemblance to the glamorous creature on posters plastered all over town. Several women were excitedly discussing going to see *Full Circle* the following night, as I slid further down into my seat, pulling the cap over my eyes.

Us thespians are a superstitious lot, because of the many 'accidents', physical or otherwise, that can happen during a live show. Therefore, many of us have idiosyncratic little customs we carry out before the curtain goes up, ranging from sensible warm-ups to sometimes outlandish behaviours. Nickolas Grace, for example, insisted every night on touching or kissing me before I went on. One night he was so late that he tore through backstage just as I was making my entrance and managed to just barely brush me with his lips, but the commotion and unexpected kiss rattled me so that I dropped every single prop I was carrying – I think it was the most jocular 'entrance round' of applause I ever received.

Imagine my surprise then, when the *New York Times* reporter, a Mr Wong, who interviewed me on the last flight of Concorde, referred to me as 'former actress Joan Collins' – shame on you, sir, and I hereby emphasise my indignity with a particularly grand, 'Don't you know who I am??' I demand a retraction, a personal apology and if possible, his head on a platter. Although, it could have been worse. At least he didn't call me a 'former female actor'.

A friend who manages several theatres in the West End was regaling us with the regulations he is forced to abide by in order to mollify the over-paid, under-worked bureaucrats in charge of enforcing the ridiculous 'elf'n'safety rules. It seems that the general population has become so moronic nowadays that they are complaining about the lack of signage in theatres to alert them well in advance that the aisle veers slightly to the right or to the left. In addition, he is being forced to replace the traditional red EXIT signs with placards displaying a little green man running like the clappers out of a burning building. Clearly this is not the message we want to convey in a crowded theatre. It reminded me of an 'In case of fire' placard backstage upon which a wit had crossed out the instructions and replaced them with the word 'PANIC'. The topping on the cake came when this extremely officious inspector turned to my friend after scrutinising every inch of his theatre and remarked, 'You do realise that stairs are dangerous, don't you?'

Several times in my life, I have been roundly criticised by some of the press for 'deserting' to the United States. The boring truth of the matter is that I have always been fortunate enough to keep a place in the US. This was the case when I was away working on a daily soap opera called *Guiding Light*.

Acting in a serial in which fifty-five minutes (or more, depending on who's going on holiday) of taped film must be shot daily in the minimum amount of time is the show business equivalent of boot camp. I haven't worked so hard or felt so pressured since I was raising my children by myself. I had thought that a prime-time serial like *Dynasty* was reasonably tough, since we had to get fifty minutes of film in the can in six days, but that was a sun-kissed holiday on the Riviera compared to 'Daytime'.

To commit to memory anywhere from fifteen to forty-five pages of dialogue *every day*, you need the mind-bending concentration of Uri Geller and the stamina of an SAS operative. There is no proper rehearsal time, which as any actor knows is essential, and when the time comes for blocking camera moves, the mayhem from the lighting crew and technicians manning the cameras makes concentrating on not getting clocked by the boom mic an imperative. We'd then 'dress rehearse' three or four or five scenes which took place on the same set and immediately shoot these scenes one after another without a break. This is like performing half of the first act of a play without rehearsals, and it is admirable that the wonderful actors with whom I worked do it seemingly effortlessly. I consider it a great accomplishment personally that I was able to keep up from day one (well, day two, really, there is a learning curve). 'You almost get used to it after a while,' grinned Ron Raines, who at that time had been in *Guiding Light* for nine years. 'You train your short-term memory to learn all this stuff real fast and then by the next day you've forgotten it, but even after nine years it's still pretty tough.'

Pretty tough indeed. When I told another actress who was on *Coronation Street* for over twenty years about our schedule, she was aghast. 'It's not possible,' she said. 'On "Corrie" we shoot five *half-hour* episodes in six days and sometimes we shoot until midnight, until we get it right. How can you possibly remember all that dialogue?'

'Because of strict labour regulations, American soaps can only shoot for a limited amount of time, about four to five hours. We tape on the first take and, unless you fall flat on your face, they'll use it,' I replied.

She couldn't believe it, which further justifies my feelings of awe at the professionalism and dedication of the actors I was privileged to work with.

I was shocked to hear recently that some actresses on *Bridgerton* and other period shows were refusing to wear corsets not only because of 'elf'n'safety, but because they were too tight! It is an actor's job to show the public how they lived in the past, and women have worn corsets for thousands of years. If this trend continues, actors will not be allowed to use swords or guns, as surely they are more dangerous to 'elf'n'safety than a mere corset?

There have been several incidents of someone dying on set from a gun, including one of my nicer leading men, Jon-Erik Hexum. When feeling bored to tears while waiting to be called on to set, he jokingly put the prop gun to his temple and fired it. It killed him instantly. And let's not forget the shooting on the set of *Rust*, of the unfortunate young technician. I don't think anyone's ever died from wearing a corset.

Percy and I are constantly searching for entertaining content on TV and streaming services. Some of the serials and movies are so juvenile, vulgar or violent that we struggle to stay tuned even for ten minutes.

At the BFI Luminous Awards recently, all the speeches centred on making more movies with diverse content, unique and original qualities, and using new and younger talent both before and behind the camera. At the same event, another presenter announced that cinema attendance in the past year was down 37 per cent. The juxtaposition of these two facts explained *a lot*.

When I heard about a new series on Paramount Plus called *The Offer*, about the making of one of the all-time greatest movies, *The Godfather*, I couldn't wait to see it. Having not seen a word of publicity or media buzz about this series, I was naturally sceptical, but Percy and I nevertheless went ahead and turned it on. We were riveted for the entire ten episodes.

The show opened on the backlot of Paramount studios, drenched in sunshine, and photographed in bright true-life colour. A good-looking, dark-haired, beautifully dressed man walked towards another and announced, 'Hi, I'm Bob Evans. Welcome to my studio.'

'Oh, God, he looks *just* like Bob Evans,' I gasped. I'd known Robert since we were both contract actors at Twentieth Century-Fox. We had dated briefly but remained good friends. I was at his house after attending Sharon Tate's memorial following the notorious quadruple Hollywood murders. Suddenly, Robert had quipped, 'Right! Shall we attend the second feature?' That was his decidedly non-PC way of saying that we couldn't miss Jay Sebring's funeral later that day.

So many things and people resonated with me in *The Offer*, apart from Matthew Goode's brilliant portrayal of the famed Robert Evans (speaking of 'wolves', Bob chased me around my Beverly Hills hotel room while I giggled until he gave up, exhausted, and said, 'Well, I may not be the best lover, but at least I'm a funny fuck!'). I also knew producer Al Ruddy (played brilliantly by Miles Teller) and Charlie Bluhdorn (played equally skilfully by Burn Gorman), head of Gulf + Western, who owned Paramount and had a reputation for firing people indiscriminately. Suddenly, I blurted out to Percy, 'He fired me too!'

'From what?' asked Percy.

'I was cast opposite Michael Caine in *The Italian Job*. I was paid a good salary as I had a great agent in Sue Mengers. One day she called and informed me that Bluhdorn had fired me.'

I asked Sue why I was fired and she snapped, 'Don't know. But he's famous for it. They cast Maggie Blye.'

'Who?'

'Exactly,' she snapped back.

I don't know if Miss Blye had much of a career after *The Italian Job*, but my consolation is that I managed to keep the salary that Bluhdorn had paid me, since the contract had been signed and I had a 'pay or play' clause.

Therefore it was fascinating for me to see how Bluhdorn, in the series, screamed, 'You're fired!' hysterically and often at various employees. The other bigwigs shrugged at the hapless recipients and said, 'It's just what Charlie does.'

As for the actors who played Brando and Pacino (Justin Chambers and Anthony Ippolito), they were uncannily, almost eerily spot on, as was frankly everyone in the cast. The whole series was fabulous, and I enjoyed it immensely because it was beautifully wittily and engagingly written. As Bob Evans said, 'If it ain't on the page, it ain't going to be on the screen.'

Yet I fail to understand how a marvellously written, directed and produced series about such a massive twentieth-century phenomenon failed to catch the public's attention, or even get nominated for an Emmy. Has the public's taste declined so far? Would Bob Evans be able to produce *Rosemary's Baby*, *Love Story*, *The Odd Couple*, *Midnight Cowboy* and *Marathon Man* in today's climate? We would have missed some of the seminal movies of 1970s American cinema – and that's without mentioning *The Italian Job*. What would England be without 'You were only supposed to blow the bloody doors off!'

22

Well, He's Still Here!

Of all the parties I've been to, and I've been to many, I have to modestly admit that I enjoy the ones Percy and I throw the best. One of the greatest nights of my life was our twentieth wedding anniversary in February 2022.

Held at Claridge's hotel, where we originally married, it was the most perfect evening – elegant, stylish and full of joy. During the misery of COVID lockdown, we had been planning every detail for the past three years and I had spent the last two weeks before the event carefully organising the perfect placement for all 125 guests.

We had decided to essentially re-enact our wedding, so chose the same menu and the same guest list, most of whom were able to come – Christopher Biggins, Frederick Forsyth, the Fennells (all of them), the Delevingnes (also all of them).

Sadly, several good friends had died in those two decades since the wedding. Roger Moore, Cilla Black, Arlene Dahl and several others were much missed. But we had a wonderful group of new friends including Elizabeth Hurley and her son Damian, the Duchess of York, Simon Cowell, Simon and Yasmin Le Bon, James Blunt, David and Gabrielle Peacock, Amanda Wakeley and Hugh Morrison, as well as some co-stars from *Dynasty*, like Stephanie Beacham and Emma Samms and of course my family.

Many people congratulated us for providing the 'first time that they had been able to come out and enjoy themselves since lockdown'. It was the first time that my oldest friend Evie Bricusse, still mourning the recent death of her beloved husband Leslie, had dressed up in three years.

Percy and I decided the theme of the party would be 'art deco': white tie for the men, long dress for the ladies. Most women I know love to get dressed up and men like white tie because it makes them all look handsome. Into the beautifully decorated anteroom covered in orchids they came, fast and furious, everyone looking tip-top glorious. Poppy Delevingne was elegant in black flowing chiffon. Sarah Ferguson, the Duchess of York, wore a sheer black sleeved dress with a sparkly belt around the waist, and Evie Bricusse in a velvet emerald green dress I designed for her.

As we mingled with old friends, reunited after a long isolation, our guests enjoyed cocktails and the most scrumptious canapés: my favourite, caviar on tiny potatoes, and Percy's favourite, pigs in blankets. I gasped with delight entering the ballroom, where the tables were decorated with fabulous tall foliage and exquisite lilies and peonies. I always want table centrepieces to be tall so that guests can still see each other across the tables.

Instead of numbered tables, which seem so elitist and frankly boring, I'd named the fourteen tables after some of my favourite stars of the golden age of Hollywood: Gable, Hepburn, Dietrich, Chaplin, Harlow. Our table was named for my favourite singer, Sinatra. The band played a medley of his songs, which started the party in full swing.

The menu was a delicious entrée of pâté de foie gras on a bed of lightly dressed French beans, followed by a succulent tenderloin, accompanied by the most delectable Domaine du Clos des Pivotins Sancerre and a robust Margaux du Château. Pudding was a sweet treacle tart with lashings of thick cream. Not a good day for a diet. As we listened to the strains of Joe Pettitt's swing orchestra playing a variety of classics from the 1930s and 40s, we were transported back in time to the more elegant and romantic pre-war days.

'I wish I had lived then,' I whispered to Percy.

'Then you'd be dead now,' he whispered back.

The speeches were led by Biggins, who had the crowd in hysterics as he joked about my appearance as a judge on the *Masked Singer*, saying I was 'beautiful, sexy and completely bewildered'. Theo Fennell paid a special tribute to us and described Percy as an 'extraordinary human being', and then my proud husband stood up. The audience loved Percy, who thanked everyone for travelling from far and wide and referred to me as 'My Angel who came from heaven . . .' He added, 'It feels like only twenty minutes ago we took our vows. We have had lots of laughter, that has kept me going every day,' and said that I was still his 'accomplice, counsellor, fearless leader, loyal supporter and very best friend'.

This was too wonderful. My eyes filled with tears as I stood up and gave my speech, which had the crowd in stitches. At the end, as the guests wiped away tears of emotion and laughter, sequin-clad chorus girls danced onto the stage and performed a fantastic swing dance routine, choreographed by our friend Paul Robinson, elegant in his white tie. The evening ended with a DJ playing our favourite dance songs.

We were excited to show everybody the gifts that we gave each other. My husband and Theo Fennell had designed a stunning pair of emerald and opal heart-shaped earrings surrounding 'P Loves J' and we laughed when we realised that I'd had Theo design a pair of gorgeous silver and opal cufflinks shaped in the Roman numerals XX with our initials inside!

The only slightly upsetting moment was receiving calls late that afternoon from three people cancelling. That left me scurrying around changing place cards and asking some friends to come at the last minute, which they kindly did! Now *that's* friendship.

Our twentieth anniversary was a spectacular event: just perfect. Loads of fun, incredibly elegant, stylish, smart, fun friends, joyful, happy, full of kindness, empathy, good food, good wine, and good dancing. I want to share the speech I gave with you . . .

Well, he's still here. It's a miracle, a wonderful miracle to have been so happily married for twenty years to this wonderful man – with never a cross word . . . well, show me a partnership with no cross words and I'll show you a liar.

When I look around tonight at all you beautiful people, I am so thankful to see so many old friends and many new friends as well. Sadly, too many of our great friends, who were with us on that fabulous February day in 2002, are no longer with us; there are too many to mention but more recently, we lost the fabulous Johnny Gold, friend to everyone, and my dearest friend Leslie Bricusse. However, I'm glad to say that Leslie's beautiful wife Evie is here tonight and celebrating a very special day, her birthday, so let's raise a glass and wish a Happy Birthday to Evie and many, many more.

When I met Percy Gibson for the first time, he was with a colleague who was working with us on the play *Love Letters*. I remarked to the other man, 'Oh, you look terribly young.'

'What about me?' asked Percy.

I looked him up and down and replied, 'You'll do.'

He has certainly proved 'He'll do' over and over again!

Percy is a man of many talents and abilities, he can do anything and everything – and can be quite bossy about it. For example, I used to cook, not in Nigella's class, but after Percy started 'helping' and gently pushing me out of the way as I stirred a steaming pot of 'spag bol', it seemed easier to just let him get on with it, which he now does. He seems to actually enjoy it. He spoils me by bringing me delicious coffee in bed every morning along with the papers and if he goes for his run before I wake up, he leaves me little notes under the kettle.

I've always been a lucky person, but I consider myself so lucky to have found my soul mate. I think we were meant for each other, as for twenty years we have hardly ever spent a day apart, I am always there for him and he for me, we're together 24/7 without driving each other mad, even though sometimes we snap at each other like little Pekinese dogs, particularly when he's driving too fast.

I call him 'Perfect Percy' (which he hates) or 'Big Dog' (which he likes). In many ways we're totally different, I'm able to do five things at once, he can only concentrate on one, but that 'one' is always more precise and accurate than mine. They say with marriages it's 'third time lucky'. Well, in my case it's fifth time lucky! I believe that a good marriage is like a beautiful garden: if you look after it and give it love and attention, it will thrive and grow, and if not, it will wither and die. I also believe having separate bathrooms helps! Percy and I have not just a good marriage – we have a magical one, he is my life partner.

Darling, I am so proud that you're my husband.

And I am so proud to be your wife.

Life is never all plain sailing.

It was around our sixth wedding anniversary that my husband started acting suspiciously. We had just moved into our new apartment in Hollywood and, preoccupied as I was with moving, buying furniture and household stuff, and constantly arranging things, I didn't notice that he was spending a great deal of time with the doors firmly shut in his office. Whenever I came in, he would hastily hang up on whoever he was talking to or say, 'What do you want? I'm talking to the accountant/lawyer/ business manager about your taxes' which, as usual, terrified me so much I hastily retreated to shove my head in the sand and continue to play 'dolls' house' in my new surroundings.

Perhaps a person of a more jealous bent might have suspected Percy of having an affair, but it never crossed my mind. I completely trusted him.

We flew back to the UK, and when Percy casually asked me what I wanted to do on my upcoming birthday in May, I told him I really didn't know, but I would like to be in the South of France with my children.

'But I realise it won't be possible as Sacha has to be in New York and Tara's kids are at school and she is in the country and Katy is working so hard right now,' I hastily added, to avoid any potential let-downs, 'so a lovely day with you will be fine.'

I never gave it much thought and we flew to Saint-Tropez a few days before my birthday. Returning from a bibulous lunch at Club 55, where the rosé went down even more smoothly than usual, I was perplexed by the sight of several cars at our front door. I thought perhaps they were burglars when Percy pointed out that it was unlikely burglars would drive up and park their cars outside the house in broad daylight. My knees buckled and my mouth gaped when I saw Tara, her two children and her fiancé shouting 'Surprise!' at the front door. I gulped, 'Why aren't the children at school?'

'Yes, we'll talk about that, Mummy, but not right now,' Tara answered. 'We couldn't miss being with you on your birthday!'

'How on earth did you manage it?' I asked Percy, who was obviously relieved that his secret surprise had been pulled off.

The next few days were filled with fun in the sun (although there was rain and thunder too) and frolicking in the pool with the children. Two days before my birthday, we all went to Sénéquier, a popular café, where I was surprised to see my brother Bill and his wife Hazel sitting there with our friends Johnny and Jan Gold, and Simon and Joyce Reuben. 'Why didn't you tell me you were here?' I asked. 'We just got here,' Bill said. 'But we can't see you because we're going to Monaco for the Grand Prix tomorrow.' Seemed a good enough excuse to me, I reasoned. But I love my brother and wanted him to be at my birthday too, so I was a bit put out by his cool reply.

The next evening, I had decided to teach our cook Lynette my special spaghetti bolognese recipe: 'It feeds twenty but we'll freeze the leftover sauce,' I told her. I slaved over a hot stove all afternoon, after which Percy and I settled down to a fierce game of Scrabble, when suddenly the doorbell rang. 'Who on earth is that at seven-thirty?' I moaned. 'No idea,' Percy answered innocently. At the front door, to my utter amazement, stood my son Sacha with his wife Angela and four-year-old daughter Ava Grace, beaming with joy. Yells of 'Surprise!' yet again rang out throughout the house.

'I thought you were in New York!' I gasped, 'I *can't* believe you're here!!' Sacha smiled sheepishly and said, 'The amount of lying we've had to do . . .'

It's true, I had kept asking about their plans and saying what a pity they couldn't come to the South of France for my birthday, and they just sympathised forlornly, yet all the while they were planning to make the trip! Thank God I had made enough spaghetti bolognese to feed them all.

Fifteen minutes later the doorbell rang again and this time, to my astonishment, my best friend Judy Bryer was standing there, having just flown in from Las Vegas. 'You are such a liar!' I said to her, since we had spoken almost daily about the fact that she was supposed to arrive two weeks later for her own birthday. 'It was very hard to keep my mouth shut,' she concurred.

'You really pulled this off,' I said to Percy, who smiled mysteriously but said nothing. I was completely bowled over and stunned by all the surprise arrivals – practically all my immediate family and my best friend were joining me for my birthday. But what were we all going to do and where?

On the day of my birthday, having recovered from all the thrill ('I don't know how much more surprise I can take,' I had said to Percy), I received a call from my youngest daughter Katy, really excited to know how all the arrivals went. She had been due to arrive the night before but in circumstances completely beyond her control her passport had been lost.

Later that morning I suggested lunch at Club 55, but everyone vehemently disagreed and said it would be much more fun to stay at home and take advantage of the good weather by the pool. It sounded so reasonable that I happily complied, but I did notice everyone seemed rather concerned about the weather for some reason.

My friend Joyce called and said, 'I didn't realise it was your birthday and we've persuaded your brother and Johnny and Jan to stay – would you like to come to dinner at our house?'

'Perfect,' I said. For once, everyone agreed.

I was quite looking forward to a small dinner as we pulled up to the Reubens' villa. It was quiet and peaceful at their place, and our hostess met us, behaving quite naturally. I took some photos of the children in front of the house, and dawdled looking at paintings as we headed into her living room. It didn't strike me at the time that my three grand children all had their hands on their hips and were looking quite impatient.

When Joyce opened the door to her living room, there stood a large crowd of my really good friends from England and France yelling 'Surprise!!'

I'm not one for the cliché, but you could have knocked me down with the proverbial feather. Frankly, I don't remember much about what happened within those few moments – I may well have fainted – but I started to regain memories of kissing and hugging everyone while trying to hold back tears.

'How did you manage to do it?!' I asked Percy. 'It's a miracle!'

He grinned, 'I've been planning it for years.'

'Now I *know* why I haven't heard from any of you on my birthday!!' I announced to the congregation.

'Are you *sure* you didn't know?' many of my friends asked. 'You must have known *something* was happening.'

As I told them, I honest-to-God thought my surprise had been my family and Judy, and that was more than enough. 'More to come,' said Percy mysteriously. We sat down at the tables, beautifully decorated with what felt like hundreds of candles and gorgeous lilac and orchid arrangements, overlooking the glorious Saint-Tropez bay on a clear and moonlit evening. Then, after the superb dinner of slow-cooked lamb and Mediterranean vegetables, Percy led us down the lawn to the edge of the terrace to admire the most astounding display of fireworks, accompanied by Frank Sinatra crooning 'Witchcraft' (our first song) and 'oohs' and 'aahs' from everyone except me – all I could do by now was continue to sob with happiness.

Then five chefs appeared in front of us carrying the most ornate swan-shaped chocolate cake surrounded by sparkling Roman candles and lovingly decorated with a picture of my entire family.

I'm not sure how I mustered the ability to speak again, but I'm told I blubbered an ebullient thank you to everyone for being so good at dissimulation and bald-faced lying. In response, I was then treated to a series of loving toasts from assembled guests. I remember Theo Fennell's clearly: 'As Shakespeare put it – and Joan would have heard it originally from him – "Age shall not wither her nor custom stale her infinite variety".' It all just made me choke up again and think to myself that I must have done something good in my life to receive such love.

We then danced and danced to all of my favourite music, under the starry skies . . . Yes, I know it reads like chick-lit, but I can't even explain how magical it was without choking up.

Percy pulled out all the stops to give me the most wonderful, memorable day of my life. 'Your husband has raised the bar for spoiling a wife,' Sarah Standing told me. 'I don't think any of the men here will ever speak to him again and it'll be hard to top this fabulous birthday bash.'

'I couldn't agree more. Percy's a prince,' I said, 'and I'm one lucky lady to have someone care so much.'

Although I'm much travelled, I had never been to Peru, the land of my husband's birth. Since we tied the knot, Percy and I had planned to go several times but never managed it, so I was delighted that we spent several days in Lima on our way to Sydney via Santiago, Chile. Yes, I know – it was jet lag extraordinaire.

Percy had filled me in on the beauty of the country and the abundance of gorgeous plants and foliage like rampant bougainvillea and palm trees. However, as we drove down the main drag of Javier Prado, I couldn't see the trees for the wood. Because impaled on every tree, fence and lamppost were humungous posters of politicians vying to become the next MP, representative, councillor, and God knows what else. The sheer volume of rival candidates made our UK local elections look positively parsimonious.

But meeting Percy's family and friends was sheer joy. Their

generous hospitality was boundless. Every day there were lusciously long lunches lasting four or five hours and packed with superb dishes – Peruvian cuisine is remarkably good – which segued into equally wonderful dinners thrown by Percy's seemingly endless parade of bountiful friends and family. It's a wonder they get any work done! I discovered the local antidote to this bacchanalia when I woke up early one morning to discover the park surrounding our hotel a seething mass of joggers, giving a whole new meaning to the phrase 'eat and run'.

We culminated our stay by visiting Calle Percy Gibson – a street named after Percy's grandfather, a famous poet and not, as scurrilous wags have said, named after Percy for marrying me. It was a marvellous trip but, oh, my waistline will never recover!

23
Camping It Up

The first (and only!) time I was invited to the Metropolitan Museum of New York's famous 'Met Gala', in aid of their celebrated costume institute, my first thought was *What shall I wear??*

As one of the most iconic fashion events in the world, the Met Gala attracts the most fabulous models and actresses and famous designers like moths to the fashion flame. Not only is the prospect daunting but the theme of the ball in 2019 was camp – what the hell could that entail? The dictionary defines camp as 'deliberately exaggerated and theatrical in style, typically for humorous effect'.

It was a daunting prospect to compete with high-powered style and glamour, but I was comforted by the fact that the new wunderkind of Valentino, Pier Paolo Piccioli, head designer of the iconic fashion house, was going to design a dress for me.

As I wondered what that design would be, my PR Jeffrey Lane, who was coordinating with Valentino's people, soothed my fevered brow: 'They said leave it all to him. Pier Paolo will send you the sketches.'

Six weeks passed and no sketches arrived.

'Don't worry,' counselled Kate, the Valentino PR. 'We can organise a dress in a week – we did it last year for Lady Gaga.'

Yet another month passed and now I was in full-blown panic. I called Carlos De Souza, the head of PR for the Valentino empire, who assured me all was well and that Pier Paolo, who was in Milan, would be in touch 'soon'.

Finally, they arrived – five beautiful fashion sketches, exquisitely packed in Valentino boxes trimmed with white ribbon – of dresses that were . . . oh, dear me . . . a bit too 'ingénue' for me. Pier Paolo and I went into full 'collaboration' mode from that moment on, with texts, emails, photos, hand drawings, hasty calls placed at various hours of the day to account for the time difference from LA to Rome. With only four weeks to go before the grand event, another Valentino box arrived, hand-couriered from Rome to London. Inside was a stunning design of a dress in heavy white faille silk ruffles with a crinoline absolutely covered in feathers. I loved the fact that feathers embodied the 'camp' styles as referenced in Susan Sontag's 'Notes on Camp', the inspiration for this year's theme, so I decided that I'd 'camp' it up some more with diamonds by the yard.

I wasn't about to borrow from any of the jewellers, as that would entail being shadowed by security officers in scenes reminiscent of *Ocean's Eight*, so my LA stylist Rene Horsch and I went to a fabulous wholesale shop in downtown LA that specialised in gorgeous costume jewellery. There we chose several necklaces, bracelets and, the zenith of camp – a tiara. Rene sourced a fabulous diamanté necklace which he soldered to the top of it, and the combination sparkled as much as the one the Queen wore at her coronation.

Percy and I arrived in NY on the Thursday before the big day, the first Monday in May. On Friday and Saturday I had the final fitting with the great designer himself – Pier Paolo Piccioli.

'Call me Pee-Pee,' he insisted.

'I'll try,' I replied, casting a furtive glance at Jeffrey and Percy, who remained impressively stone-faced.

Pee-Pee was great fun. A wonderfully receptive designer who appreciated my feedback even when I said, 'More feathers, please!' He took in the bodice as I'd lost weight since the last fitting and added more and more feathers. On the night, I did my own hair and make-up and I fixed the tiara gently on top of my head.

Our group mustered in the main lobby of the Pierre Hotel – beautiful and talented Julianne Moore resplendent in shimmering green, Chinese musical phenom Lay Zhang, American musical legend Mark Ronson, waiflike warbler Likke Li and the glorious and striking model Adut Akech. Led by the energetic Carlos De Souza, we all stepped into the courtyard of the Pierre to what felt like an opening night with about two hundred fans gathered around, whooping and cheering, and dozens of paparazzi snapping jauntily.

We piled into two massive SUVs of the type that Donald Trump uses for his flotilla – not easy to do in a massive crinoline skirt – and set off, rather late, I thought, to the event. The traffic was an utter nightmare with bumper-to-bumper jams, so we passed the time watching the arrivals on *Vogue*'s Instagram feed on Carlos' phone. We saw Lady Gaga doing her camp striptease on the pink carpet, arriving in a huge, hooded outfit with a cape, surrounded by male dancers in tuxedos brandishing black umbrellas. She strutted and posed for the cameras then stripped down to a black strapless sheath, in which she also posed extensively.

She did about ten minutes of this, so I asked, 'What about all the other celebrities waiting in line to go on the carpet?'

'She's Lady G, she gets away with everything,' Carlos laughed. She certainly made the time stuck in the traffic go much faster. Then Lady G stripped off the black sheath to reveal a pink sheath and finally pulled that off to reveal a black bra and panties with fishnet tights and boots. She primped and posed, kissed the designer and draped herself down on the stairs with her bottom sticking out. I've never seen anything so *not* introverted. Seventeen minutes had gone by, and we were thoroughly entertained. Dear Lady G – thanks for lightening the tedium of NY traffic jams.

Then . . . Hello! Billy Porter arrived dressed as Cleopatra, held aloft by a half-dozen, half-naked men. He was completely covered in gold sequins, sporting golden wings. Billy was followed by Serena Williams, wearing yellow sneakers – smart, I thought.

Still in the car, and after a heated discussion as to what 'camp' really meant, we decided that the purpose was to 'put a smile on our faces and a warm glow in our hearts'. Apparently, this trend usually surges at times of social and political instability.

We finally arrived at the traditional and austere facade of the Metropolitan Museum – a vision decorated in pink flowers, pink feathers and gigantic pink flamingos, which, according to the doyenne of *Vogue*, fashion editor and chair of the ball Anna Wintour, are the quintessence of camp.

We shuffled along impatiently in a long queue before we were allowed onto the red (no, pink!) carpet.

In front of us, J-Lo flaunted a twenty-foot white fur and sequin train which prompted us to perform some sprightly jumping out of the way as her attendants slowly manoeuvred it. I also had to duck an army of make-up and hair experts all tweaking bits of their clients. I didn't even have lipstick on me, as my tiny minaudière was in Pier Paolo's pocket.

It was a bit like standing in line at the Waitrose checkout on a lunchtime rush, except we were surrounded by the likes of Kim and Kanye West, Kendall Jenner, Harry Styles in a black chiffon embroidered blouse with a huge pussycat bow, Idris Elba, handsome in a heavily embroidered jacket, and 6' 5" RuPaul, clad in a gaudy, multicoloured sequin pantsuit.

Tom Ford, looking extremely elegant and soigné in a simple dinner jacket accessorised with a white gardenia, gave me a big hug and then went to attend to the gorgeous Gemma Chan, who was wearing his impossibly chic silvery dress and cape, topped with a glorious silver concoction reminiscent of Elizabeth Taylor in *Boom!*

Then the diva of divas and the last of our Valentino team, the stunningly beautiful Naomi Campbell, joined us, glittering in a pink lace Valentino bodysuit topped with a huge floating pink plumed cape and train. A man, holding a piece of plastic, knelt behind her fanning her feathers so they fluttered prettily. A human wind machine – clever.

We all hit the pink carpet together. The photographers whooped then ordered us around as we all stood arm in arm. Pier Paolo, Carlos, Julianne, Naomi, Mark, Lay, Likke, Adut. To say it was surreal would be a gross understatement. Naomi put her arms around my shoulders for a hug and I almost toppled over. I don't know how Victorian ladies managed their corsets and crinolines, but I consoled myself with the thought that they didn't have to wear six-inch stilettoes and have five thousand cameras trained on them, while hordes of fans yelled and screamed either side of the stairs.

When our little band of brothers, and sisters, finally arrived at the top of the thirty or so steps (it felt like a thousand) we paid our respects to the hosts. Anna Wintour looked regal in sequins and a plumed ombré cape. I congratulated her on her damehood, and she graciously replied that she was delighted to have me. Lady Gaga, in her cerise sheath, and I reminisced about our meeting for the first time at the *Vanity Fair* party with my sister Jackie. Serena Williams wore a yellow embroidered ball gown with sneakers – I congratulated her on the arrival of her new baby boy. Harry Styles, still in his see-through blouse, was followed by Alessandro Michele, the CEO of Gucci, who had donated five million dollars to the Met for the ball. He was a vision of cyclamen ruffles from top to toe. We consoled each other over the missed opportunity for me to front their handbags and shoes advertisements: 'They only offered it to me a week after I had signed with Kurt Geiger,' I told him. Mr Michele promised to take up the opportunity again as soon as possible (which I am still waiting for).

I was gasping for a drink by now and worried we were late to sit down, as it seemed we had been on the pink carpet for at least two hours. I clutched onto Pier Paolo for dear life as we ran down a long corridor, then up another flight of stairs, arriving at a tiny room where a group of brilliantly costumed guests were all swigging cocktails and looking relaxed.

'A glass of white wine, please,' I croaked to a waiter. I said hello to Demi Moore, chic in a YSL tuxedo; the Delevingne sisters, Poppy and Cara, the latter wearing the highest platform shoes I've ever seen; and Kate Moss, looking gorgeous in silver sequins. Lily Collins and I laughed about the days we lived in the same building in LA, where the postman constantly mis-directed our mail to the wrong Collins.

As I took a grateful gulp of my wine, Carlos took me by the arm to be interviewed by *Vogue, Women's Wear Daily* and Associated Press. After only one sip he dragged me off again – to dinner, I hoped.

But yet another queue of major celebrities were crammed together in a dark, narrow passage covered in pink peonies. I stood behind Jenifer Lopez, wearing a few strategically placed silver bugle beads with matching helmet, accompanied by Alex

Rodriguez. We discussed the merits of Craig's, our joint favourite restaurant in LA, but the couple didn't seem terribly happy
with each other.

Several actresses whose names I didn't know but whose faces
and *embonpoint* I recognised chatted excitedly while manoeuvring their trains and huge headdresses as we moved agonisingly
slowly, one by one, negotiating yet another set of pink-carpeted
steps. I was fascinated how Katy Perry managed her chandelier
costume so gracefully then disappeared into the bathroom to
return for dinner dressed as a hamburger.

Finally, we arrived at the dining room – an exquisite pano-
rama of pink. I managed to stumble to our table, my feet now
throbbing. Pier Paolo and Carlos were videoing everything
and everyone, so I finally got my phone out of Carlos' pocket
to text Percy that 'I think we'll be a little late for the Gucci
after-party'.

Leslie Grossman from *American Horror Story* came over to
say hello, dressed in feathers and diamonds, channelling Zsa
Zsa Gabor, and I waved to Sarah Paulson, who was in Mo-
schino black satin, and Donatella Versace wearing . . . Well,
what else?

'Hurry up and eat – Anna likes to get things going so we can
watch the entertainment,' whispered Carlos. I rushed through
my delicious tomato tartlet but was unable to face the fillet steak,
which I knew from past experience would haunt me for the rest
of the evening.

Then an ominous crash of music preceded Lady Gaga onstage. She was casually dressed in a bra, panties and fishnets (as
you do) and gave a speech about loving each other, inclusion
and diversity and embracing your 'inner camp'. She introduced
the stars of *Pose*, Ryan Murphy's new television series about
the Trans movement in 1980s Manhattan. Ryan himself was

wearing top-to-toe sequins, channelling Liberace perfectly. It was rumoured that he suggested the theme for this year, so he certainly 'walked the walk' of which he talked.

As dancers filled the stage, the curtains parted to reveal the icon of icons – Cher. This was a great and delightful surprise as the entertainment is a closely guarded secret. But with so many hairdressers and stylists in the know, how closely can one guard a secret?

Nevertheless, the sophisticated crowd went mad for her, standing up whooping and cheering. The legend was dressed down in ripped jeans, a tiny top, an anorak, and a long blonde wig – the complete opposite of camp, but nevertheless wonderfully ageless.

Bette Midler, wearing a top hat and tailcoat in glittery black sequins, came to our table and boogied with Julianne Moore, and I glimpsed Gwyneth Paltrow and Katie Holmes doing the same.

Cher left after her first number then came back wearing her original Bob Mackie-style sleek black embroidered bodysuit and a massive black curly wig to sing 'Believe'. Harry Styles jumped on the table in front of us, obscuring our view, and took no notice of our entreaties to 'get down, we can't see'.

Then people started to get up to leave – and fast! Bella Hadid, chic and exquisite in a black sheath with long beaded gloves, Zendaya, Lupita Nyong'o, Emma Roberts and Karlie Kloss led the troops in the massive exodus. Managing to ooze past this wall of names, pandemonium reigned as everyone tried to find their PRs and their limos outside. It was a frenzy. Freezing, Pier Paolo lent me his jacket as I chatted to two of New York's finest – the policemen tasked with protecting us all – who were absolutely *loving* the whole event and genuinely thrilled to be there. Billy Porter came over, looking a little bit more normal after losing the gold wings, and we had a great chat about *American Horror Story*, which we both starred in.

I finally arrived at Hunter College, the venue for the Gucci after-party, where Percy and Jeffrey had been waiting for hours while being entertained by the various arrivals and seeing the efficiency with which the guards turned away anyone who was not on the list.

We were escorted by a security officer to a basketball gymnasium, the scores of the last game still posted on the board and 'Go Hawks!' posters on the walls. We said hello to Rosie Huntington-Whiteley and then sat down with our Valentino group to watch the world go by. Within a minute someone fell over the table, which tipped my glass of wine all over my feathers.

'Time to leave!' said Percy firmly, to which I agreed weakly, thinking *My feet will never be the same again.* I must have walked five miles. 'Let's forget the after parties.'

But what an experience it was. I loved my first Met Ball, and I would certainly go again in a heartbeat – although at $30,000 a seat, I'll wait to be invited!

24

Oscar Night

Awards season is always an odd time in the year's calendar. There are numerous parties before, after and even during awards ceremonies. Two months before the Oscars, there are so many other award shows that by the time the 'Big O' comes around, the likely winners in all categories have been locked in by the bookies. But, nevertheless, there's the odd surprise or two every year.

Percy and I watched the 2018 Oscar ceremony in the private dining room of the Annenberg Center. I was lucky enough to sit next to my friend, the super-suave and brilliant designer Tom Ford, and Percy got the short straw with his dinner partner, the notorious Monica Lewinsky, she of stained dress fame. While Tom was an amusing, fascinating conversationalist and a most attentive dinner companion, Percy had a tougher time with Miss Lewinsky. She kept looking around and appeared much more interested in flitting around the room, cultivating movers and shakers. A miniseries was in preparation about her time with President Clinton and she seemed eager to let everyone know about it.

We were feeling quite bored after the seemingly endless Oscar ceremony finally concluded with the tiresome *The Shape of Water* winning Best Picture. We left to stroll around the cocktail area, saying hello to acquaintances like Sofia Vergara and James Corden, who was always good for a laugh about the awards. But this event didn't begin to compare with the star power of previous ceremonies.

I've been taking my Oscar voter responsibilities seriously since I attended my first ceremony in 1957 with my close friend Joanne Woodward and her movie-star husband Paul Newman. I tottered down the red carpet at the Pantages Theatre in vertiginous pink satin heels and a pink balloon-skirted gown I had designed myself. I was majorly excited because one of the nominees for the Best Actress award was Joanne, in recognition of her staggering performance in *The Three Faces of Eve*, but facing tough competition from Deborah Kerr, Anna Magnani, Elizabeth Taylor and Lana Turner. Joanne had styled her own hair for this, the biggest night in Hollywood, as had I, and we had applied our own make-up and worn our own jewellery – those were the days! But Joanne had one up on me and all the other guests that evening in that she had designed, cut and *sewn* her own dress! 'Shocking,' shrieked the tough, outspoken grand dame Joan Crawford. 'By making her own clothes Joanne Woodward has set Hollywood glamour back twenty years.' Well, Miss Crawford, you should see what some starlets are wearing today. Cut to the crotch, boobs barely contained, legs akimbo, many frocks seem attached to their wearer by tooth floss. I'm sure she'd turn in her grave.

However, Joanne was mighty proud of her intricate green velvet dress with matching coat, and it looked brilliant when, to our whoops and cheers, she won Best Actress. 'I'm keeping the dress,' she said when a museum in her hometown asked for it to be displayed. 'I'm almost as proud of that dress as I am of my Oscar.' She had been beavering away at it all through the film we had been making together with Paul, *Rally 'Round the Flag, Boys*.

Marlon Brando also won, and he clowned with Bob Hope pretending to fight over his statuette. That was quite a turnabout for Marlon from a few weeks earlier when he sat in my living room eating ice cream out of the carton and declaiming Bob as 'a big fake who would go to the opening of a petrol station'.

Bob Hope was the MC of the 1958 awards ceremony and he was, as always, brilliant, trading quips with the likes of John Wayne, Burt Lancaster and Kirk Douglas. These were some of the most superb, charismatic actors of what is now called the 'golden age' of cinema and, being an avid moviegoer, I was more than star-struck to see Burt and Kirk perform a hilarious song and dance routine called 'It's Great Not to be Nominated', a ditty which poked fun at some of the male nominees. The number ended with a spectacular stunt when Kirk stood on Burt's shoulders, who held him aloft as they danced jauntily off the stage.

The number was such a success that, to my surprise, I was asked to perform a 'cod' version the following year with two other British actresses – Angela Lansbury and Dana Wynter. Legendary lyricist Sammy Cahn wrote the lyrics to 'It's Bully Not to be Nominated', which we performed in exaggerated English accents. Angela and Dana wore slinky satin sheaths, but I opted for a tight gold lamé number which, again, I had designed myself, since I considered the old-school Hollywood designers too fussy and complicated. The next day, to our horror, we found out that all the nominated actresses were insulted by our jocular japes and had taken them personally. Granted, the words were pretty appalling and unfunny, but at least we got a grin from Shirley when we hissed 'Shirley MacLaine's a talent that's rare, if you like juvenile delinquent hair.' Rosalind Russell glowered as we made reference to her age – ageist jokes don't go down well in Hollywood. (I was surprised to see Jimmy Kimmel, in his first year as host in 2020, crack a feeble joke about eighty-eight-year-old Christopher Plummer, for instance, and was glad they booed him!) I was sorry Rosalind Russell took the skits personally, as she and I got along quite well the year before, exchanging quips when I presented Best Cinematography to Jack Hildyard. She asked me to explain what a cinematographer does, and I said, 'He's the one who shows up first on set before anyone is there, fixes the lens, adjusts the lights, peers through the viewfinder at you and then stands up and asks "So, what were *you* up to last night?"' At that year's after party, held at the Beverly Hills Hotel, I chatted with the witty and urbane David Niven who had won for *Separate Tables*. That was also the year the show was too short for the telecast (an historical occasion, never repeated). A bemused Jerry Lewis got the news and asked the presenters, winners and nominees to come up on stage while he grabbed the conductor's baton and conducted a frantic waltz. He screamed at us, 'Keep dancing, kids, keep dancing!'

For ten excruciating minutes, a host of stars like Dean Martin (about who Jerry quipped, 'You never thought Dean and I would be onstage together again!'), Natalie Wood, Robert Wagner, Maurice Chevalier and little me had to awkwardly take each other's hands and prance around, waltzing horribly whilst Jerry frantically encouraged us!

In 1974, I saw Niven at the Oscars again when my then-husband Ron Kass was nominated for best documentary for *Naked Yoga*, a film he had produced. True to the title, a streaker shot past security and paraded naked on stage in front of David.

He had the wit and presence of mind to quip, 'Isn't it fascinating to think that probably the only laugh that man will ever get in life is by stripping off and showing his shortcomings?' The audience burst into hysterics.

As the 1980s dawned, stylists to the stars came into vogue.

When I hosted the technical awards with Arnold Schwarzenegger for the 1984 Oscars, there was a designer on board who was rigorous in her insistence that I wear a strange melange of styles, 'to go with the theme of the night'. This confection consisted of a long black skirt and a bright-red sequin beaded top, backless and almost frontless, which I wasn't happy about as it was much too revealing. Arnold seemed quite taken with the outfit and several times put his arms around me during filming, in what would today be called 'inappropriate touching'. So, I touched him back. I squeezed a massive bicep, which was solid as steel. 'Wow,' I said, 'you're hard!' He winked at me. Shortly after, he became governor of California and had a child with his housekeeper.

As the 1980s powered on, it was considered rather tacky to not wear anything but designer duds, and as I was then working on *Dynasty* I was lucky enough to be able to borrow several outfits I'd worn on the show. Around this time, the legendary super-agent Irving 'Swifty' Lazar started hosting his fabulous Oscar-night viewing parties at the trendy Spago restaurant on Sunset Boulevard. Most stars who weren't nominated or presenting awards preferred to go to Swifty's party rather than face the hassle of the red-carpet madness at the actual ceremony.

Swifty's parties were the hottest and most coveted ticket in town, as he was meticulous about who he invited. Competition to be asked was fierce and Swifty had to fend off hundreds of wannabe invitees. Jackie and I were honoured to always be invited, along with major luminaries and legends like Billy Wilder, Robert Mitchum and Cary Grant – it was a veritable Who's Who of Hollywood and an evening of complete magic.

In 1992, I went to my table at Spago escorted by Swifty's right-hand man and my future agent, Alan Nevins. I noticed that he was seated next to someone called Ms Ciccone. 'Who's that?' I enquired.

'Me,' said a little voice. I turned to see Madonna herself wearing a black beret, string of pearls and a simple blue top. She was with Rosie O'Donnell and they never stopped talking during the show, and left shortly after it ended, much to Swifty's fury. I wore a long black lace dress which I had bought myself, unlike most of the actresses on the red carpet, who were loaned their designer dresses. Today, the top actresses actually get *paid* to wear a particular designer's dress and jewellery, sometimes even more than $25,000.

Swifty kept his parties private and became enraged if people took photos inside. Each year, Spago's Oscar decorations became more and more spectacular. That year, each table flaunted a massive plastic star in the centre covered in tiny gold stars, atop of which was an arrangement of black and gold ribbon fashioned to look like rolls of film. In front of each of our placements was a tiny gold Oscar, and I have kept mine to this day, since I know it's the only one I'll ever get!

Swifty even forbade any of his guests to stand and mingle during the telecast, and one year he even banned Raquel Welch because she was socialising too much and sat on Robert Mitchum's knee. Swifty died in 1993 and his legendary parties were taken over by Graydon Carter, editor of *Vanity Fair* magazine.

This iconic *Vanity Fair* party started at Morton's restaurant, then moved to Cecconi's (which was great because Elton's AIDS Foundation party was across the street and people could walk back and forth between the two), then it moved to the Sunset Tower Hotel and finally became so big that they had to erect a tent across the main thoroughfare, to connect it to the vast Annenberg Center.

Jackie and I went to all the parties every year, and we always had the most brilliant time. The first time Percy and I went together, I realised to my horror that my place card was next to a man who had written the most horrible article about me. I hissed to Percy, 'Quick! Change my place card!'

'Um, OK,' he said. 'Who do I change it with?'

'There's Dominick Dunne across the table, put me next to him, please,' I begged.

He dutifully did what I asked, but sharp-eyed Dominick noticed the commotion.

'Hey there, young man, what do you think you're doing?'

'Erm, Dom . . . er, Mr Dunne sorry, my wife, Joan . . . I'm sure you know her – Joan Collins – asked me to change her place card.'

'Do you realise that that's just NOT done? It is absolutely the worst manners.'

Poor Percy explained the gravity of the situation to Dominick, who charmingly relented. He was a great writer and also a really good friend.

Vanity Fair parties are always fun, and you never know who you are going to meet. At once such party, Paris Hilton popped over to our table wearing a fairy frock and tiara. She explained that she goes to 'tons of parties', and that she often gets paid for attending – sometimes up to $100,000 – by organizers who want their grand opening, New Years' gig or plain party to be the hottest one in town. She produced her cell phone, on which there was a picture of her and her sister Nicky mirroring a famous photograph of my sister Jackie and I, taken by the legendary Annie Leibowitz for *Vanity Fair*. What a compliment!

A historic fact is that the Oscar itself was named when Bette Davis observed how closely the statuette's buttocks resembled her husband's! Harmon Oscar Nelson's derriere is without a doubt the most coveted and prestigious of all awards.

*

In 2011, at yet another *Vanity Fair* party, I wore a very tight gown. I had squeezed myself into a beautiful creation of purple and lilac satin with appliqued flowers and crystals by Georges Hobeika. It fitted so well that I was resigned to not being able to eat too much. I was also on a course of antibiotics for the flu so already wasn't feeling great.

Percy and I sat with my sister, George and Jolene Schlatter of *Laugh-In* fame, and Leonard and Wendy Goldberg, producers of *Dynasty* and now helming *Charlie's Angels*, TV's *Blue Bloods* and my friend Liam Neeson. At one point, I dared to shush Anderson Cooper's table because they were making too much noise during Natalie Portman's acceptance speech, and they shot daggers – I somehow never learned to get on the good side of the media. Major studio execs and socialites filled the rest of the room to the brim, giving me pause to wonder who would get first billing if it burned down.

The stars of the night arrived from the Governors Ball around 9 p.m., after we'd been socialising for about four hours, and my dress was getting progressively tighter. By 10.30 p.m. there were about eight hundred people milling about and I started feeling slightly dizzy, so Percy and I walked outside to get some fresh air. Next thing I knew, I was lying on a gurney surrounded by some rather attractive firefighters who were asking me questions like, 'What's your name?' (*as if* they didn't know) and 'How old are you?' (which I refused to answer.) Apparently, I had fainted in Percy's arms and he, in a panic, had asked security to call an ambulance.

In my delirium, I was terrified that the paparazzi would get pictures of me lying dazed on a stretcher, being carried to an ambulance. It would have earned the paps a pretty penny. But I needn't have worried – on a gossip newscast the next day they thought I was Janet Jackson!

I was ignominiously whisked into an ambulance to Cedars Sinai Hospital, where half my dress was cut off me despite my horrified screams of protest and attempts to cover my modesty.

'I'm not wearing knickers,' I screamed.

'It doesn't matter, lady. We need to see your abdomen.'

Not quite how I expected to end this glamorous night, I nevertheless put myself in the care of professionals at the A&E. After an hour of tests, the doctors discharged me with admonishments not to wear such tight dresses and to eat beforehand in future, if I was expected to last more than seven hours at the party!

My mother used to irritate me by asking me who I had met at whatever party I had attended that evening and then enquiring, 'Did you *cultivate* them?' Horrified, I would usually reply, 'No, I didn't,' and that I wasn't a horticulturist. But as I grew older, I saw the wisdom in her words (as rebellious daughters usually do!). If I hadn't attended a particular party in LA in the late 1970s, I wouldn't have been cast in Aaron Spelling's *Love Boat*, which in turn led to *Dynasty*. So, I've learned the lesson that you never know who you are going to meet at parties, and what it could lead to ... At the *Vanity Fair* party in 2017, I noticed a group of people clustered around a drinks table. An attractive woman who looked familiar waved and smiled and beckoned us over. 'That's Sarah Paulson,' I whispered to Percy. 'She was so brilliant as Marcia Clark in *The People v. O.J. Simpson*.'

Sarah introduced us to her life partner Holland Taylor – another brilliant actor – then to an important-looking man. 'This is Ryan Murphy,' said Sarah, and I recalled he was known as 'The Three Hundred Million Dollar Man' due to his enormous recent contract with Netflix.

'I'm a great fan,' said Mr Murphy. 'Maybe we should do something together.'

I murmured a thank you. I was used to people saying this and I never expected anything to come of it, let alone an actual offer. We chatted amicably and I told Ryan how much I admired his amazing talent and innovative TV shows, particularly *The Assassination of Gianni Versace*, a six-part series about the tragic events involving the fabled Italian designer.

'I'd love you to do something on *American Horror Story*,' he said. 'Would you be interested?'

'Absolutely,' I replied. 'Can I play a witch?'

25

My American Horror Story

One of the most popular American TV shows, *American Horror Story*, was a mysteriously scary but fascinating series of interconnecting stories created, produced and written by TV's latest wunderkind. In the past decade, Ryan Murphy was the brilliance behind such hits as *Nip/Tuck*, *Glee*, the mesmerising *The People v. O.J. Simpson*, and my favourite, *Feud*, a study of the enmity between two great legends of the silver screen, Bette Davis and Joan Crawford. So Mr Murphy had 'legs', as they say, and I was excited to meet him.

'I'll write a great role for you,' Ryan smiled that night at the *Vanity Fair* party. He seemed genuinely interested in the idea, but I didn't think much would happen – until two weeks later, after attending a Barbra Streisand concert, backstage in her dressing room, Ryan was there too. (I first met Barbra in 1963, when my then husband Anthony Newley was appearing in *Stop the World: I Want to Get Off*. Everyone was talking about this brilliant nineteen-year-old performing at a club downtown. She was magnetic and we became friends. When she did *Funny Girl*, her first movie, she even asked my advice on make-up and lighting.)

'You should get our offer at the end of the week,' Ryan said. 'I've talked to your agent – it's with the lawyers now. You'll love the role.'

I was amazed. Deals in Hollywood usually move super-slowly. It's almost unheard of for a project to come to fruition in just a couple of months. But, lo and behold, my agent called the next day, saying the deal was almost done. The problem was that I had committed to my daughter Tara, her husband Nick and all my grandchildren coming to visit us in the South of France in the middle of August. The *American Horror Story* people weren't happy with this, as it meant I was not available for three weeks, but I needed that time and I have always insisted family has to come first, so this was potentially a deal breaker. When I was doing *Dynasty*, I managed every three or four weeks to hop on a British Airways flight to visit Katy and Tara in London (luckily, I had a deal with British Airways at the time!).

But, happily, *American Horror Story* did happen and I went on to play the dual role of selfish socialite Evie Gallant and one of a coven of witches, a film-star witch amusingly called Bubbles McGee. I adored the name and the part, for which I wore a silver-white bouffant wig redolent of Jean Harlow. After my death scene (actors die a LOT in *American Horror Story*), the fake nails embedded in my skull from the 'nail bomb' and the 'blood' splattered all over my face took three days to get rid of.

I loved working with such talented actresses as Sarah Paulson, Emma Roberts and Billie Lourd, as we witched and shivered our way through the freezing dark sound stages at Twentieth Century-Fox. I particularly adored the wonderful Kathy Bates, Oscar winner and a truly great actress, who I respect enormously. After we played our first scene together, Kathy was extremely complimentary, and we pledged undying friendship.

Evan Peters, who played the horrific eponymous role in *Monster: The Jeffrey Dahmer Story* a few years later, had the dubious honour of killing Evie Gallant – me – in the most horrible way. I wasn't looking forward to this so I went on set a couple of days before we were to shoot it to find out how it was to be staged.

The description in the script was terrifying. Mr Gallant (Evan), described as an eccentric gay hairdresser, plunges a machete several times into Evie's body as she lies asleep in bed. She screams loudly as blood and guts spill everywhere. She shudders and, as Evan's face is shown vengefully, she dies! Well, I hadn't been Queen of the Horror Flicks all those years ago in England without knowing that these barbaric effects can be easily faked, so I wasn't too worried. On the day, I breezed onto the set in a diaphanous mauve negligee. With me were Percy and my grand-daughter Miel.

On my bed I saw a sort of coffin, and lying on top of it a facsimile of my body dressed in a copy of my negligee. At the bottom of the mannequin was a pair of grotesque feet. They were enormous and greyish, with arthritic toes painted a vile orange peeking out.

'Don't tell me those are supposed to be MY feet?' I huffed to the prop man. 'My feet are quite nice. And small,' I added.

'Sorry, Joan,' he said. 'Too late. Is the body OK though?'

I nodded. What choice did I have? At least it wasn't fat.

'OK, Joan, get in,' called the director. 'Let's do this thing.'

I crawled in underneath the fake body. It was hot, heavy and uncomfortable as the crew adjusted my own head to fit on top of the body.

Fiddling with the lights and sound seemed to take forever, and I was getting nervous about my 'murder', when suddenly the assistant director called out, 'OK, people. Take ten!' and all the grips, props, camera and wardrobe people who had been clustering and fussing around me disappeared in a flash, including Percy and Miel! I lay alone on the darkened stage, the faint smell of offal emanating from a bucket near me. My intestines, no doubt, I thought. I could vaguely see shapes in the distance, but I was trapped under seventy-five pounds of fibreglass and stuffing.

'Percy?' I called softly. 'Miel? Can you come and talk to me, please?' No answer – they were all obviously enjoying a nice cup of java while my throat became so dry it felt as if I was in the Mojave Desert. After what seemed an eternity, everyone returned, jaunty, jolly, well-fed and watered.

We rehearsed without offal. The director gave Evan and me a few notes: 'Don't forget – raise that machete really high and plunge it in Joan really HARD!' Then he called 'Action'!

Evan Peters was a true apostle of method acting. He lunged towards me with a hideously menacing expression on his face, brandishing his weapon high above his head. Then he swung the machete and crashed it hard into my 'body'. A huge mass of offal, intestines and fake blood came shooting out like a volcanic eruption, spraying all over my face. When Evan hit me the second time I shuddered with real terror as it reverberated through me.

'Don't move, Joan – just lay still,' yelled the director, seeing my total horror and discomfort. 'Close your eyes, honey. You're *dead*, honey – stay dead, honey. Do not move.'

I lay still as stone, the stink of pigs' blood, liver and intestines getting up my nose and in my ears, while the camera zoomed in for a close-up of my 'dead' face.

'Cut!' yelled the director. 'Beautiful, Joan, honey, we got it. It's a wrap, boys and girls, it's a wrap.'

I managed to scrape off some of the animal detritus which had actually seeped through to my nightdress. 'The intestines were the worst,' I murmured to Percy, slipping and sliding on the 'blood', as I staggered off the set to my dressing room, followed by Miel, who said excitedly, 'Ooh, it looked so *real*.'

'It felt real too,' I moaned. 'But I'm never going to eat liver or sausages again!'

26

Sibling Rivalry

Although the press and gossipmongers have ruminated about the relationship between my sister Jackie and myself, I like to think it was simply normal 'sibling rivalry'. It is quite common between brothers and sisters, including recently between Princes William and Harry and don't forget the Bouvier sisters.

My sister's 2021 documentary, *Lady Boss*, pointed the finger to the moment that I decided to write a novel as when she became upset with me. Although Jackie was very successful and her books were top of the bestseller list, several 'talking heads' in the documentary reported our rivalry..

I had already written my bestselling autobiography, *Past Imperfect*, which Jackie seemed to accept strangely. We never discussed my books, and she pretended she had never read them.

At the height of *Dynasty*, I needed to pursue all avenues for income. Having been through it once, I'd learned that fame is illusory, and income based on fame is fleeting. I have always believed, as Michael Caine said, 'an actor needs to have other strings to his bow'. Acting is the most precarious profession, so to ensure I could continue to make a good living after *Dynasty* finished, I started to write inspirational beauty books and novels, which also became bestsellers. I'm very glad I did, as I learned to my great shock and horror that, after working on it for nine years, I would not be getting any residuals from *Dynasty*, which I had been hoping would be my annuity.

I figured Jackie wouldn't mind that I wrote books when *Dynasty* ended, since when she was young I had encouraged and helped her with her acting ambitions when she wanted to follow in my footsteps and become an actress. However, because we never faced each other with the facts, was resentment really festering in my little sister now?

I helped Jackie to try and realise her dreams. When she stayed with me in Hollywood, I always invited her to industry parties with me, introducing her to casting agents and directors, all of whom might help her career. Her documentary only acknowledged this briefly.

My agent Swifty Lazar believed my writing was good enough for me to become a novelist. I had always been top of my class in English composition, essays and writing, so therefore it seemed quite natural to follow in my sister's footsteps, much as she had in mine. But, sadly, Jackie's documentary revealed that she had resented being promoted as my 'little sister' in her film and theatre career. So much so, that she insisted on always being called Jackie Lerman. However, she realised that she wouldn't be able to sell books under that name, so 'Jackie Collins' she became and faced all the publicity as 'Joan's little sister'.

I told this to her and Oscar later. 'You've been Jackie Lerman for years because you didn't want to be known as my sister. Do you realise that in all the interviews you do they are going to ask you about me?' Oscar agreed but said, 'We want the book to be a bestseller. It doesn't matter how we do it.'

Maybe I should look at things through the prism of my relationships. Jackie hated my fourth husband, the Swede, Peter, and told me she'd 'never speak to me again' if I married him. As it turns out, she was quite right, because I divorced him a year later.

Similarly, we went through a period of coolness later when I was seeing my English boyfriend Robin, who was often sarcastically rude to her, correcting her pronunciation and commenting on her taste. Maybe that explains why she didn't attend my wedding to my now-husband, Percy. But Jackie and I never confronted each other about our problems, and it was only when I married Percy and she grew to love him that our rift finally healed.

Maybe I didn't give Jackie enough credit for 'rescuing' my career with *The Stud*, as some 'talking heads' in her documentary bluntly stated? I have always given her credit for writing an excellent book and script which she very generously allowed me to try and sell for a movie. But I had to schlep *The Stud* script around for two years, pitched it tirelessly, and finally persuaded George Walker to produce it.

I cannot deny that, like all siblings, we had our spats and ups and downs (but we never became anywhere near as cataclysmic as the Windsor boys!). But there were hurts. When I had to sell my Beverly Hills house and needed to come to LA for business, I hinted to Jackie that perhaps we could stay in her fabulous guest suite in her Beverly Drive mansion. My brother and sister-in-law and several of our mutual friends regularly stayed there, but she didn't offer, so I stayed in a hotel.

Sometimes, things were so cool between us that when we went to parties we would not even speak to each other. Allegedly, she was hurt when I'd once come to LA but not told her, but it was only for three days! I know I was extremely upset, and so was our brother Bill, when Jackie refused to come to London for our father's funeral. I could never understand why she hated our father. Granted, he was a strict disciplinarian, but he never hit us or was ever violent or cruel. Yes, I suspect, maybe he was a bit of a philanderer during the war, but he never abandoned us, and he was a good provider and he adored our mother.

None of these issues were ever discussed, nor, I'm convinced, did Jackie ever fully explain any of them to other people. Yet why should she? Are we supposed to be endlessly devoted to each other, and never disagree or do anything that might upset the other, just because we're sisters?

No one – not our friends, not our closest family – will really know everything we shared together, our bond over an entire lifetime, and the deep abiding love that always existed between us and that I still feel.

When Jackie died, Percy and I, like our brother Bill, Jackie's three daughters, six grandchildren, three sons-in-law and count-less other friends and family, were bereft. Jackie was so loved and admired by so many that her death was headline news across the world. She even made the cover of *People* magazine – she would have loved that! We grieved and tried to comfort each other, but Jackie's death left a void in all our lives that was impossible to fill.

27

Diana and Dodi and Other Royals

When Princess Margaret was introduced to my then fiancé Warren Beatty at a Hollywood party in the early 1960s, her eyes lit up. Having always had an eye for a handsome face, she and Warren were soon locked in animated conversation, and who knows what else happened? I had been introduced to Princess Margaret at a royal premiere the previous year and Warren had remarked on her beautiful blue eyes and vivacious personality.

I had a chance to sample her vivacious personality several times in the following years, most memorably when she came to see Keith Baxter and me in Noël Coward's *Private Lives* at the Aldwych Theatre in 1991. One night the company manager excitedly informed us before the performance that Princess Margaret was coming to the show with seven friends.

'Will she come backstage after?' I asked.

'Only if she likes the first act,' he replied. 'She may even leave if she doesn't like it – she has been known to.'

'Oh dear, we better give sparkling performances tonight,' I told the cast.

After the first act, in which we all did our darnedest, the company manager informed us that Princess Margaret 'loved it' and would like to meet the whole company onstage.

After the show we stood stiffly as Princess Margaret entered stage right, tiny and regal in a tight-waisted cocktail frock and mink stole. She was sipping a large drink in a small glass, which she gave to an equerry whenever she shook hands with one of the cast. In her other gloved hand she held a cigarette in a long, amber holder.

'I liked the performance enormously,' she chirped to me in her high-pitched voice. 'I read the play again this afternoon and this production is quite true to dear Noël's concept.'

I was most impressed by her diligence in not only reading the play but also understanding all the nuances. But then she threw me for a loop when she announced in her piercing tone, 'But the girl, Sybil, where's the girl? Her voice is far too high-pitched. I can hardly understand a word.'

Talk about pot calling kettle. Young Sara Crowe was summoned to the royal presence and sternly admonished to lower her voice. Sara looked understandably flummoxed by this critique but, since she had received excellent reviews (some better than mine!), she left her performance as it was.

In the early 90s, I was collecting some interesting *objets* for my new flat in Belgravia when my friend, the property developer Ned Ryan, brought over two gorgeous silver boxes.

'A very distinguished lady wants to sell them,' he said. 'Are you interested?'

Well, the price was right, so I bought them both and displayed them to good effect in my drawing room. Later, when I was polishing one of them, a very large cigar box, I opened it to find inside a card with these words: 'To Princess Margaret and Lord Snowdon on the occasion of their visit.'

Wow, I thought, that certainly is a very distinguished lady, but I still left the box out on the table. At my Christmas party a few months later, Ned Ryan, who had been invited but couldn't come due to a previous engagement with Princess Margaret, rang at about 10.30 p.m. 'I'm with Bryan and Nanette Forbes and Princess Margaret and they're all bored, so could we come over to your party?'

'Of course,' I said, 'come on over.'

When Princess Margaret arrived with her entourage, she stood in the hallway chatting to Roger Moore, who almost fell over as he bowed. She asked for a glass of Famous Grouse, which luckily I had – 'In a small glass please,' she commanded, 'as I have tiny hands.'

As the waiter scuttled away I realised that Roger was now ushering Princess Margaret into the very room where her silver box shone like a beacon on the coffee table. I tried to head her off at the pass while hissing to Ned sotto voce, 'Hide the damn box, for God's sake.' He didn't need to be told twice. If she had seen it, he could have been sent to the Tower for selling royal artifacts! Luckily, she enjoyed my party and being lionised by some of the glitterati of show business, so she never clocked the incriminating silver box.

I admired Princess Margaret for the way she lived her some-what hedonistic life by her own rules. It must have been difficult being the younger sister of the Queen, but I think she had a ball and lived her life to the fullest.

Princess Diana was undoubtedly the most fascinating young woman of her generation too, and I was not alone in my admir-ation of her style and charm. When she married her prince in 1981, Katy and I sat enthralled in front of the TV, watching the beautiful twenty-year-old walk down the aisle in her flouncy, fabulous Emanuel gown.

A few years later, I met her at a charity ball where we were both wearing Bruce Oldfield gowns. Diana was exquisite in a silver lamé gown with big shoulder pads, and I wore a white silk jersey, also featuring shoulder pads, for which I was becoming quite well known. We chatted briefly while the paps papped and the tabloids the following day screeched, 'Dynasty Di meets Alexis'.

When I began working with Nolan Miller, *Dynasty*'s designer, we started copying some of Princess Diana's more outrageous outfits. When she visited Russia she wore a fitted grey wool coat and an astrakhan muff, so when Alexis went to Moldavia she wore an almost identical outfit complete with muff, matching hat and knee-length suede boots.

The second time I met Princess Diana was in Palm Beach at a charity benefit given by the philanthropist Armand Hammer. I had hit it big in *Dynasty* and she had been married to Prince Charles for about two years, but it seemed that the honeymoon period was waning. I stood in line to be presented to her and was surprised when Princess Diana whispered, 'How do you stand it? How do you stand the attention of the press and paparazzi all the time?'

I was somewhat bemused but replied, 'Well, I think you just have to try and ignore them as much as possible.'

'Not much chance of that.' She pointed towards the batch of international photographers in the bleachers whose long, intrusive lenses were trained on the beautiful young princess. 'They follow me everywhere. It's as if I'm in a goldfish bowl. Do they do that to you too?'

'Thankfully not that much,' I answered, 'but I agree it must be very difficult for you.'

'It's horrid,' she shrugged, 'but I suppose it's part of the job.'

When I moved down the line to meet Prince Charles, he made his usual remark and one that is always used by his brother, Prince Andrew, too: 'What are *you* doing here?'

'I was invited, sir,' I said, curtsying gaily.

Later, Prince Charles sent an equerry over to my table to request a dance and, under the eyes of a thousand snapping lenses, we waltzed together while our future king talked animatedly in his beautifully modulated voice about how important philanthropy was. Suddenly, to my astonishment, my then husband Peter Holm stalked over to Princess Diana and asked her to dance, which she did! A cartoon of the four of us appeared in a tabloid a few days later with Prince Charles saying to me in the caption: 'Take it from me, Joan, the age gap won't spoil anything.'

Diana was always a complete model of good manners. When she visited the theatre to see me in *Private Lives*, she was utterly charming and interested to hear me talk about Noël Coward. When I sent her a copy of my beauty book, she sent me a glowing handwritten letter of thanks in spite of the fact that she had just returned from a gruelling trip to Australia.

Our paths crossed several times during the years up until her death. After her divorce, I heard that she and Dodi Fayed were in a relationship. I was quite surprised. I had known Dodi for years, as he was a regular at Tramp, the nightclub co-owned by Johnny Gold and Oscar Lerman, Jackie's husband, where I used to often hang out.

One day, my then husband (#3), Ron Kass announced, 'I've asked Dodi to stay with us.'

'Who's Dodi?' I asked, sitting on the sofa, playing with Katy.

'You know, the young guy we see at Tramp all the time. He's always hanging around Jackie and Oscar's table.'

'Oh – isn't he Mohamed Al-Fayed's son?' I asked. 'The one who does coke?'

Ron looked innocent. 'Does he? I didn't know. Anyway, he wants to get into show business and become a producer, so he sort of wants to follow me around a bit – study how it's done while we're shooting *The Optimists*.'

Privately, I thought that although Ron had helmed The Beat-les' Apple company for a while, he didn't really know a lot about how to be a film producer. I also wasn't thrilled to have another person living in our small, rented house in South Street, May-fair. Katy and my two children by Tony Newley, Tara and Sacha, were also living there.

'It's ridiculous,' I said. 'I'm not going to have Dodi sleeping on the sofa, and he'll probably want to hang out with all his coke-sniffing friends.'

'Don't worry,' Ron tried to soothe me. 'He'll sleep in the basement.'

'On the waterbed?' I asked in amazement.

'Yes, might as well put it to some use.'

I had been gifted a huge waterbed and had wanted to chuck it out, but Ron thought it would be great to put it in the big base-ment for when one of his three sons came to visit. Consequently, with the help of my interior designer friend Robin Guild, the basement had become a sexy hideaway. Dark-blue and purple paisley drapes hid the walls, and the place was eerily lit by exotic Middle Eastern lamps. It was supposed to be a getaway for Ron, but Tara and Sacha and their friends loved to bounce up and down on the waterbed, giggling at the squashy noises it made.

'Well, how long does this Dodi have to stay?' I asked.

'A couple of months, just so he can come with me to the set every day and eventually find his own pad.'

'OK,' I grumbled. 'But I'm not too happy about this at all, Ron.' Baby Katy gurgled contentedly.

'But you like him, don't you?'

'He's OK. He seems a nice boy, very quiet and reserved.' Must be the coke, I thought.

'Well, he won't disturb us. The basement has its own entrance. And after all, his father has promised to put some money into our film.' Ron was an associate producer on *The Optimists of Nine Elms* starring our mate, the brilliant Peter Sellers. Playing the cameo role of 'The Baby' in the film was my darling one-year-old infant Katy Kass, and I was delighted to take her to the set when she was called. She would do her bit by looking adorable and cute and the crew applauded.

Several nights during the shooting Ron would return to South Street with Peter and Dodi in tow. They would come in the back door into 'the waterbed room', as the kids called it, and stay there for hours. I would be involved in feeding Katy and putting her to bed in her bedroom on the top floor, but even there the smell of marijuana wafted up the stairs.

When I asked Ron what was going on down there, he dismissively said, 'Peter always wants more script discussions.' Like King Charles III, I loathe confrontation (quite the opposite of my Alexis character, who thrived on it), so apart from making some rebukes, I just got on with the business of being a mother to my three children – and sometimes six kids when Ron's boys came to visit.

I was glad when Dodi finally left, leaving Tara and Sacha free to jump up and down on the waterbed again, but I realised soon after that the residue of Dodi's visit was that my then-husband Ron Kass had formed a serious cocaine habit. Sadly I believe that eventually destroyed him.

Many years later I was travelling on British Airways from LA to London, and there in the aisle seat next to me was Dodi. We were pleased to see each other and after exchanging reminiscences and pleasantries I asked him what he was going to be doing in London.

'I'm looking for a new girlfriend,' he smiled. 'Do you know anyone?'

'No, I'll ask around,' I laughed. 'But I thought you already had one?'

He shrugged, then quipped, 'There's always room for one more.'

Some weeks later a picture appeared in a tabloid of Dodi and Princess Diana, intimating they were an item. From then on it was non-stop media attention for the couple.

If Princess Diana thought she had been stalked by the paparazzi during her marriage to Charles, it was nothing compared to the furore her relationship with Dodi Fayed caused.

However, in the beginning he was able to provide a certain amount of protection because of his great wealth. In July of 1997, I was in Saint-Tropez on Valentino's boat when Giancarlo Giammetti, Valentino's business partner, spotted the Fayed yacht, *Kalizna*, moored nearby.

Bringing out his binoculars, he scanned the ship and announced, 'I think I see Diana; I'll go and invite her for lunch or dinner.' Jumping on his water scooter, he shot over to the boat.

But as Giancarlo arrived, three burly sailors in white uniforms appeared on the deck holding what looked like Kalashnikov rifles in Giancarlo's direction.

'I'd like to speak to the princess,' he shouted.

'Go away,' yelled a guard. 'They don't want to be disturbed.'

'But we're friends of Princess Diana's,' he yelled.

The guns were raised menacingly and a guard yelled, 'Go away! You better leave right now.' A crestfallen Giancarlo scooted back to the boat while we all craned our necks hoping to catch a glimpse of the new young couple smooching!

How tragic that it was a few weeks later, when I was woken at 6 a.m. in the South of France by my agent, calling to tell me the awful news of Princess Diana's tragic death.

My friend Stella Wilson and I sat in front of the TV for two days watching the dreadful events unfold as the short, sad saga of Princess Diana's life came to a close. I often wonder if she would have been happy with Dodi.

28

Queenly

When Nicholas Coleridge, the ex-CEO of Condé Nast, asked me if I would consider being a part of the Queen's Platinum Jubilee procession to be held in June 2022, I had no hesitation in saying yes. This was the previous summer at a party at Lady Annabel Goldsmith's house, when people were finally starting to venture out into the real world after two horrible years of hiding from COVID.

A staunch monarchist ever since childhood, the thought of being part of a proposed tribute to Her Majesty's unfailing contribution to the monarchy was very appealing, but I had no idea what it would entail.

I sat at dinner between Nicholas and TV personality Gyles Brandreth, whose enthusiasm about the project was contagious, but I still didn't receive a definitive answer about what my role would be.

'Your event is going to be called "Dames in Jags",' said Nicholas excitedly. 'It will feature you, Dame Judi, Dame Maggie and Dame Shirley Bassey being driven in vintage Jaguars down the Mall.'

'Do we have to *drive* them?' I asked.

'No, no, you will just be sitting there smiling and waving to the crowds.'

'Like the Queen Mother!' I quipped.

'Of course,' smiled Nicholas. 'So don't forget the white gloves.'

I didn't hear from Nicholas for several months until early January, when he informed me that Dames Judi, Maggie and Shirley were unable to attend but that Dames Twiggy, Zandra Rhodes, Darcey Bussell and Floella Benjamin could. But apparently he still didn't know exactly what would happen on the actual day.

Meanwhile, I had to start thinking sartorially. An open-topped car in early June sounds like fun, but what if it rained, as it did for the Queen's Diamond Jubilee in 2012? I remembered watching the event as our brave but forlorn-looking monarch, with stoic Philip by her side, sailed down the Thames. For one and a half hours they stood in a specially decorated royal barge in pouring freezing rain, while Percy and I, and friends, watched from the balcony of Leslie and Evie Bricusse's riverside flat. We were wrapped in anoraks and huddled together for warmth, but the Queen was not.

'Oh, it won't rain,' Nicholas assured me. 'And if it does, you'll have umbrellas and rugs.' I suddenly thought of the movie *D-Day, The 6th of June* about the Allies' beach invasion in France. The weather was so appalling that it actually enabled them to open a second front and finally win. Percy calculated that the trip from Trafalgar Square to Buckingham Palace would probably take at least one hour, maybe more.

I needed to plan an outfit. I was in LA and, with my stylist friend Rene Horsch, spent several days combing the department stores of Neiman Marcus and Saks as well as the boutiques of Valentino and Tom Ford. However, none of them had anything suitable for a trip down the Mall in an open vintage Jaguar. Undaunted, I decided to have my dressmaker copy a Roland Mouret dress and an Amanda Wakeley cape. I wanted to wear peach, my favourite colour, and it needed to be a particular fabric.

We hit gold at the excellent emporium Beverly Hills Silks and Woollens, one of my go-to places ever since *Dynasty*. Yards of peach-coloured silk were uncovered and I triumphantly returned to London with my spoils.

I consulted my favourite milliner, Philip Treacy, and he designed a beautiful but rather large peach creation, with a mass of feathers sticking out.

'Don't you think it might be a bit much?' I ventured.

'Not for you, dear,' smiled Philip.

I recalled in the early days of *Dynasty*, when I wore a big hat in my first scene, the producer Aaron Spelling told the executives, 'We gotta put a lotta hats on that gal!'

My outfit was set. Now I just needed to know the details of what was going to happen, as I still hadn't heard from Nicholas.

As the great day grew nearer and the papers were hysterically announcing all the forthcoming events, excitement in the capital and all of the UK was palpable. During one final fitting with Philip for the hat, as we were deciding where to place the veil, I received a message from Nicholas Coleridge. 'All the Dames are invited to the Royal Box after their part in the procession is over, but the Palace doesn't want anyone to wear a hat or medals.'

'You're kidding?' I said.

'They don't want the Royal Box to look too "Ascot-ey",' Nicholas replied.

I was disappointed. The beautiful hat I was planning to wear would now be redundant, as would my lovely shiny DBE decoration, which I'd seldom worn.

'But I *have* to wear a hat, or my hair will be a horrible mess!' I told Philip.

I had called Dame Lesley (AKA Twiggy) the previous day and told her I would be wearing a hat.

'I'm not – I hate hats,' she replied.

'But what about your DBE medal? Will you wear that?' I asked.

'Oh, I don't know where it is!' she squawked. 'Probably in the safe.'

'Well, since this is one of the few occasions we can wear our honours, I'll wear mine in the procession and take it off for the Royal Box.'

'OK,' said Twigs, 'so will I.'

Then I received a call from Dame Zandra enquiring about the same things.

'I'm wearing a hat,' she announced, 'but it's a small one.'

'OK,' I said, 'so will I,' and bustled over to Philip Treacy to cancel the big one and order a small chapeau. He soon created a more modest beret with a veil.

The final plans for the day were incredibly complicated. All roads in Central London were closed, so we had to be at St George's House by 10 a.m., where we were to hang out and be ready to leave by bus to the starting point at 1.30 p.m.

The venue was all hustle and bustle. Celebrities and actors jostled and mixed with each other as we all queued for lunch in a giant hall, gossiping and giggling with acquaintances we hadn't seen for years. They included Juliet and Hayley Mills, Maxwell Caulfield, Esther Rantzen, Angela Rippon, Cliff Richard and Anita Harris. Then we were off!

We were whisked into one car, then into a giant car park where we dodged JCB tractors and double-decker buses with murals of the decades on each side, representing the 1950s to the present.

I was delighted to see my picture on the side of the 1970s bus, and also on the 1980s – an iconic shot of me as Alexis descending from a private jet wearing a small hat with a veil! 'How apt,' I thought.

I was escorted to a 1940s open-top white Jaguar, already oc-cupied by Dame Darcey Bussell (no hat – no medal – simple frock). I felt overdressed. She was being interviewed for the BBC and I joined her.

'My God, it's cold,' I said to Darcey, who was in short sleeves. Rugs appeared as if by magic, along with bottles of water.

After telling our interviewer how joyous and thrilled we were to be there, and how much we loved Her Majesty the Queen, Percy and I moved to our Jag. We waved at the 1950s bus as it rolled by, containing all our friends. I shrieked like a banshee, 'There's my friend Juliet!' and she shrieked back. Then along came another bus featuring Charlotte Tilbury, Kate Moss wear-ing a Union Jack jacket, and Naomi Campbell (resplendent in strapless couture, even though it was about 50 degrees). They screamed, 'Joan, Joan!' and we screamed back 'Naomi! Charlotte! . . . Patsy?' I didn't expect to see Patsy Kensit there too!

A loudspeaker announced that all Dames must get into their own cars so, like drivers at Le Mans, we scrambled over, stop-ping for selfies and 'Hello, darlings'. The petrol fumes from the cars in front were overwhelming and the wind was frigid, but the bonhomie and goodwill were contagious. We set off at two miles an hour, with our young chauffer driving.

There was something magical and terrifically emotional driving down the Mall. It was covered with Union Jack flags and lined with well-wishers on either side. They were waving banners and flags, smiling and laughing, holding pictures of the Queen. Many of them shouted merrily, 'Joan, we love you!'

'That should really warm your heart,' Percy smiled.

As we proceeded along the route behind the double-deckers, I felt so very patriotic. I waved graciously, but cautiously, as I was nursing a torn tendon in my bicep, but I hope I gave a passable impression of our dear Queen's royal gesture.

Finally, we arrived outside the Royal Box, which was packed with royals and relatives of the Queen. As we descended from the Jaguar, trying to look presentable after two hours in the freezing wind, Princess Beatrice and her husband Eduardo waved at us excitedly. Then he nudged Princess Anne, who nudged Prince Charles and Camilla, and they all waved, smiled at us, and mouthed, 'Well done!' Very gratifying indeed.

Shown to the green retiring room behind the box, I collapsed onto a sofa and was offered a cup of tea. Suddenly, a vision appeared in a red dress. Catherine, the Duchess of Cambridge, with her two young children in tow.

'Hello, Joan,' she said sweetly, holding out her hand.

'Hello, ma'am,' I gulped, forgetting to curtsy.

'This is Charlotte, and this is Louis,' she said, and both little people held out their tiny hands politely for a handshake.

When we returned to the back of the Royal Box, we sat next to Andrew and Madeleine Lloyd Webber. 'I'm freezing,' he whispered. 'I'm even colder here than in the Jag.' I whispered back. 'Are you staying to sing "God Save the Queen" with everyone at the end?'

'I don't think so,' said Andrew. 'Our car is miles away and we'll probably get caught in the crowds.'

'I'm not sure where our car is,' said Percy. 'We weren't exactly told the end game or how to leave here.'

'Nicholas told us the crowds afterwards would be humungous so it will be every man for himself,' I said.

We tried not to laugh as poor Dame Prue Leith's Jag stuttered then broke down right in front of the Royal Box, then we decided to sneak away, leaving the rest of the pomp and pageantry to the royal family.

Scrambling down from the back of the Royal Box, Percy and I found ourselves in a muddy back road, surrounded by policemen,

TV equipment and officials, none of whom could give us a clue as to where we should go to find our car. I was wearing peach lace Louboutins heels, now the worse for wear from the mud and hellish to walk in. I'd sensibly worn wedges in the car. As I limped dejectedly down the road, bitterly cold, I must have looked pathetic, because a nice cop in a golf cart zoomed up and took pity on us, saying, 'Hello, Joan! Even though it's against the rules, I'm a big fan, I'll take you to where your car is.'

He drove us to the end of Constitution Hill, where our car and driver had been waiting faithfully for seven hours. I do hope he went to get a coffee!

Arriving back at the sanctuary of our flat, I received a text from Charlotte Tilbury, saying, 'Darling, Kate and Naomi are so looking forward to seeing you at my party later tonight, as am I.'

'Oh, no way, I can't go,' I said to Percy. 'My toes have gone to sleep; I have to thaw them out, I think they're frostbitten!'

We snuggled under the covers to watch the rest of the fabulous procession on TV. I was stunned by the beauty and elegance of the golden state coach – empty today, but how well I remembered the young Queen Elizabeth riding shyly in it for her coronation seventy years ago. There were over a hundred thousand people at this amazing parade and it was much, much more exciting and joyful than anything we could have imagined.

It was thrilling to see our Queen, a seemingly robust ninety-six-year-old, appear at the balcony to the frenzied cheers of the crowd. She was chicly dressed all in green, with her immediate family around her. I was absolutely certain that she would make it to one hundred, and was so sad when she didn't.

29

What Was Your Secret, Ma'am?

I awoke on 8 September 2022 feeling completely exhausted and utterly bereft. I had spent practically all my waking hours the previous day glued to the television with Percy and my daughter Katy. At lunchtime, when the newscaster announced that the Queen was not well, we realised it was probably code speak for 'close to death'. We were extremely worried.

I first became aware of the then Princess Elizabeth when I was a young evacuee in Ilfracombe. In my parents' sudden, mad rush from London to escape the Blitz, unnecessary things like toys were left behind. I entertained myself by reading, by playing with conkers and skipping with an old frayed rope, but it was all rather boring. Then the woman next door produced a treasure. She gave me an old cutting-out book from the 1937 coronation of King George VI.

Inside were two wonderfully pretty cardboard figures of the two young princesses, Elizabeth and Margaret Rose, aged eleven and seven. How lovely the figures were in their dainty, modest undies, and how much fun it was to press the cardboard cutouts from the book and carefully try on the many adorable and stylish outfits. I whiled away hours dressing them up in their little kilts and pale jumpers and cardigans or lacy party frocks, having imaginary conversations with them. By the time the

Doodlebugs stopped raining on London, and we were taken back home again, the little cardboard princesses and their paper outfits were in total tatters.

I thought about those long-ago days when, with dreadful finality, the TV announcer intoned sorrowfully, 'We regret to announce that Her Majesty Queen Elizabeth has died.' Katy, Percy and I burst into tears. 'The world will never be the same,' I sobbed.

My fascination with Princess Elizabeth began in earnest in 1947, during the exciting preparations for her wedding to Prince Philip, or 'Phil the Greek' as my father rudely referred to him. I, however, thought that Prince Philip was as handsome as any movie star as I cut and pasted pictures from newspapers and magazines of Philip and Elizabeth into a special scrapbook I kept just for them.

The pre-wedding preparations were so outstandingly glamorous in an England still suffering from post-war austerity and rationing that I, my fellow schoolmates and, indeed, the whole country were gripped and completely fascinated by the splendour, the like of which we had never experienced.

Young Princess Elizabeth looked radiant in her engagement pictures, glowing with happiness, and we all wanted to be just like her when we grew up – to marry a handsome prince and live happily ever after.

The wedding day was another fairy tale. It was especially moving when it was reported that the princess had saved up all her clothing coupons to buy the fabric for her magnificent gown. I also loved watching her coronation from the window of a friend's house. One unforgettable moment was seeing a carriage pass by, containing a very large woman and a very small man. Noël Coward reportedly was asked, 'Who's that woman?'

'The queen of Tonga,' he replied.

'And who is the man sitting beside her?'

'Her lunch,' retorted Noël in his typically droll manner.

In the 1950s, Princess Elizabeth and Princess Margaret Rose became the pin-up girls of the media, setting the example for the future Princess Diana and Catherine, Princess of Wales. Everything they did became tabloid fodder, and Elizabeth and Philip were the golden couple of the time.

What can one say about our Queen Elizabeth that hasn't been said a million times? Everyone was aware of her numerous good points: her incredible energy, dedication, commitment and dignity; even under scrutiny, she seemed to have no bad points whatsoever. That is more than can be said for some of the heads of state who she met. With the graciousness and charm for which she was always famous, Queen Elizabeth bestowed a friendly handshake and a benign smile even to several leaders whose abuse of human rights and democracy was notorious.

Some were shocked that our Queen, a model of propriety and good manners, should have had to entertain such obvious villains but, sadly, she had little say on these matters. She had to always remain democratic and maintain the tradition of the 'stiff upper lip' at all times, a quality for which she was most admired and loved.

I was lucky enough to meet the Queen several times and she was always extremely friendly, giving me a firm handshake and a lovely smile. On one memorable occasion at the Royal Academy, I gave one of the worst curtsies I've ever executed, but she just smiled.

The first time I ever met the Queen was in 1962, at a Royal Command Performance at the Leicester Square Theatre, when my date was a then unknown actor by the name of Warren Beatty.

In the following years, I attended several other royal premieres. When I met the Queen Mother in 1983, she enquired why I wasn't working on *Dynasty*. I told her I was on hiatus, then tentatively asked her if she hated me in the show, to which she replied with a smile, 'Oh, no, my dear, we ALL love you!' I envisioned the female members of 'The Firm', including the Queen, spending every Wednesday night huddled in front of the TV having cups of tea and watching the antics of Krystle and Alexis with glee.

Few people know what taste the Queen had in popular culture. When she attended Royal Variety Performances, she looked suitably engaged. She even laughed at some of the better comedians and never frowned at some of the ghastly ones. She was surely riveted by 'Pudsey', the performing dog, and perhaps thought about what new tricks to teach her corgis.

I was presented to Queen Elizabeth and the Duke of Edinburgh again at the Royal Albert Hall in 1982 at a concert to celebrate The Beatles' twentieth anniversary. I was quite nervous. A series of events had conspired to make me tense, but it didn't show in the now-iconic picture by Richard Young. In the photo, my nine-year-old daughter Katy had just presented a bouquet to the Queen and was looking at her lovingly as I curtsied demurely, and the Queen and the Duke smiled.

I had just spoken the lyrics to John Lennon's 'Imagine', accompanied by the entire Royal Philharmonic Orchestra (as one does!). That in and of itself was numbingly scary, in front of not only the royals but five thousand other elite members of the audience, and I had also been the mistress of ceremonies. On top of that, as I entered through the stage door earlier, I had been accosted and served with a writ for not paying for a hire car that Ron Kass had leased three years previously (which had actually been returned long ago). It was terribly embarrassing, particularly as several photographers snapped away as I tried to enter the Albert Hall.

The Queen, of course, knew nothing about the writ as I curtsied, my knees trembling. I was wearing the 'Dynasty Diamonds', a parure of rubies and diamonds that were, of course, totally fake, like all of Alexis' jewels. I wondered if Her Majesty could tell the difference between those and the magnificent diamond necklace that she was wearing – I bet she did. The following day, when the picture was printed, the headlines were horrifying: 'Royal star Joan Gets Writ'; 'A Writ on Joan's Big Night'. I sincerely hoped the Queen didn't see them but apparently she read all the papers.

At the Royal Variety Performances in 1985, I shared a dressing room with, among others, the salty-tongued Lauren Bacall. She was wearing a plain black pantsuit and I was done up in a beaded full-length gown with a matching feather-trimmed cape. When I was called onstage, Bacall said, 'Eighty-six the feathers, Collins.'

'What?' I spluttered. 'Why?'

'Over the top, honey,' she said. 'Too much for the Queen.'

Since I knew the Queen was tiaraed and diamond necklaced and 'brooched' to the nines, I chose to ignore Miss Bacall. The following day, all the papers featured my feathers and me meeting the Queen, with Miss Bacall in her pantsuit just a blurry figure in the background!

A more relaxed occasion for me was when the Queen bestowed upon me an OBE in 1997. She greeted me with such a warm smile that I felt as though we were really good acquaintances.

At a lunch in Windsor Castle in 1998, an extremely animated monarch talked with Michael Caine, Shirley Bassey and me, fascinating us with stories about some of the interesting artwork hanging on the hallowed walls. The Queen was full of enthusiasm and seemed younger than a woman in her seventies.

One of my fondest memories took place at Buckingham Palace in 2014. I was invited to see a performance of George Bernard

Shaw's *Pygmalion*, given by RADA students to mark sixty years of the monarch's patronage of the drama school. After the show, the Queen walked around the room greeting and chatting to her many celebrity guests. She was holding a glass in her hand, but whether it was wine or water, I didn't dare ask. When she came to me, she mentioned having bestowed my OBE, which I told her was perhaps the biggest highlight of my life, other than giving birth to my children. We talked about the play, and she was incredibly knowledgeable about it and its adaptation to *My Fair Lady* in the 1950s.

Then 'my fair lady' herself joined us to say hello to me – the beautiful and elegant Duchess of Cambridge, or, as she was still called, Kate Middleton. We talked about our children and she said she was looking forward to having more after her son George.

It was a star-studded group in attendance. Among the luminaries, many of whom like me were graduates of RADA, were Ralph Fiennes, Hugh Laurie, Richard E. Grant, Trevor Eve, Helen Mirren and Helena Bonham Carter. Altogether a wonderful 'luvvie' evening which we all enjoyed, but by far the biggest luminary there was Our Majesty the Queen.

A hundred years ago, if a woman lived to be in her nineties, she would be feeble, bedridden and arthritic. Our Queen was in such robust health and had such vibrant energy that people took for granted the gruelling four-hundred-or-so engagements schedule she had to complete each year. As for that trip down the Thames in the pouring rain on her Diamond Jubilee in 2012 – if you allowed *your* grandmother to stand in the rain and freezing cold, you would probably be arrested for abuse!

The Queen's role entailed a great deal of hand-shaking in her time, and much of it none too gentle, as I can vouch. I observed some hand-shakers close up at the Royal Academy. I thought that she must have extremely strong fingers to survive some of those bone-crushers. Don't tell me shaking hands with over four thousand people a year, standing still for hours on end without showing a flicker of discomfort, and attending over four hundred functions without revealing the faintest hint of ennui is not an outstanding achievement in itself.

The Queen always looked immaculate and was impeccably composed. No lipstick on the teeth, a heel caught in a hem, or a dress that blew up in the wind, which happens to most mere mortals. She neither fidgeted nor looked bored, she never yawned or sneezed, and there was never ever a hair out of place beneath a stylish hat. I often wonder what hairspray she used to guarantee that those well-coiffed curls didn't move. I would have loved to know her beauty and make-up regime. Her skin was admirably free of any freckles or sun damage at all, even though her face often had to be exposed to the full glare of the sun (she could never wear sunglasses to protect her eyes, as the public had to be able to see her) and, in fact, to the elements in all weathers.

A question that often surprises me is, 'Why are you still working? Wouldn't you like to just lie around and put your feet up?' The very idea! I'm sure no one would have dared address such a fatuous remark to the Queen. Instead, people should have demanded, 'What's your secret, ma'am?'

Our royal family is the envy of the world, and America, in particular, laps up anything to do with our monarchy: their memorabilia collectors are zealous; the royal wedding of William and Catherine was almost a public holiday, with endless coverage throughout the day; and the film *The Queen* even received an Oscar! The monarchies of Norway, Sweden, Spain, Jordan, not to mention some of the US presidents, are no doubt more than slightly envious of the pomp and ceremony and the effortless attention our Queen attracted, and frankly they should be.

There was simply no one in the world like Her Majesty Queen Elizabeth II, and there never will be.

30
Kids These Days

Gone are the days when children were seen and not heard; today children are seen and heard all too vociferously. Within the space of a mere generation, it seems that kids have been catapulted into the realm of top dog, and helmsman of the household. On summer holidays, I marvelled at the way their parents seemed to minister to my young grandchildren's every need. The quiet of my rural idyll in the hills of the South of France was punctuated by the sound of children's voices raised high above the entreating voices of their parents, who followed them around the pool and garden with a supplicant air. At the risk of offending everybody under the age of fifteen, I must admit that today's little darlings could learn a lot from generations past.

For example, when I was a girl, I was lucky if my parents actually acknowledged my existence, let alone followed me around, eager to please me. I was lucky to get one present at Christmas, and the same for my birthday, when the entertainment usually consisted of having a couple of school friends over for tea, a cucumber sandwich and a piece of cake; if it was very special, a candle might be added. Thousands of pounds are often spent on children's parties now, apparently. I know of one cleaning lady who spent £2,000 on birthday presents for her daughter.

When I was growing up, Christmas wasn't even thought

about until the second week of December. There were no shops brimming with every imaginable gadget, toy or decoration. We would all marvel at the church nativity scene and ponder on the spirituality of the occasion. Today, Christmas is all about what you can get, instead of what it means to give. Surely this is the important message we should be instilling in our children?

My youthful entertainment consisted of a record player, a radio, a couple of jigsaw puzzles, a few dolls and a dolls' house, whose furniture I made myself out of conkers, wool and bits of old wood. When I visit my own grandchildren's homes, the mountains and mountains of toys astound me. When I gently suggest it might be good to donate a few to a children's hospital, outraged faces stared back at me in horror.

While today's youngsters idle away hours in front of their devices or the television set, I was fortunate if I was allowed two visits to the cinema a week. On one particular occasion, I remember coming home from the cinema to be greeted by my father, who announced that we would be going to the pictures as a treat that evening. I, not realising there was a limit on amusements, happily declared what a fine day this was turning into, as I had already seen one movie earlier that afternoon with my mother. My father curtly informed me I had therefore had my quota of fun and stimulation and would not be going to the pictures that evening after all. I would never have dreamed of questioning his authority – it was taken as given that Daddy had the final word on all things.

Yet today's 'mini-me's seem to take their parents' orders as an opener to a debate. Pleas and supplications turn into manoeuvring and cajoling, until out-and-out crying or faces of utter misery convince their buckling parents of their desperate need for the thing at hand.

I watched my own children crumble in the face of their

children's opposition and wondered how so much could have changed in so little time.

Moreover, the parent-child relationship seems to have been turned on its head and it's the children now informing parents (and what must seem as hopelessly out-of-touch grandparents) what the ground rules are. Watching a popular dance show on TV alongside my granddaughter, I commented on a woman, who was performing badly, as 'the girl in the pink dress'.

'You can't say *that*,' the teenager squeaked indignantly, 'it's sexist and incorrect.'

'What should I say?' I asked.

'The individual in the pink dress,' she replied. 'We can't assume how she identifies.'

If I admitted I was ever bored as a child, my parents had a credo: 'People who are bored are boring!' I will never forget it. And, according to my daughter Tara, to whom I repeated the same mantra, neither has she; it was ingrained in her brain, and she used it on her own children. Video games, TikTok, Instagram, iPhones, iPads – it's a brave new world of technological wonders and amusements, yet they still whine that they're bored!

The brains of these young creatures are firmly lodged in cyberspace. When I asked my granddaughter how I could bid for something on eBay, she logged on in a fraction of the time it had taken me to work out exactly what on earth eBay was.

The dexterity of my grandchildren's fingers as they fly across the computer keys astounds me. I never even learned to type, and although the majority of these young cyber kittens have never been taught either, they use their two index fingers with astonishing speed.

In my naivete, I imagined I was ahead of the game when my husband Percy bought me this new technological marvel, an iPad, but I have quickly been reminded of my limitations by the fish-to-water aptitudes of this younger generation. Their fingers seem shaped to accommodate the keys of most new-fangled technologies – unlike mine. But I've found an answer – Siri!

Words like megabyte, gigs, Skype, blog, Twitter and YouTube are double-Dutch to me but roll off young people's tongues.

However, while my six-year-old grandson was still grappling with the basic concepts of reading, at the tender age of five I was reading Enid Blyton's *Famous Five*. Then again, why should they bother to learn to read when the magic of the internet and television is at their disposal twenty-four hours a day, not to mention the plethora of kids' movies. How could a boring old book compare to that?

Plus, it seems that the very act of learning to read has been complicated by the new style of alphabetical teaching which seems so odd to me: no longer a, b, c, but phonetically sounded in what appears to be a foreign dialect. I couldn't help them even if I wanted to!

And yet, when it comes to manners, it seems that Ps and Qs are just letters of the alphabet. As a child, I wouldn't dream of leaving the table before my parents, not to mention leaving anything on my plate, because, as my parents would remind me, 'the children are starving in India'.

These words still ring in my brain, so that I always feel guilty if I leave anything on my plate (portion control is the answer). But the pickiness of this generation is something else! One child is a vegetarian, one doesn't eat fish, one refuses anything green, another only wants meat, another only wants pasta with butter, another only wants pasta with cheese. How do the parents cope?

There's a pertinent scene in that biopic of Joan Crawford, *Mommie Dearest*. When her daughter refuses to finish her dinner, Crawford insists that it is served to her at every mealtime for the next two days (not a technique I would advocate, but one that easily illustrates how times have changed). The amount of food that is thrown into our rubbish bins on a daily basis could feed a family of four for a week.

As I silently tut-tut beneath my breath, raising my eyes to the ceiling in supplication, and wondering why the long-suffering parents of today seem to have no control, I ponder where my generation went wrong. Or was it our children who went wrong, as they tried to revolt against the strict Edwardian attitudes that I inherited and that our parents in turn inherited from theirs?

I was told what to wear until the age of fifteen – no two ways about it. My mother bought me sensible skirts, and sensible shoes from Clarks (so I now have feet without corns or bunions).

There is no doubt that the fashion houses now cater to the young when, in the past, there was no such thing as pre-teen and teenage fashion.

My own children, born in the late 1960s and 1970s, were attired in matching smocks, gingham knee-length frocks, and sensible shorts, and I always insisted on socks and shoes.

Today, looking at the clothes in the stores, you could be forgiven for thinking 'Are these for tiny tots or tiny tarts?'

Sequined bikinis with hearts on the nether region, sundresses cut out to the navel, and lots of gothic black, and this is for four-year-olds! The outfits are emblazoned with messages such as 'Born to shop' or 'Money is what parents are for'.

We used to hold after-dinner 'disco' nights in our living room, where the children displayed an almost frightening propensity for adult dance moves, straight out of MTV. They were completely unselfconscious and when they performed Geri Halliwell's 'It's Raining Men' with appropriate gestures, I wondered if they really knew what they were implying.

But at the same time, watching them perform to all the latest hits with so much confidence, charm and sophistication, I

reflected on how I, as an insecure, shy child, was never compli-
mented by my parents, rarely told I was clever, pretty or talented,
and basically told to shut up if I expressed my opinions.

So, as I wandered around my Riviera villa, picking up soaking-
wet towels and bathing suits and avoiding tripping over the
several toys scattered around my normally pristine infinity pool,
I have to admit that watching them jump and jiggle around the
pool all afternoon afforded me some of the greatest pleasures of
my already lucky life.

It's my grandchildren's happiness and their freedom that's
so infectious, and whatever I may think about the differences
between their generation and mine, in all honesty I wouldn't
change my gorgeous grandchildren for the world.

Epilogue

Looking back at my life and career, I think that I have had an extremely lucky and happy life. Firstly, I believe I have inherited the 'happy gene' from my paternal grandmother Hetty and from my own dear mother Elsa. They always managed to see the bright side of life even through the darkest days of the Second World War. I have survived four gruelling divorces, multiple family dramas, several court cases and many financial setbacks.

Luckily, my acting career took off with minimum effort – RADA, Rank, Hollywood – just like that! It is said that, to have a career in showbusiness, you need resilience, talent and luck. Well, I certainly had the latter, and I believe I had the talent to sustain me through a career spanning over seven decades. Luckily, I've also had the resilience to withstand the endless waiting for the phone to ring with the next job, not allowing my mind to catastrophise while in enforced 'resting' and instead working to create the next opportunity.

It helps me to never stay still. My mother called me 'Miss Perpetual Motion' because, as a child, I was always doing *something*. So, I keep on working because I love being busy. I love writing, performing my one-woman show, pitching ideas for new projects, and occasionally picking up the odd award for 'lifetime achievement'. I dragged the script of *The Stud* around for years and pitched it to producers at the various parties, award shows and industry events I attended. I did the same with various other projects I successfully made. I'm still doing that with a project about Wallis, Duchess of Windsor, which I'm passionate about.

But I'm also lucky to have a wonderful life while, like many actors, I am 'resting'. I wake up when I want and read the UK papers in bed wherever I am. Percy usually makes me a delicious cup of coffee and then I keep up with my friends and family by phone, email and Instagram. I enjoy Instagram, although I'm not a huge fan of social media in general.

One would think that my decade at Twentieth Century-Fox, garnering top billing with Richard Burton, Bette Davis, Gregory Peck, Paul Newman, Bob Hope and Bing Crosby, and eventually Gene Kelly and Elizabeth Taylor, or controlling the global TV screens for almost a decade as the fascinating Alexis in *Dynasty*, would be achievement enough. But life is long, and success is not. 'Success is not final, and failure is not fatal. It is the courage to continue that counts,' said Winston Churchill.

So I try and live by certain similar credos: 'Forget your age and live your life'; 'Live each day as if it's your last, and someday you'll be right!'; 'Life is a banquet, and most poor suckers are starving to death.' And my favourite, 'Eat life, or life will eat you.'

But I ultimately realise how stupendously lucky my life has been. I was so lucky to meet my husband – my best friend, my accomplice, and my partner for life. Percy has been a godsend, and my children and grandchildren all love him. Through thick and thin, Percy has performed above and beyond the call of 'in sickness and in health, for richer, for poorer'. He is the best husband and the best man – I am one lucky wife and a very lucky woman.

So, do I deserve this lucky life? Well, my husband, my family and my friends have told me so. I certainly hope I've earned it. And I shall continue to do so. Onward!